MAYA ANGELOU

Singin' and Swingin' and Gettin' Merry Like Christmas

virago

VIRAGO

First published by Virago Press 1985
This edition published by Virago Press in 2008

9 11 13 15 17 19 20 18 16 14 12 10

First published in the USA by Random House 1976

Grateful acknowledgement is made to the following for permission
to reprint previously published material:

Chappell & Co., Inc.: For eight lines of lyrics from the song 'Street Song' by George Gershwin
(p. 178), and three lines of lyrics from 'There's a Boat That's Leavin' Soon for New York'
by George Gershwin (p. 146).
Copyright © Gershwin Publishing Corp 1935
Copyright renewed. All rights reserved. International Copyright Secured.

Harper & Row Publishers, Inc.: For lines from the poem 'For a Lady I Know' from *On These I
Stand* by Countee Cullen (p. 142). Copyright © 1925
Harper & Row Publishers, Inc: renewed 1953 by Ida M. Cullen.

Northern Music Company: For four lines of lyrics from the song 'Stone Cold
Dead in the Market (He Had It Coming)', words and music by Wilmoth Houdini (p. 89).
Copyright © Northern Music Company 1945, 1946. All rights reserved.

A CIP catalogue record for this book is available from the British Library.

ISBN 978-1-84408-503-3

Typeset in Goudy by M Rules
Printed and bound in Great Britain by
Clays Ltd, St Ives plc

Papers used by Virago are from well-managed forests
and other responsible sources.

MIX
Paper from
responsible sources
FSC® C104740

Virago Press
An imprint of
Little, Brown Book Group
Carmelite House
50 Victoria Embankment
London EC4Y 0DZ

An Hachette UK Company
www.hachette.co.uk

www.virago.co.uk

Acknowledgments

Thanks to the
BELLAGIO STUDY AND CONFERENCE CENTER
of the
ROCKEFELLER FOUNDATION,
particularly
BILL AND BETSY OLSEN
A special thanks to my friend and secretary,
SEL BERKOWITZ

For
MARTHA and LILLIAN
NED and BEY
for the laughter,
the love and the music

Singin' and Swingin'
and Gettin' Merry
Like Christmas

1

'Don't the moon look lonesome shining through the trees?
Ah, don't the moon look lonesome shining through the trees?
Don't your house look lonesome when your baby pack up to
    leave?'

Music was my refuge. I could crawl into the spaces between
the notes and curl my back to loneliness.

In my rented room (cooking privileges down the hall), I
would play a record, then put my arms around the shoulders of
the song. As we danced, glued together, I would nuzzle into its
neck, kissing the skin, and rubbing its cheek with my own.

The Melrose Record Shop on Fillmore was a center for
music, musicians, music lovers and record collectors. Blasts
from its loudspeaker poured out into the street with all the
insistence of a false mourner at a graveside. Along one wall of
its dark interior, stalls were arranged like open telephone
booths. Customers stood playing their selections on turntables
and listening through earphones. I had two hours between

3

jobs. Occasionally I went to the library or, if the hours coincided, to a free dance class at the YWCA. But most often I directed myself to the melodious Melrose Record Store, where I could wallow, rutting in music.

Louise Cox, a short blonde who was part owner of the store, flitted between customers like a fickle butterfly in a rose garden. She was white, wore perfume and smiled openly with the Negro customers, so I knew she was sophisticated. Other people's sophistication tended to make me nervous and I stayed shy of Louise. My music tastes seesawed between the blues of John Lee Hooker and the bubbling silver sounds of Charlie Parker. For a year I had been collecting their records.

On one visit to the store, Louise came over to the booth where I was listening to a record.

'Hi, I'm Louise. What's your name?'

I thought of 'Puddin' in tame. Ask me again, I'll tell you the same.' That was a cruel childhood rhyme meant to insult.

The last white woman who had asked me anything other than 'May I help you?' had been my high school teacher. I looked at the little woman, at her cashmere sweater and pearls, at her slick hair and pink lips, and decided she couldn't hurt me, so I'd give her the name I had given to all white people.

'Marguerite Annie Johnson.' I had been named for two grandmothers.

'Marguerite? That's a pretty name.'

I was surprised. She pronounced it like my grandmother. Not Margarite, but Marg-you-reet.

'A new Charlie Parker came in last week. I saved it for you.'

That showed her good business sense.

'I know you like John Lee Hooker, but I've got somebody I want you to hear.' She stopped the turntable and removed my record and put on another in its place.

'Lord I wonder, do she ever think of me,
Lord I wonder, do she ever think of me,
I wonder, I wonder, will my baby come back to me?'

The singer's voice groaned a longing I seemed to have known my life long. But I couldn't say that to Louise. She watched my face and I forced it still.

'Well, I ain't got no special reason here,
No, I ain't got no special reason here,
I'm gonna leave 'cause I don't feel welcome here.'

The music fitted me like tailor-made clothes.

She said, 'That's Arthur Crudup. Isn't he great?'; excitement lighted her face.

'It's nice. Thank you for letting me hear it.'

It wasn't wise to reveal one's real feelings to strangers. And nothing on earth was stranger to me than a friendly white woman.

'Shall I wrap it for you? Along with the Bird?'

My salary from the little real estate office and the dress shop downtown barely paid rent and my son's baby-sitter.

'I'll pick them both up next week. Thank you for thinking of me.' Courtesy cost nothing as long as one had dignity. My grandmother, Annie Henderson, had taught me that.

She turned and walked back to the counter, taking the

record with her. I counseled myself not to feel badly. I hadn't rejected an offer of friendship, I had simply fielded a commercial come-on.

I walked to the counter.

'Thank you, Louise. See you next week.' When I laid the record on the counter, she pushed a wrapped package toward me.

'Take these, Marg-you-reet. I've started an account for you.' She turned to another customer. I couldn't refuse because I didn't know how to do so gracefully.

Outside on the evening street, I examined the woman's intention. What did I have that she wanted? Why did she allow me to walk away with her property? She didn't know me. Even my name might have been constructed on the spot. She couldn't have been seeking friendship; after all she was white, and as far as I knew, white women were never lonely, except in books. White men adored them, black men desired them and black women worked for them. There was no ready explanation for her gesture of trust.

At home I squeezed enough from the emergency money I kept in a drawer to repay her. Back at the store, she accepted the money and said, 'Thanks, Marg-you-reet. But you didn't have to make a special trip. I trust you.'

'Why?' That ought to get her. 'You don't know me.'

'Because I like you.'

'But you don't know me. How can you like someone you don't know?'

'Because my heart tells me and I trust my heart.'

For weeks I pondered over Louise Cox. What could I possibly have that she could possibly want? My mind, it was certain, was a well-oiled mechanism which worked swiftly and seminoiselessly. I often competed with radio contestants on quiz programs and usually won hands down in my living room. Oh, my mental machine could have excited anyone. I meant anyone interested in a person who had memorized the Presidents of the United States in chronological order, the capitals of the world, the minerals of the earth and the generic names of various species. There weren't too many callers for those qualifications and I had to admit that I was greatly lacking in the popular attractions of physical beauty and womanly wiles.

All my life, my body had been in successful rebellion against my finer nature. I was too tall and raw-skinny. My large extroverted teeth protruded in an excitement to be seen, and I, attempting to thwart their success, rarely smiled. Although I lathered Dixie Peach in my hair, the thick black mass crinkled and kinked and resisted the smothering pomade to burst free around my head like a cloud of angry bees. No, in support of truth, I had to admit Louise Cox was not friendly to me because of my beauty.

Maybe she offered friendship because she pitied me. The idea was a string winding at first frayed and loose, then tightening, binding into my consciousness. My spirit started at the intrusion. A white woman? Feeling sorry for me? She wouldn't dare. I would go to the store and show her. I would roll her distasteful pity into a ball and throw it in her face. I would smash her nose deep into the unasked-for sympathy until her eyes dribbled tears and she learned that I was a queen, not to be approached by peasants like her, even on bended knees, and wailing.

7

Louise was bent over the counter talking to a small black boy. She didn't interrupt her conversation to acknowledge my entrance.

'Exactly how many boxes have you folded, J.C.?' Her intonation was sober.

'Eighteen.' The boy's answer matched her seriousness. His head barely reached the counter top. She took a small box from a shelf behind her.

'Then here's eighteen cents.' She pushed the coins around counting them, then poured them into his cupped palms.

'O.K.' He turned on unsure young legs and collided with me. He mumbled 'Thank you.'

Louise rounded the counter, following the little voice. She ran past me and caught the door a second after he slammed it.

'J.C.' She stood, arms akimbo on the sidewalk, and raised her voice. 'J.C., I'll see you next Saturday.' She came back into the store and looked at me.

'Hi, Marg-you-reet. Boy, am I glad to see you. Excuse that scene. I had to pay off one of my workers.'

I waited for her to continue. Waited for her to tell me how precious he was and how poor and wasn't it all a shame. She went behind the counter and began slipping records into paper jackets.

'When I first opened the shop, all the neighborhood kids came in. They either demanded that I "gi' them a penny"' – I hated whites' imitation of the black accent – 'or play records for them. I explained that the only way I'd give them anything was if they worked for it and that I'd play records for their parents, but not for them until they were tall enough to reach the turntables.'

8

'So I let them fold empty record boxes for a penny apiece.'
She went on, 'I'm glad to see you because I want to offer you
a job.'

I had done many things to make a living, but I drew the
line at cleaning white folks' houses. I had tried that and lasted
only one day. The waxed tables, cut flowers, closets of other
people's clothes totally disoriented me. I hated the figured carpets, tiled kitchens and refrigerators filled with someone else's
dinner leftovers.

'Really?' The ice in my voice turned my accent to upper-
class Vivien Leigh (before *Gone With the Wind*).

'My sister has been helping me in the shop, but she's going
back to school. I thought you'd be perfect to take her place.'

My resolve began to knuckle under me like weak knees.

'I don't know if you know it, but I have a large clientele
and try to keep in stock a supply, however small, of every
record by Negro artists. And if I don't have something, there's
a comprehensive catalog and I can order it. What do you
think?'

Her face was open and her smile simple. I pried into her
eyes for hidden meaning and found nothing. Even so, I had to
show my own strength.

'I don't like to hear white folks imitate Negroes. Did the
children really ask you to "gi' them a penny"? Oh, come now.'

She said, 'You are right – they didn't ask. They demanded
that I "gi' them a penny."' The smile left her face. 'You say it.'

'Give me a penny.' My teeth pressed my bottom lip, stress-
ing the *v*.

She reached for the box and handed me a coin. 'Don't
forget that you've been to school and let neither of us forget

9

that we're both grown-up. I'd be pleased if you'd take the job.'
She told me the salary, the hours and what my duties would
be.

'Thank you very much for the offer. I'll think about it.' I
left the shop, head up, back straight. I tried to exude indifference, like octopus ink, to camouflage my excitement.

I had to talk to Ivonne Broadnax, the Realist. She was my
closest friend. Ivonne had escaped the hindrance of romantic
blindness, which was my lifelong affliction. She had the clear,
clean eyes of a born survivor. I went to her Ellis Street house,
where she, at twenty-five, was bringing up an eight-year-old
daughter and a fifteen-year-old sister.

'Vonne, you know that woman that runs the record store?'

'That short white woman with the crooked smile?' Her
voice was small and keen and the sound had to force itself past
white, even teeth.

'Yes.'

'Why?'

'She offered me a job.'

'Doing what?' I knew I could count on her cynicism.

'Salesgirl.'

'Why?'

'That's what I've been trying to figure out. Why? And why
me?'

Ivonne sat very still, thinking. She possessed a great beauty
which she carried nonchalantly. Her cupid's-bow lips pursed,
and when she raised her head her face was flushed pink and
cream from the racing blood.

'Is she funny that way?'

We both knew that was the only logical explanation.

10

'No. I'm sure that she's not.'

Ivonne bent her head again. She raised it and looked at me. 'Did you ask her?'

'No.'

'I mean did you ask her for the job?'

'No. She offered it.' I added just a little indignation to my answer.

Ivonne said, 'You know white people are strange. I don't even know if they know why they do things.' Ivonne had grown up in a small Mississippi town, and I, in a smaller town in Arkansas. Whites were as constant in our history as the seasons and as unfamiliar as affluence.

'Maybe she's trying to prove something.' She waited. 'What kind of pay she offering?'

'Enough so I can quit both jobs and bring the baby home.'

'Well, take it.'

'I'll have to order records and take inventories and all that.' The odor of an improvement in my life had barely touched my nostrils and it made me jittery.

'Come on, Maya' (she called me by the family name). 'If you could run a hook shop, you can run a record shop.'

Once when I was eighteen in San Diego I had managed a house of prostitution, where two qualified workers entertained and I, as financial backer, took a percentage. I had since layered that experience over and over in my mind with forgiveness and a conscious affectation of innocence. But it was true, I did have a certain talent for administration.

'Tell her you'll take the job and then watch her like a hawk. You know white women. They pull off their drawers, lay down first, then scream rape. If you're not careful, she'll get weak and faint on you, then before you know it you'll be washing windows, and scrubbing the floor.' We cackled like two old crones, remembering a secret past. The laughter was sour and not really directed at white women. It was a traditional ruse that was used to shield the black vulnerability; we laughed to keep from crying.

I took the job, but kept Louise under constant surveillance. None of her actions went unheeded, no conversation unrecorded. The question was not if she would divulge her racism but when and how the revelation would occur. For a few months I was a character in a living thriller plot. I listened to her intonations and trailed her glances.

On Sundays, when the older people came in after church services to listen to the Reverend Joe May's sermons on 78 rpm records, I trembled with the chase's excitement. Large, corseted women gathered around the record players, their bosoms bloated with religious fervor, while their dark-suited husbands leaned into the music, faces blank in surrender to the spirit, their black and brown fingers restive on clutched Bibles.

Louise offered folding chairs to the ladies and moved back behind the counter to her books. I waited for one smirk, one roll of her eyes to the besieged heavens and I would have my evidence that she thought her whiteness was a superior quality which she and God had contrived for their own convenience.

After two months, vigilance had exhausted me and I had found no thread of prejudice. I began to relax and enjoy the wealth of a world of music. Early mornings were given over to Bartok and Schoenberg. Midmorning I treated myself to the vocals of Billy Eckstine, Billie Holiday, Nat Cole, Louis Jordan and Bull Moose Jackson. A piroshki from the Russian delicatessen next door was lunch and then the giants of bebop flipped through the air. Charlie Parker and Max Roach, Dizzy Gillespie, Sarah Vaughan and Al Haig and Howard McGhee. Blues belonged to late afternoons and the singers' lyrics of lost love spoke to my solitude.

I ordered stock and played records on request, emptied ashtrays and dusted the windows' cardboard displays. Louise and her partner, David Rosenbaum, showed their pleasure by giving me a raise, and although I was grateful to them for the job and my first introduction to an amiable black-white relationship, I could exhibit my feelings only by being punctual in coming to the shop and being efficient at work and coolly, grayly respectful.

At home, however, life shimmered with beautiful colors. I picked up my son from the baby-sitter's every evening. He was five years old and so beautiful his smile could break the back of a brute.

For two years we had spun like water spiders in a relentless eddy. I had to be free to work for our support, but the baby-sitters were so expensive I had to have two jobs to pay their fees and my own rent. I boarded him out six days and five nights a week.

On the eve of my day off, I would go to the baby-sitter's house. First he'd grab the hem of my dress, then wrap his arms around my legs and hold on screaming as I paid the weekly bill. I would pry his arms loose, then pick him up and walk down the street. For blocks, as I walked, he would scream. When we were far enough away, he'd relax his strangle hold on my neck and I could put him down. We'd spend the evening in my room. He followed my every turn and didn't trust me to go to the bathroom and return. After dinner, cooked in the communal kitchen, I would read to him and allow him to try to read to me.

The next day was always spent at the park, the zoo, the San Francisco Museum of Art, a cartoon movie house or any cheap or free place of entertainment. Then, on our second evening he would fight sleep like an old person fighting death. By morning, not quite awake, he would jerk and make hurtful noises like a wounded animal. I would still my heart and wake him. When he was dressed, we headed back to the sitter's house. He would begin to cry a few blocks from our destination. My own tears stayed in check until his screams stabbed from behind the closed doors and stuck like spearheads in my heart.

The regularity of misery did nothing to lessen it. I examined alternatives. If I were married, 'my husband' (the words sounded as unreal as 'my bank account') would set me up in a fine house, which my good taste would develop into a home. My son and I could spend whole days together and then I could have two more children who would be named Deirdre and Craig, and I would grow roses and beautiful zinnias. I would wear too-large gardening gloves so that when I removed them my hands would look dainty and my manicure fresh. We would all play chess and Chinese checkers and twenty questions and whist. We would be a large, loving, hilarious family like the people in *Cheaper by the Dozen*.

Or I could go on welfare.

There wasn't a shadow of a husband-caliber man on my

horizon. Indeed, no men at all seemed attracted to me. Possibly my façade of cool control turned them away or just possibly my need, which I thought well disguised, was so obvious that it frightened them. No, husbands were rarer than common garden variety unicorns.

And welfare was absolutely forbidden. My pride had been starched by a family who assumed unlimited authority in its own affairs. A grandmother, who raised me, my brother and her own two sons, owned a general merchandise store. She had begun her business in the early 1900's in Stamps, Arkansas, by selling meat pies to saw men in a lumber mill, then racing across town in time to feed workers in a cotton-gin mill four miles away.

My brother, Bailey, who was a year older than I and seven inches shorter, had drummed in my youthful years: 'You are as intelligent as I am' – we both agreed that he was a genius – 'and beautiful. And you can do anything.'

My beautiful mother, who ran businesses and men with autocratic power, taught me to row my own boat, paddle my own canoe, hoist my own sail. She warned, in fact, 'If you want something done, do it yourself.'

I hadn't asked them for help (I couldn't risk their refusal) and they loved me. There was no motive on earth which would bring me, bowed, to beg for aid from an institution which scorned me and a government which ignored me. It had seemed that I would be locked in the two jobs and the weekly baby-sitter terror until my life was done. Now with a good salary, my son and I could move back into my mother's house.

A smile struck her face like lightning when I told her I had retrieved my son and we were ready to come home. There was a glaze over her eyes. It was unnerving. My mother was anything, everything, but sentimental. I admired how quickly she pulled her old self back in charge. Typically she asked only direct questions.

'How long will you all stay this time?'

'Until I can get a house for us.'

'That sounds good. Your room is pretty much as you left it and Clyde can have the little room in back.'

I decided that a little bragging was in order. 'I've been working at the record shop on Fillmore and the people down there gave me a raise. I'll pay rent to you and help with the food.'

'How much are they paying you?'

When I told her, she quickly worked out a percentage. 'O.K. You pay me that amount and buy a portion of food every week.'

I handed her some cash. She counted it carefully. 'All right, this is a month's rent. I'll remember.'

She handed the money back to me. 'Take this downtown and buy yourself some clothes.'

I hesitated.

'This is a gift, not a loan. You should know I don't do business slipshod.'

To Vivian Baxter business was business, and I was her daughter; one thing did not influence the other.

'You know that I'm no baby-sitter, but Poppa Ford is still with me looking after the house. He can keep an eye on Clyde. Of course you ought to give him a little something every week. Not as much as you pay the baby-sitters, but

16

something. Remember, you may not always get what you pay for, but you will definitely pay for what you get.'

'Yes, Mother.' I was home.

For months life was a pleasure ring and we walked safely inside its perimeter. My son was in school, reading very well, and encouraged by me, drifting into a love affair with books. He was healthy. The old fears that I would leave him were dissolving. I read Thorne Smith to him and recited Paul Laurence Dunbar's poems in a thick black Southern accent.

On an evening walk along Fillmore, Clyde and I heard loud shouting and saw a group of people crowded around a man on the corner across the street. We stopped where we were to listen.

'Lord, we your children. We come to you just like newborn babies. Silver and gold have we none. But O Lord!'

Clyde grabbed my hand and started to pull me in the opposite direction.

'Come on, Mom. Come on.'

I bent down to him. 'Why?'

'That man is crazy.' Distaste wrinkled his little face.

'Why do you say that?'

'Because he's shouting in the street like that.'

I stooped to my son giving no attention to the passers-by. 'That's one of the ways people praise God. Some praise in church, some in the streets and some in their hearts.'

'But Mom, is there really a God? And what does He do all the time?'

The question deserved a better answer than I could think of in the middle of the street. I said, 'We'll talk about that later, but now let's go over and listen. Think of the sermon as a poem and the singing as great music.'

He came along and I worked my way through the crowd so he could have a clear view. The antics of the preacher and the crowd's responses embarrassed him. I was stunned. I had grown up in a Chris-tian Methodist Episcopal Church where my uncle was superintendent of Sunday School, and my grandmother was Mother of the Church. Until I was thirteen and left Arkansas for California, each Sunday I spent a mini-mum of six hours in church. Monday evenings Momma took me to Usher Board Meeting; Tuesdays the Mothers of the Church met; Wednesday was for prayer meeting; Thursday, the Deacons congregated; Fridays and Saturdays were spent in preparation for Sunday. And my son asked me if there was a God. To whom had I been praying all my life?

That night I taught him 'Joshua Fit the Battle of Jericho.'

2

My life was an assemblage of strivings and my energies were directed toward acquiring more than the basic needs. I was as much a part of the acquisitive, security-conscious fifties as the quiet young white girls who lived their pastel Peter Pan-collared days in clean, middle-class neighborhoods. In the black communities, girls, whose clothes struck with gay colors and whose laughter crinkled the air, flashed streetwise smirks and longed for one picket fence. We startled with our overt flirtations and dreamed of being 'one man's woman.' We found ourselves too often unmarried, bearing lonely pregnancies and wishing for two and a half children each who would gurgle happily behind that picket fence while we drove our men to work in our friendly-looking station wagons.

I had loved one man and dramatized my losing him with all the exaggerated wailing of a wronged seventeen-year-old. I had wanted others in a ferocious desperation, believing that marriage would give me a world free from danger, disease and want.

In the record store, I lived fantasy lives through the maudlin melodies of the forties and fifties.

'You'd be so nice to come home to.'

Whoever you were.

'I'm walking by the river
'cause I'm meeting someone there tonight.'

Anyone – that is, anyone taller than I and who wanted to get married. To me. Billy Eckstine sang,

'Our little dream castle with everything gone
Is lonely and silent, the shades are all drawn
My heart is heavy as I gaze upon
A cottage for sale.'

That was my house and it was vacant. If Mr. Right would come along right now, soon we could move in and truly begin to live.

Louise Cox and her mother were practicing Christian Scientists. I accepted an invitation to visit their church. The interior's severity, the mass of quiet, well-dressed whites and the lack of emotion unsettled me. I took particular notice of the few blacks in the congregation. They appeared as soberly affluent and emotionally reserved as their fellow white parishioners. I had known churches to be temples where one made 'a joyful noise unto the Lord' and quite a lot of it.

In the First Church of Christ, Scientist, the congregation wordlessly praised the Almighty. No stamping of feet or clapping of hands accompanied the worship. For the whole service, time seemed suspended and reality was just beyond the simple and expensive heavy doors.

'Did you like it?'

We sat in Louise's kitchen, eating her mother's homemade-from-scratch biscuits.

'I don't know. I didn't understand it.'

After a year of relentless observation, I trusted her to think me unexposed, rather than ignorant.

Her mother gave me a copy of Mary Baker Eddy's *Science and Health*. I began to wrestle with new concepts.

The tough texture of poverty in my life had been more real than sand wedged between my teeth, yet Mary Baker Eddy encouraged me to think myself prosperous. Every evening I went home to a fourteen-room house where my son and seventy-five-year-old Poppa Ford awaited my arrival. Mother usually was out dining with friends, drinking with acquaintances or gambling with strangers. Had she been there, her presence would not have greatly diminished my loneliness. My brother, who had been my ally, my first friend, had left home and closed himself to me. We had found safety in numbers when we were young, but adulthood had severed the bonds and we drifted apart over deep and dangerous seas, unanchored.

In Mother's house, after dinner, I would read my son to sleep and return to the kitchen. Most often, the old man dreamt over an outsized cup of heavily sugared coffee. I would watch his aged ivory face, wrinkled under ghostly memories, then go to my room where solitude gaped whale-jawed wide to swallow me entire.

Science and Health told me I was never alone. 'There is no place God is not.' But I couldn't make the affirmation real for me.

The sailor wandered around the store. He was reading the bulletins and scanning the posters. His dark hair and oval, sensual face reminded me of Italian Renaissance paintings. It was strange to see a white military man in the black area in broad daylight. I decided that he had gotten lost. He walked to the counter.

'Good morning.'

'Have you got "Cheers"?'

Maybe he wasn't lost, just found himself in our neighborhood and decided to buy some records. 'Cheers'? I thought of all the white singers – Jo Stafford, Helen O'Connell, Margaret Whiting, Dinah Shore, Frank Sinatra, Bob Crosby, Bing Crosby and Bob Eberle. Tex Beneke. None had recorded a song entitled 'Cheers.' I ran my mind over Anita O'Day, Mel Tormé, June Christy. No 'Cheers' there. He had looked like a vocal man, but then maybe he was looking for a white Big Band instrumental. Stan Kenton, Neal Hefti, Billy May. No 'Cheers' in their catalogs.

'I don't know if we have it. Who cut it?' I smiled. 'Cut it' showed that I was so much a part of the record business that I wouldn't say 'Who recorded it?'

The man looked at me and said dryly, 'Charlie Parker.'

Although I lived in a large city, in truth I lived in a small town within that city's preserves. The few whites I knew who were aware of Charlie Parker were my brother's friends and were wrapped away from me in a worldly remoteness. I stumbled to get the record. When I shucked the jacket off he said, 'You don't have to play it.' He went on, 'I'll take "Well You Needn't" by Thelonius Monk and "Night in Tunisia" by Dizzy Gillespie.'

My brain didn't want to accept the burden of my ears. Was that a white man talking? I looked to see if maybe he was a Creole. Many Negroes from the bayou country could and did pass for white. They, too, had hank-straight black hair, dark eyes and shell-cream skin.

There was nothing like a straight question: 'Are you from Louisiana?'

'No, I'm from Portland.'

There is a textured grain that colors the black voice which was missing when he spoke. I wrapped his selections and he paid for them and left. I wondered that he had been neither amiable nor rude and that he didn't remind me of anyone I'd ever met.

My two employers and Louise's handsome friend, Fred E. Pierson, cabdriver and painter, were the only whites I knew, liked and partially understood. When I met Fred, his friendliness had caused my old survival apparatus to begin meshing its gears. I suspected him (perhaps hopefully) of being personally (which meant romantically) interested in me. He helped me to paint the seven downstairs rooms at Mother's house and told me of his great and sad and lost love affair and that he liked having me for a friend.

The next weekend the sailor returned. He browsed for a

while, then came to the counter and interrupted my preoccupation with papers.

'Hi.'

I looked up as if startled. 'Hello.'

'Have you any Dexter Gordon?'

'Yes, "Dexter's Blues".' Another Negro musician.

'I'll take that.'

I asked, 'How about a Dave Brubeck?'

'No. Thanks, anyway.' Brubeck was white. 'But anything by Prez? Do you have "Lester Leaps In"?'

'Yes.'

He waited. 'Do you know of any jam sessions around here?'

'Oh, you're a musician.' That would explain it. Members from the large white jazz orchestras visited black after-hours joints. They would ask to sit in on the jam sessions. Black musicians often refused, saying, 'The white boys come, smoke up all the pot, steal the chord changes, then go back to their good paying jobs and keep us black musicians out of the union.'

He said, 'No, I just like jazz. My name is Tosh. What's yours?'

'Marguerite. What kind of name is Tosh?'

'It's Greek for Thomas – Enistasious. The short of it is Tosh. Are there any good jazz clubs here? Any place to meet some groovy people?'

There was Jimbo's, a blue-lighted basement where people moved in the slow-motion air like denizens of a large aquarium, floating effortlessly in their own element.

Ivonne and I went to the night spot as often as possible. She would take money from her catering business and I from my savings; we would put on our finest clothes, and hiding behind dignified façades, enter the always crowded room. Unfortunately, our attitudes were counterproductive. We projected ourselves as coolly indifferent and distant, but the blatant truth was we were out to find any handsome, single, intelligent, interested men.

I told Tosh I didn't know of any places like that in my neighborhood. When he left the store, I was certain he'd find his way to the downtown area, where he would be more welcome.

Louise continued encouraging me toward Christian Science. I gingerly poked into its precepts, unwilling to immerse myself in the depths because, after all, Christian Science was an intellectual religion and the God its members worshiped seemed to me all broth and no bones. The God of my childhood was an old, white, Vandyck-bearded Father Time, who roared up thunder, then puffed out His cheeks and blew down hurricanes on His errant children. He could be placated only if one fell prostrate, groveled and begged for mercy. I didn't like that God, but He did seem more real than a Maker who was just thought and spirit. I wished for a Someone in between.

Louise's partner was Jewish, so I spoke to him of my need and asked him about Judaism. He smiled until he sensed my seriousness, then said he attended Beth Emanu-El. He told me that there was a new rabbi who was very young and extremely modern. A black singer had recorded 'Eli Eli' and I listened to the song carefully. The beautiful high melodies and the low moaning sounded very close to the hymns of my youth. It was just possible that Judaism was going to answer my need. The Torah couldn't be as foreign as *Science and Health*.

For hundreds of years, the black American slaves had seen the parallels between their oppression and that of the Jews in Biblical times.

> 'Go down Moses
> Way down in Egypt land
> Tell old Pharaoh
> To let my people go.'

The Prophets of Israel inhabited our songs:

> 'Didn't my Lord deliver Daniel?
> Then why not every man?
> Ezekiel saw the wheel, up in the middle of the air.
> Little David play on your harp.'

The Hebrew children in the fiery furnace elicited constant sympathy from the black community because our American experience mirrored their ancient tribulation. With that familiarity, I figured Judaism was going to be a snap!

Beth Emanu-El looked like a Tyrone Power movie set. Great arches of salmon-pink rose over a Moorish courtyard. Well-dressed children scuttled from shul and down the wide stairs.

I explained to a receptionist that I wanted to speak to Rabbi Fine.

'Why?' Her question really was, What are you doing within my hallowed halls? She repeated, 'Why?'

'I want to talk to him about Judaism.'

She picked up the phone and spoke urgently.

'This way.' Stiff-legged and stiff-backed, she guided me to the end of a hall. Her gaze rested on me for a still second before she opened the door.

Rabbi Alvin I. Fine looked like a young physical education teacher dressed up for an open house at school. I had thought all rabbis had to be old and bearded, just as all priests were Irish, collared and composites of Bing Crosby and Barry Fitzgerald. He invited me in and offered a seat.

'You want to discuss Judaism?' There wasn't a hint of a snicker in his voice. He could have been asking a question of a fellow rabbi. I liked him.

'I don't know anything about it, so I can't discuss it.'

'Do you want to become a Jew?'

'I don't know. I'd just like to read up on your faith, but I don't know the titles of any books.'

'What is the faith of your fathers?'

'Methodist.'

'And what is it not giving you that you think Judaism would provide?'

'I don't know what Judaism's got.'

'Can you say you have applied yourself to a careful study of the Methodist tenets?'

'No.'

'Would you say you have totally applied the dictates of the Methodist church?'

'No.'

'But you want to study Judaism, an ancient faith of a foreign people?'

He was systematically driving me to defense. If he wanted debate, I'd give him debate.

I said, 'I want to read about it, I didn't say I wanted to join your church. I like the music in the C.M.E. Church and I like the praying, but I don't like the idea of a God so frightening that I'd be afraid to meet Him.'

'Why does your God frighten you?'

It would sound too childish to say that when my minister threatened fire and brimstone, I could smell my flesh frying and see my skin as crisp as pork cracklings. I told him a less personal truth. 'Because I'm afraid to die.'

I expected the bromide: If a person lived a good life free of sin, he or she can die easy.

Rabbi Fine said, 'Judaism will not save you from death. Visit a Jewish cemetery.'

I looked at him and felt the full force of my silliness in being there.

He said, 'I'll give you a list of books. Read them. Think about them. Argue with the writers and the ideas, then come back to see me.' He bent over his desk to write. I knew I would enjoy talking with him about Life, Love, Hate and mostly Death. He gave me the paper and smiled for the first time and looked even more boyish. I thanked him and left, certain that we would continue our discussion soon. I took a year to buy or borrow and read the books, but twenty years were to pass before I would see Rabbi Fine again.

3

Tosh became such a regular in the store that his arrivals raised no eyebrows and black customers even began saying hello to him, although he only nodded a response. He had been discharged from the Navy and found a job in an electrical appliance shop. He had taken a room in the Negro neighborhood and came to the record store every day. We talked long over the spinning records. He said he liked to talk to me because I didn't lie.

I asked how he had come to like black people so much.

'I don't like black people,' he said, dead serious. 'And I don't like Italians or Jews or Irish or Orientals. I'm Greek and I don't like them either.'

I thought he was crazy. It was one thing to be introverted, but another to admit to me that he disliked black people.

'Why do you dislike people?'

'I didn't say I disliked people. Not to like people isn't the same as to dislike them.'

He sounded profound and I needed time to mull over that idea.

I asked if he liked children. He said he liked some children.

I told him about my son, how bright he was and pretty and funny and sweet.

'Does he play baseball?'

I hadn't thought about the physical games Clyde could share with a father. A new world appeared with the question. In my next castle-building session, I would dream about a husband who would take our sons to the park to play baseball, football, basketball and tennis, while our daughter and I made cookies and other refreshments ready for their return.

'No, he doesn't play ball yet.'

'Let's go to the park on your day off. I'll teach him what I know.'

I had not really examined Tosh before. He had thick black hair and the slow, sloe eyes of Mediterranean people. His face was gentle and had an air of privacy. He was handsome, but he fell some distance from the mark I had set for a husband. He was two inches shorter than I and White. My own husband was going to come handsome, six feet three inches and black. I snatched myself away from the vague reflection and set a date for the three of us to go to Golden Gate Park.

My son and Tosh liked each other. They played handball, and after a picnic lunch, Tosh took a portable set from a package and began to teach my son chess. The day ended at my house, where I introduced Tosh to my mother. She was hospitable, just.

'How did you come to meet Maya? Where are you from?' and 'When are you going back?' Tosh held his own before that whirlwind of a woman. He looked directly at her, ignored the implied queries, answering only what he was asked outright. When he left, Mother asked me my intentions.

'He's just a friend.'

She said, 'Well, remember that white folks have taken advantage of black people for centuries.'

I reminded her: 'You know a lot of white people. There's Aunt Linda and Aunt Josie and Uncle Blackie. Those are your friends. And Bailey has those friends Harry and Paul, the table tennis expert.'

'That's what I'm saying to you. They are friends. And that's all. There's a world of difference between laughing together and loving together.'

A few days later I agreed to allow Tosh to take Clyde out alone. They came to the store as I was leaving and Clyde was full of his afternoon.

'We rode on the cable cars and went to Fisherman's Wharf. I'm going to be a ship's captain or a cable car conductor.' His eyes jumped like targets in a game of marbles. 'Mr. Angelos is going to take me to the zoo next week. I'm going to feed the animals. I might become a lion tamer.' He examined my face and added, 'He said I could.'

Although Tosh had said nothing romantic to me, I realized that through my son he was courting me as surely as Abelard courted Héloïse. I couldn't let him know I knew. The knowledge had to remain inside me, unrevealed, or I would have to make a decision, and that decision had been made for me by the centuries of slavery, the violation of my people, the violence of whites. Anger and guilt decided before my birth that Black was Black and White was White and although the two might share sex, they must never exchange love. But the true nature of the human heart is as whimsical as spring weather. All signals may aim toward a fall of rain when suddenly the skies will clear.

31

Tosh grew up in a Greek community, where even Italians were considered foreign. His contact with blacks had been restricted to the Negro sailors on his base and the music of the bebop originators.

I would never forget the slavery tales, or my Southern past, where all whites, including the poor and ignorant, had the right to speak rudely to and even physically abuse any Negro they met. I knew the ugliness of white prejudice. Obviously there was no common ground on which Tosh and I might meet.

I began to await his visits to the shop with an eagerness held in close control. We went to parks, the beach and dinners together. He loved W.C. Fields and adored Mae West, and the three of us howled our laughter into the quiet dark air of art movie houses.

One night, after I had put my son to bed, we sat having coffee in the large kitchen. He asked me if I could read fortunes and put his hand in mine.

I said, 'Of course, you are going to be a great musician and be very wealthy and live a long, rich life.' I laid his hand on the table, palm open.

He asked, 'Do you see where I'm going to be married?'

I was thrust through with disappointment. While I hadn't ever seen him in the 'my husband' role, his attention had been a balm for my loneliness. Now he was saying he was planning marriage. Some childhood sweetheart would arrive on the scene. I would be expected to be kind to her, and gracious.

I looked at the shadowy lines in his hand and spitefully said, 'Your love line is very faint. I don't see a happy marriage in your future.'

He caught my hand and squeezed it. 'I am going to be married, and I'm going to marry you.'

The sounds refused to come together and convey meaning. I am going to marry you. He had to be talking about me, since he was addressing me, yet the two words 'you' and 'marry' had never been said to me before.

Even after I accepted the content of his statement, I found nothing to say.

'A white man? A poor white man? How can you even consider it?' Disbelief struggled across her face. My mother's diamond winked at me as her hand flew about in the air. 'A white man without a pot to piss in or a window to throw it out.'

She was famous for temperamental explosions but she had never been angry enough at me to hurl her full thunderbolt of rage. Now, when I told her of Tosh's proposal, she was accelerating from an 'ing bing' (her phrase for a minor riot) to a full-out tantrum. With alarming speed her pretty butter-colored face became tight and reddened.

'Think of your life. You're young. What's going to happen to you?'

I hoped not much more than had happened already. At three years old I had been sent by train from California to Arkansas, accompanied only by my four year-old brother; raped at seven and returned to California at thirteen. My son was born when I was sixteen, and determined to raise him, I had worked as a shake dancer in night clubs, fry cook in hamburger joints, dinner cook in a Creole restaurant and once had a job in a mechanic's shop, taking the paint off cars with my hands.

33

'Think ahead. What the hell is he bringing you? The contempt of his people and the distrust of your own. That's a hell of a wedding gift.'

And, of course, I was bringing him a mind crammed with a volatile mixture of insecurities and stubbornness, and a five-year-old son who had never known a father's discipline.

'Do you love him? I admit I'd find that hard to believe. But then I know love goes where it's sent, even in a dog's behind. Do you love him? Answer me.'

I didn't answer.

'Then tell me why. Just why are you going to marry him?'

I knew Vivian Baxter appreciated honesty above all other virtues. I told her, 'Because he asked me, Mother.'

She looked at me until her eyes softened and her lips relaxed. She nodded, 'All right. All right.' She turned on her high heels and strutted up the hall to her bedroom.

Bailey came to the house at my invitation. He sat in the kitchen with Tosh as I made an evening meal. They spoke about jazz musicians and the literary virtues of Philip Wylie and Aldous Huxley. Tosh had studied literature at Reed College in Oregon and Bailey had dropped out of high school in the eleventh grade. My brother had continued to read, however, spending his days on the Southern Pacific run waiting table in the dining cars and his nights with Thomas Wolfe, Huxley and Wylie. After dinner, Bailey wished Tosh a good night and asked to speak to me. We stood in the dim doorway.

'You invited me over for something more than dinner, didn't you?'

I had never been successful in keeping anything from Bailey.

'I guess so.'

'He's in love with you. Did you know that?'

I said he hadn't told me.

Bailey leaned against the door; his dark, round face in the shadow was broken open by a white smile. 'A smart man only tells half of what he thinks. He's a nice cat, Maya.'

Bailey had been my protector, guide and guard since we were tots, and I knew, despite the disparity in our sizes, that he would remain my big brother as long as we lived.

'Bail, do you think it's all right if I marry him?'

'Did he ask you?'

'Yes.'

'Do you want to?'

'Yes.'

'What are you waiting for?'

'People will talk about me.'

'Marry him, Maya. Be happy and prove them all fools and liars.'

He gave me a typically sloppy Bailey kiss on the cheek and left.

Tosh and I were married in the Courthouse on a clear Monday morning. To show her displeasure, Mother moved her fourteen rooms of furniture to Los Angeles three days before the ceremony.

We rented a large flat, and on Tosh's orders I quit my job. At last I was a housewife, legally a member of that enviable tribe of consumers whom security made fat as butter and who under no circumstances considered living by bread alone, because their husbands brought home the bacon. I had a son, a father for him, a husband and a pretty home for us to live in. My life began to resemble a *Good Housekeeping* advertisement. I cooked well-balanced meals and molded fabulous jello desserts. My floors were dangerous with daily applications of wax and our furniture slick with polish.

Clyde was sprouting with independence and opinions. Tosh told him often and with feeling that he was absolutely the most intelligent child in the world. Clyde began calling Tosh 'Daddy,' although I had concocted and given him a dramatic tale during his younger years. The story told how his own father had died on the sands of some Pacific island fighting for his life and his country. I would cry at the telling of the fiction, wishing so hard it had been true.

Tosh was a better husband than I had dared to dream. He was intelligent, kind and reliable. He told me I was beautiful (I decided that he was blinded by my color) and a brilliant conversationalist. Conversation was easy. He brought flowers for me and held my hand in the living room. My cooking received his highest praise and he laughed at my wit.

Our home life was an Eden of constant spring, but Tosh was certain the serpent lay coiled just beyond our gate. Only two former Navy friends (white), one jazz pianist (black) and Ivonne were allowed to visit our domestic paradise. He explained that the people I liked or had known or thought I liked were all stupid and beneath me. Those I might meet, if allowed to venture out alone, beyond our catacomb, couldn't be trusted. Clyde was the brightest, most winning boy in the world, but his friends weren't welcome in our house because

36

they were not worthy of his time. We had tickets to silent movies and the early talkies, and on some Sundays, took our trash to the town dump. I came to love Tosh because he wrapped us in a cocoon of safety, and I made no protest at the bonds that were closing around my existence.

After a year, I saw the first evidence of a reptilian presence in my garden. Tosh told Clyde that there was no God. When I contradicted him, he asked me to prove His presence. I countered that we could not discuss an Entity which didn't exist. He had been a debater at his university and told me that he could have argued either side with the same power; however, he knew for a fact there was no God, so I should surrender the discussion.

I knew I was a child of a God who existed but also the wife of a husband who was angered at my belief. I surrendered.

I tucked away the memory of my great-grandmother (who had been a slave), who told me of praying silently under old wash pots, and of secret meetings deep in the woods to praise God ('For where two or three are gathered together in my name, there am I in the midst of them'). Her owner wouldn't allow his Negroes to worship God (it might give them ideas) and they did so on pain of being lashed.

I planned a secret crawl through neighborhood churches. First I took a nice dress to Ivonne's house and left it, explaining my intent. Then, on at least one Sunday a month, I would prepare a good breakfast for my family and an equally good lie in order to get out of the house. Leaving Clyde at home (he hadn't the experience to lie), I would hurry to Ivonne's, put on the Sunday dress and rush to church. I changed sites each month, afraid that too many repeated visits would familiarize my face and that on some promenade with Tosh I would be stopped by a church member and possibly asked about last week's sermon.

The spirituals and gospel songs were sweeter than sugar. I wanted to keep my mouth full of them and the sounds of my people singing fell like sweet oil in my ears. When the polyrhythmic hand-clapping began and the feet started tapping, when one old lady in a corner raised her voice to scream 'O Lord, Lordy Jesus,' I could hardly keep my seat. The ceremony drove into my body, to my fingers, toes, neck and thighs. My extremities shook under the emotional possession. I imposed my will on their quivering and kept them fairly still. I was terrified that once loose, once I lifted or lost my control, I would rise from my seat and dance like a puppet, up and down the aisles. I would open my mouth, and screams, shouts and field hollers would tear out my tongue in their rush to be free.

I was elated that I could wallow in the ceremonies and never forsake control. After each service I would join the church, adding my maiden name to the roster in an attempt to repay the preacher and parishioners for the joyful experience. On the street I felt cleansed, purged and new. Then I would hurry to Ivonne's, change clothes and go back to my own clean house and pretty, though ungodly, family.

After watching the multicolored people in church dressed in their gay Sunday finery and praising their Maker with loud voices and sensual movements, Tosh and my house looked very pale. Van Gogh and Klee posters which would please me a day later seemed irrelevant. The scatter rugs, placed so artfully the day before, appeared pretentious. For the first few hours at home I kept as tight a check on my thoughts as I had held over my body in church. By the evening meal, I was ready again for cerebral exercises and intellectual exchange.

4

During the first year of marriage I was so enchanted with security and living with a person whose color or lack of it could startle me on an early-morning waking, and I was so busy keeping a spotless house, teaching myself to cook and serve gourmet meals and managing a happy, rambunctious growing boy that I had little time to notice public reactions to us. Awareness gradually grew in my mind that people stared, nudged each other and frowned when we three walked in the parks or went to the movies. The distaste on their faces called me back to a history of discrimination and murders of every type. Tosh, I told myself, was Greek, not white American; therefore I needn't feel I had betrayed my race by marrying one of the enemy, nor could white Americans believe that I had so forgiven them the past that I was ready to love a member of their tribe. I never admitted that I made the same kind of rationalization about all the other non-blacks I liked. Louise was white American (but she was a woman). David was white (but he was Jewish). Jack Simpson, Tosh's only friend, was plain white (but he was young and shy). I stared back hard at whites in the street trying to scrape the look of effrontery off their cruel faces. But I dropped my eyes when we met Negroes. I couldn't explain to all of them that my husband had not been a part of our degradation. I fought against the guilt which was slipping into my closed life as insidiously as gas escaping into a sealed room.

I clung to Tosh, surrendering more of my territory, my independence. I would ignore the straightness of his hair which worried my fingers. I would be an obedient, dutiful wife, restricting our arguments to semantic differences, never contradicting the substance of his views.

Clyde stood flinching as I combed his thick snarled hair. His face was screwed into a frown.

'Mom – ouch – when am I going to grow up – ouch – and have good hair like Dad's?'

The mixed marriage bludgeoned home. My son thought that the whites' straight hair was better than his natural abundant curls.

'You are going to have hair like mine. Isn't that good?' I counted on his love to keep him loyal.

'It's good for you, but mine hurts. I don't like hurting hair.'

I promised to have the barber give him a close cut on our next visit and told him how beautiful and rich he looked with his own hair. He looked at me, half disbelieving, so I told him about a little African prince named Hannibal, who had hair just like his. I felt a dislike for Tosh's hair because of my son's envy.

I began scheming. There was only one way I could keep my marriage balanced and make my son have a healthy respect for his own looks and race: I had to devote all my time and intelligence to my family. I needed to become a historian, sociologist and anthropologist. I would begin a self-improvement course at the main library. Just one last church visit, then I would totally dedicate myself to Tosh and Clyde and we would all be happy.

The Evening Star Baptist Church was crowded when I arrived and the service had begun. The members were rousing a song, urging the music to soar beyond all physical boundaries.

> 'I want to be ready
> I want to be ready
> I want to be ready
> To walk in Jerusalem, just like John.'

Over and over again the melodies lifted, pushed up by the clapping hands, kept aloft by the shaking shoulders. Then the minister stepped out away from the altar to stand at the lip of the dais. He was tall and ponderous as befitted a person heavy with the word of God.

'The bones were dry.' The simple statement sped through my mind. 'Dry Bones in the Valley' was my favorite sermon. The song that whites had come to use in mimicry of the Negro accent, 'Dem Bones' was inspired by that particular portion of the Old Testament. Their ridicule – 'De toe bone connected to de foot bone, foot bone connected to de ankle bone, ankle bone connected to de . . .' – in no way diminished my reverence for the sermon. I knew of no teaching more positive than the legend which said that will and faith caused a dismembered skeleton, dry on the desert floor, to knit back together and walk. I also knew that that sermon, properly preached, could turn me into a shouting, spinning dervish. I tried for the first few minutes to rise and leave the church, but the preacher swung his head to look at me each time I poised myself to leave. I sat again. He told the story simply at first, weaving a quiet web around us all, binding us into the wonder of faith and the power of God. His rhythm accelerated and his volume increased slowly, so slowly he caught me off guard. I had sat safe in my own authority in so many churches and waited cautiously for the point in the service when the igni- tion would be sparked, when 'the saints' would be fired with the spirit and jump in the aisles, dancing and shaking and shouting their salvation. I had always resisted becoming a part of that enchanted band.

The minister's voice boomed, 'These bones shall walk. I say these bones shall walk again.'

I found myself in the aisle and my feet were going crazy under me – slithering and snapping like two turtles shot with electricity. The choir was singing 'You brought my feet out the mire and clay and you saved my soul one day.' I loved that song and the preacher's voice over it measured my steps. There was no turning back. I gave myself to the spirit and danced my way to the pulpit. Two ushers held me in gloved hands as the sermon fell in volume and intensity around the room.

'I am opening the doors of the Church. Let him come who will be saved.' He paused as I trembled before him.

'Jesus is waiting.' He looked at me. 'Won't somebody come?'

I was within arm's reach. I nodded. He left the altar and took my hand.

'Child, what church were you formerly affiliated with?' His voice was clear over the quiet background music. I couldn't tell him I had joined the Rock of Ages Methodist Church the month before and the Lily of the Valley Baptist the month before that.

I said, 'None.'

He dropped my hand, turned to the congregation and said, 'Brothers and sisters, the Lord has been merciful unto us today. Here is a child that has never known the Lord. A young woman trying to make her way out here in this cruel world without the help of the ever-loving Jesus.' He turned to four old ladies who sat on the front row. 'Mothers of the Church, won't you come? Won't you pray with her?'

The old women rose painfully, the lace handkerchiefs pinned in their hair shook. I felt very much in need of their prayers, because I was a sinner, a liar and a hedonist, using the sacred altar to indulge my sensuality. They hobbled to me and one in a scratchy voice said, 'Kneel, child.'

Four right hands overlapped on my head as the old women began to pray. 'Lord, we come before you today, asking for a special mercy for this child.'

'Amens,' and 'Yes, Lords' sprang around the room like bouncing balls in a cartoon sing-along.

'Out, Devil,' one old lady ordered.

'She has come to you with an open heart, asking you for your special mercy.'

'Out of this baby, Devil.'

I thought about my white atheist husband and my son, who

was following in his nonbelieving footsteps, and how I had lied even in church. I added, 'Out, Devil.'

The raspy voice said, 'Stretch out, child, and let the Devil go. Make room for the Lord.'

I lay flat on the floor as the congregation prayed for my sins. The four women commenced a crippled march around my body.

They sang,

'Soon one morning when death comes walking in my room,
Soon one morning when death comes walking in my room,
Oh, my Lord,
Oh, my Lord,
What shall I do?'

They were singing of their own dread, of the promise of death whose cool hand was even then resting on their frail shoulders. I began to cry. I wept for their age and their pain. I cried for my people, who found sweet release from anguish and isolation for only a few hours on Sunday. For my fatherless son, who was growing up with a man who would never, could never, understand his need for manhood; for my mother, whom I admired but didn't understand; for my brother, whose disappointment with life was drawing him relentlessly into the clutches of death; and, finally, I cried for myself, long and loudly.

When the prayer was finished I stood up, and was enrolled into the church roster. I was so purified I forgot my cunning. I wrote down my real name, address and telephone number, shook hands with members, who welcomed me into their midst and left the church.

Midweek, Tosh stood before me, voice hard and face stony.

'Who the hell is Mother Bishop?'

I said I didn't know.

'And where the hell is the Evening Star Baptist Church?'

I didn't answer.

'A Mother Bishop called here from the Evening Star Baptist Church. She said Mrs. Angelos had joined their church last Sunday. She now must pay twelve dollars for her robe, since she will be baptized in the Crystal Pool plunge next Sunday.'

I said nothing.

'I told her no one who lived here was going to be baptized. Anywhere. At any time.'

I made no protest, gave no confession – just stood silent. And allowed a little more of my territory to be taken away.

5

The articles in the women's magazines did nothing to help explain the deterioration of my marriage. We had no infidelity; my husband was a good provider and I was a good cook. He encouraged me to resume my dance classes and I listened to him practice the saxophone without interruption. He came directly home from work each afternoon and in the evening after my son was asleep I found as much enjoyment in our marital bed as he.

The form was there, but the spirit had disappeared.

A bizarre sensation pervades a relationship of pretense. No truth seems true. A simple morning's greeting and response appear loaded with innuendo and fraught with implications.

'How are you?' Does he/she really care?

'Fine.' I'm not really. I'm miserable, but I'll never tell you.

Each nicety becomes more sterile and each withdrawal more permanent.

Bacon and coffee odors mingled with the aseptic aroma of Lifebuoy soap. Wisps of escaping gas, which were as real a part of a fifty-year-old San Francisco house as the fourteen-foot-high ceilings and the cantankerous plumbing, solidified my reality. Those were natural morning mists. The sense that order was departing my life was refuted by the daily routine. My family would awaken. I would shower and head for the kitchen to begin making breakfast. Clyde would then take over the shower as Tosh read the newspaper. Tosh would shower while Clyde dressed, collected his crayons and lunch pail for school. We would all sit at breakfast together. I would force unwanted pleasantries into my face. (My mother had taught me: 'If you have only one smile in you, give it to the people you love. Don't be surly at home, then go out in the street and start grinning "Good morning" at total strangers.')

Tosh was usually quiet and amiable. Clyde gabbled about his dreams, which had to do with Roy Rogers as Jesus and Br'er Rabbit as God. We would finish breakfast in a glow of family life and they would both leave me with kisses, off to their separate excitements.

One new morning Tosh screamed from the bathroom, 'Where in the hell are the goddamn dry towels?' The outburst caught me as unexpectedly as an upper cut. He knew that I kept the linen closet filled with towels folded as I had seen them photographed in the *Ladies' Home Journal*. More shocking than his forgetfulness, however, was his shouting. Anger generally rendered my husband morose and silent as a stone.

I went to the bathroom and handed him the thickest towel we owned.

'What's wrong, Tosh?'

'All the towels in here are wet. You know I hate fucking wet towels.'

48

I didn't know because he had never told me. I went back to the kitchen, not really knowing him, either.

At breakfast, Clyde began a recounting of Roy Rogers on his horse and Red Ryder, riding on clouds up to talk to God about some rustlers in the lower forty.

Tosh turned, looking directly at him, and said, 'Shut up, will you. I'd like a little fucking peace and quiet while I eat.'

The statement slapped Clyde quiet; he had never been spoken to with such cold anger.

Tosh looked at me. 'The eggs are like rocks. Can't you fry a decent goddamn egg? If not, I'll show you.'

I was too confounded to speak. I sat, not understanding the contempt. Clyde asked to be excused from the table. I excused him and followed him to the door.

He whispered, 'Is Dad mad at me?'

I picked up his belongings, saw him jacketed and told him, 'No, not at you. You know grownups have a lot on their minds. Sometimes they're so busy thinking they forget their manners. It's not nice, but it happens.'

He said, 'I'll go back and tell him 'bye.'

'No, I think you should just go on to school. He'll be in a better mood this evening.'

I held the front door open.

He shouted, ''Bye, Dad.'

There was no answer as I kissed him and closed the door. Fury quickened my footsteps. How could he scream at my son like that? Who the hell was he? A white-sheeted Grand Dragon of the Ku Klux Klan? I wouldn't have a white man talk to me in that tone of voice and I'd slap him with a cof-feepot before he could yell at my child again. The midnight murmuring of soft words was forgotten. His gentle hands and familiar body had become in those seconds the shelter of an enemy.

He was still sitting over coffee, brooding. I went directly to the table.

'What do you mean, screaming at us that way?'

He said nothing.

'You started, first with the towels, then it was Clyde's dream. Then my cooking. Are you going crazy?'

He said, 'I don't want to talk about it,' still looking down into a half-filled cup of near-cold coffee.

'You sure as hell will talk about it. What have I done to you? What's the matter with you?'

He left the table and headed for the door without looking at me. I followed, raising my protest, hoping to puncture his cloak of withdrawal.

'I deserve and demand an explanation.'

He held the door open and turned at last to face me. His voice was soft again and tender. 'I think I'm just tired of being married.' He pulled the door closed.

There is a shock that comes so quickly and strikes so deep that the blow is internalized even before the skin feels it. The strike must first reach bone marrow, then ascend slowly to the brain where the slowpoke intellect records the deed.

I went about cleaning my kitchen. Wash the dishes, sweep the floor, swipe the sputtered grease from the stove, make fresh coffee, put a fresh starched cloth on the table. Then I sat down. A sense of loss suffused me until I was suffocating within the vapors.

What had I done? I had placed my life within the confines

of my marriage. I was everything the magazines said a wife should be. Constant, faithful and clean. I was economical. I was compliant, never offering headaches as excuses for not sharing the marital bed.

I had generously allowed Tosh to share my son, encouraging Clyde to think of him as a permanent life fixture. And now Tosh was 'tired of being married.'

Experience had made me accustomed to make quick analyses and quick if often bad decisions. So I expected Tosh, having come to the conclusion that marriage was exhausting, to ask me for a divorce when he returned from work. My tears were for myself and my son. We would be thrown again into a maelstrom of rootlessness. I wept for our loss of security and railed at the brutality of fate. Forgotten were my own complaints of the marriage. Unadmitted was the sense of strangulation I had begun to feel, or the insidious quality of guilt for having a white husband, which surrounded me like an evil aura when we were in public.

At my table, immersed in self-pity, I saw my now dying marriage as a union made in heaven, officiated over by St. Peter and sanctioned by God. It wasn't just that my husband was leaving me, I was losing a state of perfection, of grace.

My people would nod knowingly. Again a white man had taken a black woman's body and left her hopeless, helpless and alone. But I couldn't expect their sympathy. I hadn't been ambushed on a dark country lane or raped by a group of randy white toughs. I had sworn to obey the man and had accepted his name. Anger, first at injustice, then at Tosh, stopped my tears. The same words I had used to voice my anguish I now used to fan the fires of rage. I had been a good wife, kind and

51

compliant. And that wasn't enough for him? It was better than he deserved. More than he could reasonably have expected had he married within his own race. Anyway, had he planned to leave me from the first? Had he intended in the beginning to lure me into trust, then break up our marriage and break my heart? Maybe he was a sadist, scheming to inflict pain on poor, unsuspecting me. Well, he didn't know me. I would show him. I was no helpless biddy to be beckoned, then belittled. He was tired of marriage; all right, then I would leave him.

I got up from the table and cooked dinner, placed the food in the refrigerator and dressed in my best clothes. I left the dinner pots dirty and my bed unmade and hit the streets.

The noontime bar in the popular hotel on Eddy Street was filled with just-awakened petty gamblers and drowsy whores. Pimps not yet clad in their evening air of exquisite brutality spent the whores' earnings on their fellow parasites. I was recognized by a few drinkers, because I was Clydell and Vivian's daughter, because I had worked at the popular record shop or because I was that girl who had married the white man. I knew nothing about strong liquor except the names of some cocktails. I sat down and ordered a Zombie.

I clung to the long, cold drink and examined my predicament. My marriage was over, since I believed the legal bonds were only as good as the emotional desire to make them good. If a person didn't want you, he didn't want you. I could have thrown myself and my son on Tosh's mercy; he was a kind man, and he might have tolerated us in his home and on the edges of his life. But begging had always stuck, resisting, in my throat. I thought women who accepted their husbands' inattention and sacrificed all their sovereignty for a humiliating marriage more unsavory than the prostitutes who were drinking themselves awake in the noisy bar.

A short, thickset man sat down beside me and asked if he could pay for my second Zombie. He was old enough to be my father and reminded me of a kindly old country doctor from sepia-colored B movies. He asked my name and where I lived. I told his soft, near-feminine face that my name was Clara. When I said 'No, I'm not married,' he grinned and said, 'I don't know what these young men are waiting for. If I was a few years younger, I'd give them a run for they money. Yes siree bob.' He made me feel comfortable. His Southern accent was as familiar to me as the smell of baking cornbread and the taste of wild persimmons. He asked if I was 'a, uh, a ah a fancy lady?'

I said, 'No.' Desperate, maybe. Fanciful, maybe. Fancy? No.

He told me he was a merchant marine and was staying in the hotel and asked would I like to come upstairs and have a drink with him.

I would.

I sat on the bed in the close room, sipping the bourbon diluted with tap water. He talked about Newport News and his family as I thought about mine. He had a son and daughter near my age and they were 'some kinda good children' and the girl was 'some kinda pretty.'

He noticed that I was responding to the whiskey, and came near the bed. 'Why don't you just stretch out and rest a little while? You'll feel better. I'll rest myself. Just take off your shoes and your clothes. To keep them from wrinkling up on you.'

My troubles and memories swam around, then floated out the window when I laid my head on the single pillow.

When I awakened, the dark room didn't smell familiar and my head throbbed. Confusion panicked me. I could have been picked up by an extraterrestrial being and teleported into some funky rocket ship. I jumped out of bed and fumbled along the walls, bumping until I found the light switch. My clothes were folded neatly and my shoes peeked their tidy toes from under the chair. I remembered the room and the merchant marine. I had no idea what had happened since I passed out. I examined myself and found no evidence that the old man had misused my drunkenness.

Dressing slowly, I wondered over the next move. Night had fallen on my affairs, but the sharp edges of rejection were not softened. There was a note on the dresser. I picked it up to read under the naked bulb that dangled from the ceiling; it said in effect:

Dear Clara,
    I tell you like I tell my own daughter. Be careful of
strangers. Everybody smile at you don't have to mean you no
good. I'll be back in two months from now. You be a good
girl, hear? You'll make some boy a good wife.
                                                    Abner Green

I walked through the dark streets to Ivonne's house. After I explained what had happened, she suggested I telephone home.

'Hello, Tosh?'

'Marguerite, where are you?' The strain in his voice made me smile.

He asked, 'When are you coming home? Clyde hasn't eaten.'

I knew that was a lie.

'Nor have I. I can't eat,' he said. I wasn't concerned about his appetite.

I said, 'You're tired of being married. Yes? Well, I'll be home when I get there.' I hung up before he could say more.

Ivonne said, 'Maya, you're cold. Aren't you worried about Clyde?'

'No. Tosh loves Clyde. He'll look after him. He loves me too, but I gave up too much and gave in too much. Now we'll see.'

The thought of his loneliness in the large apartment made my own less acute. I slept badly on Ivonne's sofa.

I went home the next day and we resumed a sort of marriage, but the center of power had shifted. I was no longer the dutiful wife ready with floors waxed and rugs beaten, with my finger between the pages of a cookbook and my body poised over the stove or spread-eagled on the bed.

One day my back began to hurt with a sullen ache, the kind usually visited only on the arthritic aged. My head pulsed and my side was punished by short, hot stabs of pain. The doctor advised immediate hospitalization. A simple appendectomy developed complications and it was weeks before I was released. The house was weary with failure – I told my husband that I wanted to go to Arkansas. I would stay with my grandmother until I had fully recovered. I meant in mind, as well as body.

He came close and in a hoarse whisper said, 'Marguerite. Your grandmother died the day after your operation. You were too sick. I couldn't tell you.'

Ah, Momma. I had never looked at death before, peered

into its yawning chasm for the face of a beloved. For days my mind staggered out of balance. I reeled on a precipice of knowledge that even if I were rich enough to travel all over the world, I would never find Momma. If I were as good as God's angels and as pure as the Mother of Christ, I could never have Momma's rough slow hands pat my cheek or braid my hair.

Death to the young is more than that undiscovered country; despite its inevitability, it is a place having reality only in song or in other people's grief.

6

When our marriage ended completely, a year later, I was a saner, healthier person than the young, greedy girl who had wanted a man to belong to and a life based on a Hollywood film, circa 1940.

Clyde was heartbroken by the separation. He acted as if I were the culprit and he and Tosh the injured parties. His once cheerful face was a muddle of solemnity. He grumbled and whined, asked again and again, 'Why did Dad leave us?'

My direct answer of 'Because he and I didn't love each other anymore' frightened him, and when he looked at me his eyes held the wonder: Will you stop loving me, too?

I tried to soothe him by explaining that he was my son, my child, my baby, my joy. But his good sense told him that Tosh had been my husband, my love and his father, and I had been able to sever those bonds. What safety was there for him?

A few months before the separation my mother and her close friend, Lottie Wells, returned to San Francisco from Los Angeles. They opened a café with ten tables and a ten-stool counter where they shared soul-food cooking chores. Lottie was a strong, powerfully built woman the color of freshly made coffee. She spoke softly, hardly above a whisper and was so tender it was impossible to resist loving her. She folded Clyde and me into her care and became our beloved Aunt Lottie.

At first Mother had exhibited no change in her attitude to my marriage, but when she observed my faithful husband, the good provider, and Clyde's love for Tosh, she had said, 'O.K., so I was wrong. He's good. I'm big enough to admit my mistake; are you big enough to understand that I only wanted the best for you?' When I told her later that the marriage was at an end, she only said, 'Well, as I always say, "No matter how good a fellow seems on the outside, you have to take him home to know him."'

Now that I was trying to mend the rift between me and Clyde I appreciated her indifference.

There are few barriers more difficult to breach or more pitiable to confront than that of a child's distrust. I used every wile in the mother's little homemaker kit to win my way back into my son's good graces. I paid attention to his loss and sympathized with him. I taught myself to skate so that we could go to the rink together. At home, I cooked his favorite foods, in portions that would please a cowpuncher and surrendered my reading time to play scrabble and twenty questions and any other diversion he chose. In the street we skipped over cracks in the pavement in a sport he called 'no stepping on the lines.'

Gradually we rebuilt our friendship.

As that emotional worry diminished, a practical one assumed importance. My pride had not allowed me to ask Tosh for money, but he had left me the small bank account and it was dwindling fast. I had to get a job and one that paid enough so I could afford a baby-sitter. I started looking.

Four dingy strip joints squatted cheek by jowl in San Francisco's International Settlement. The exteriors of the Garden of Allah and the Casbah were adorned with amateur drawings of veiled women, their dark eyes sultry with promise and their navels crammed with gems. The Pirates Cave and Captain's Table advertised lusty wenches and busy serving girls with hitched-up skirts and crowded cleavages, all sketched by the same wishful artist.

I stood on the pavement across from the Garden of Allah. A papier-mâché sultan with a lecherous grin winked atop the one-floor building. Around the doorway old photographs of near-nude women curled under a dirty glass façade. Large letters proclaimed BEAUTIFUL GIRLS! CONTINUOUS ENTERTAINMENT! The advertisement had read: 'Female Dancers Wanted. Good take-home pay.'

The interior was dimly lighted and smelled of beer and disinfectant. A large man behind the bar asked if I had come to audition. Most of his attention was centered on checking the bottles.

I said, 'Yes.'

He said, 'Dressing rooms downstairs. Go that way.'

I followed the path of his arm and descended a narrow stairwell. Women's voices floated up to meet me.

'Eddie's a nice Joe. I used to work here before.'

'Yeah. He don't hassle the girls.'

'Hey, Babe, who made that costume?'

'Francis.'

'Frances?'

'Nah, Francis. He male, but he's more twat than you.'

I allowed the light and sound from an open doorway to direct me. A floor-to-ceiling mirror made the four women seem like forty. They were older than I expected and all white. They were taken aback by my presence. I said hello and received hi's and hello's and then a heavy silence.

They busied themselves professionally, gluing on eyelashes and adjusting wigs and attaching little sequined cones to their nipples. Their costumes were exotic, complicated and expensive. Rhinestones twinkled, sequins shone, nets and feathers and chiffon wafted at each movement. I had brought a full leotard, which left only my hands, head and feet exposed. Obviously I couldn't compete with these voluptuous women in their glamorous clothes. I turned to go. Wrong place, wrong time.

'Hey, where ya going? This is the only dressing room.'

I turned back to see a short redhead looking at me.

She said, 'My name's Babe, what's yours?'

I stammered. I ran through all my names, Marguerite, Maya, Ritie, Sugar, Rita. The first three were too personal and the others too pretentious, but since I felt least like Rita, I said 'Rita.'

Babe said, 'You'd better get changed. The band will start soon. What's your routine?'

I had no routine. When I read the ad I had expected to audition for a revue and thought a choreographer would give me steps to do, rather like a teacher asking questions in an examination. I said defiantly, 'I do modern, rhythm, tap and flash.'

Babe looked at me as if I had answered in Latin.

'I mean what's your routine? I'm little Red Riding Hood, see?' She posed, offering her costume for my observation. She wore a red gathered see-through net skirt with folds of the same material draped across her shoulders. Clearly visible beneath the yards of cloth were a red brassiere and a red sequined belt low on her hips; panels of red satin hung from the belt to cover her crotch and the cleavage of her buttocks. A precious little poke bonnet sat on her red curls and at her feet was a cute wicker basket.

I said, 'I see.' And did.

She pointed to an older blonde, whose breasts hung heavy and uncovered.

'That's Rusty. She's Salome' (she pronounced it 'salami'). 'She does the Dance of the Seven Veils. That's Jody, she's the Merry Widow. See? Kate is the only one who's not somebody. She does acrobatics. You know? Flips and splits and things like that. So you gotta have a routine.'

None of the women looked up.

I said, 'Well, I don't have one, so I'd better go home.'

She said, 'Let me see your costume. Maybe we can make one up.'

I was unable to resist Babe's friendliness. Reluctantly I took the balled-up black leotard from my handbag.

'That's it?' Astonishment narrowed her voice into a shriek. The other women looked up for the second time since I'd entered the dressing room.

As usual when I was embarrassed, I responded with an angry stiffness. I said, 'Well, I *am* a *dancer*. I might not have a fancy costume, and I may not have a routine, but I can dance.

61

So don't try to make me look small.' I looked around at each woman as I fought back mortification. The dancers resumed picking at their flesh privately, like cats licking their fur.

Babe said, 'Wait a minute. Don't get your ass on your shoulders. They've never had a colored girl work here. Why don't you try it? I used to work at the Pirates Cave down the street and my best friend was Pat Thomas. She's colored, too.'

I thought I am expected to stand here embarrassed and listen to that old 'colored best friend' lie again. I rolled my leotard and put it in my bag.

Babe said, 'I got an idea. What size are you?'

I told her.

She said, 'I've got a G-string and bra made out of rabbit fur. I'll let you wear it, just for the audition, and you can be Jungle Bunny.'

That was out, and I told her so emphatically.

She said, 'Boy, you sure are sensitive. I didn't mean no harm.'

I said, 'I didn't mean to scream at you.' After all, she had been kind.

'Well, let me think.' Her face worked as she looked at me. She shouted, 'I know, I know.' She bent quickly and began fumbling in an open suitcase on the floor. She pulled out a blue satin set of panties and brassiere. Both pieces were studded with rhinestones and trimmed with blue-dyed feathers. 'Try these on.'

I undressed while the other women finished their make-up, their faces averted from me. I looked closely at the seat of the panties, and although they seemed clean I didn't pull it too close.

62

Babe said, 'Boy, you got yourself a pretty figure,' then she draped yards of blue tulle over me that floated and fell to the floor. 'Now you're Alice Blue Gown. That's your routine. You know the song? It's a waltz.'

The first tuning-up notes of a rhythm band reached the dressing room and the dancers started like robots jerking to attention. They picked up their purses and rushed to the stairs. Babe trailed them.

She whispered, 'They only want four girls and we are five. I hope you get the job. Be real sexy. And don't leave your purse in the dressing room.' She turned and raced for the stairs.

The figure in the mirror was strange to me. A long, mostly straight brown body clothed in a cloud of blue gauze. I would never be able to dance with all that material playing around. I took it off, folded it and laid it on Babe's tote bag. I tried to bring the lyrics of 'Alice Blue Gown' out of my memory. I couldn't remember and I knew I couldn't waltz without a partner. I went upstairs wearing the bra and G-string.

Four white men sat murmuring in the shadows in the back of the club and four black men were playing 'Tea for Two' on the bandstand. Rusty moved across the square polished floor, ridding her body of veils and indifferent to the music. Finally, as the music stopped, she was still as a statue and almost as pale. No hint of sexuality touched her body. And no applause appreciated her performance. She left the stage.

The acrobat took over next as the band began 'Smoke Gets in Your Eyes.' She wore a tasseled green G-string and brassiere and somersaulted, double-somersaulted, back-flipped, held one leg up over her head, showing the green patch that covered her vagina. As the last notes faded in the air she spun and jumped, ending in a perfect split. She jiggled short rises and allowed the floor to kiss her. There was no response from either the men watching or the men playing.

Jody walked onto the stage to the strains of 'Besame Mucho.' She wore black tulle, corseted to her body by a sparkling black waist cincher. Her black-stockinged legs and black patent shoes raced across the floor. She rushed from one side to the other, throwing wicked come-hither looks and tossing her wisps of clothes into the audience. When she finished, clad only in a black G-string and bra, she turned her back, pooched her behind up and looked over her shoulder with a pout. The music had ended, but she waited to her own drummer, then went around collecting the discarded clothing and went downstairs.

When Babe walked onto the stage, the four men fell silent. She nodded to the musicians, put one hand on her hip and held her basket aloft with the other.

The band played 'All of Me' and the woman became a sexy, taunting twelve-year-old. She pranced about the stage offering illicit sex. She stuck out her tongue in a juvenile tease, then changed the purpose by sliding it around her lips insinuatingly, curling it over the corners. Her eyes were hard and wise and her body ample and rounded. Her breasts jiggled and her hips quivered with promise. She stripped to the red G-string and cones which covered her nipples.

When the music stopped, she stood still, looking out toward the men. Her face wrinkled in a strange smile. She had been sexually exciting and knew it. Within seconds, they began their murmuring again, and Babe collected her discarded clothes and waved at the musicians, who grinned in response. She passed me saying nothing.

I waited in the dark, not quite knowing if I should introduce myself or just go up and start dancing, or be sensible, race downstairs, put my clothes on and go home.

A voice shouted, 'Where's the colored girl?'

I nearly answered 'Present.' I said, 'Here.'

'Well, let's go,' the voice ordered.

I walked onto the stage and the musicians stared their surprise. The drummer beckoned to me.

'Hi, honey. What's your routine?'

Certainly not 'Alice Blue Gown.'

I said, 'I don't know.' And added, 'I can dance, but I need something fast to dance to.'

He nodded. 'How about "Caravan"?'

'That's fine.'

He spoke to the other players, counted down four and the music began. I started dancing, rushing into movement, making up steps and changing direction. There was no story, no plan; I simply put every dance I had ever seen or known into my body and onto the stage. A little rhumba, tango, jitterbug, Susy-Q, trucking, snake hips, conga, Charleston and cha-cha-cha. When the music was finished I had exhausted my repertoire and myself. Only after the low talking resumed in the rear did I realize the men had stopped to watch me and that the other women had dressed and were sitting at a small table in the dark.

The drummer said, 'Baby, you didn't lie, you can dance.' All the brown and black faces smiled in agreement.

I thanked them and went downstairs with pride to change clothes. Babe passed me on the stairs, carrying her bag.

She asked, 'How did it go?'

I said, 'O.K. What about these things?' meaning her G-string and bra.

She said, 'Bring them up with you. I'll just put them in my purse.' They would have fit comfortably in a cigarette package.

I said, 'O.K. In a minute.'

The big bartender stood over the table after I joined the other dancers.

He said, 'Rusty, you, and Jody and Kate and—' He turned to me. 'What's your name?'

I said, 'Rita.'

'—and Rita. Start tomorrow.' He looked at Babe. 'Babe, try again. We had you here last year. The customers like new faces.'

He went back to the bar. The three women got up silently and walked over to him. I was embarrassed for Babe, and when I handed the costume to her I wanted to say something kind.

She said, 'Congrats. You've got a job. You'd better go over and talk to Eddie. He'll explain everything. How much, hours and the drinks.'

I said, 'I'm sorry you didn't make it.'

She said, 'Aw, I expected it. All these guys are down on me since last year.'

I asked, 'Why?'

She said, 'I got married. My old man is colored.'

I went to join the others, and the bartender said, 'O.K., Kate, you and the other girls know the routine. See you tomorrow night. You.' Although he didn't look at any of us, he meant me. The bartender was a fleshy man with large hands and a monotone voice. His thin, pink skin barely covered a network of broken veins.

'You worked around here before, Rita?' His eyes were focused on the edge of the bar.

'No.'

'You been a B-girl?'

'No.' I had no idea what he was talking about.

'Salary is seventy-five a week and you work the bar.'

I began to get nervous, wondering if I should tell him I knew nothing about mixing drinks.

He continued, 'If you hustle you can clear ten, fifteen bucks a night. You get a quarter for every champagne cocktail a customer buys for you and two dollars off every eight-dollar bottle of champagne.'

Eddie had given the spiel so often he no longer listened to himself. I began to pick meaning from his litany. I was expected to get men to buy drinks for me and I would get a percentage. Ten extra dollars a night sounded like riches, fur coats and steaks. I rattled around twenty-five cents into ten dollars and choked on the idea of forty cocktails per night. If I told the man I didn't drink, I'd lose the job.

'We use ginger ale and sometimes 7-Up with a lemon twist. And we got the fastest waitresses on the street. Show time is eight o'clock. Six shows a night, six times a week each one of you girls dance fifteen minutes a show.' He shifted his head, the spiel was over. I backed away, but he stopped me. 'Uh, Rita, you belong to the union?'

'No.' I had never heard of a dancers' union or a B-girls' union.

'Soon as we reopen, the AGVA representative'll be down here. Every girl has to belong to the union or we get blackballed. If you want to, we'll advance your initiation fee and you can pay it back in two weekly payments.'

'Thank you.' I was beginning to like this man who talked like a villainous Edward G. Robinson, yet was too withdrawn to look directly at my face.

'I'm only the manager, but the boss thinks that you shouldn't strip. The other girls are strippers. You just dance. And wear costumes like you wore today.' The costume I had borrowed made stripping absolutely unnecessary. 'Most girls buy their materials from Lew Serbin's Costume Company down on Ellis Street. Last thing is this, Rita: we've never had a colored girl here before, so people might say something. Don't get upset. If a customer gets out of line with any of the girls in a coming-on way, I take care of that, but uh, if they say something about your color, I can't help that. 'Cause you *are* colored. Right?' He nearly looked at me. 'And don't go home with any guy or else the police'll be down and close us up.' He turned his back and began typing on the cash register keys.

'See you at seven-thirty tomorrow.'

'Thank you.'

A showgirl. I was going to be a star shining in the firmament of show biz. Once more adventure had claimed me as its own, and the least I could do was show bravery in my strut and courage in the way I accepted the challenge. It was time to celebrate. No bus could take me back fast enough to Ivonne's house, where I had left my son. I stopped a taxi and gave the driver her address.

Ivonne grinned when I told her of my new profession and laughed outright at the salary.

'Seventy-five bones a week. What are you going to do with all that money? Buy a yacht?'

'It's going to be more than seventy-five.' I told her about the

68

drinks and the percentage. Ivonne had the talent of forcing her face absolutely still and looking so intently at an object that her eyes seemed to telescope. She sat a few moments registering my information.

'My. I know you'll try anything once, but be careful. How many Negroes are working down there?'

'Only the guys in the band, as far as I can see. I'm the first Negro dancer they've had.'

'That makes it a little different, doesn't it?' Her voice had descended to a tone just above a whisper.

'I don't see that, Vonne.'

I had always wanted to believe that things were exactly as they seemed, that secrets and furtive acts and intents always made themselves known somehow. So I acted easily or uneasily on the face rather than the hidden depth of things. 'I'm going there to dance and to make some money.'

She got up from the sofa and walked toward the kitchen. Our children's laughter floated out from a back bedroom.

'Aleasar made some spaghetti. Let's eat.'

We sat down at the wrought-iron dinette table.

I asked, 'What worries you about my working down there?'

'I'm not worried, you can take care of yourself.' A smile widened her small mouth as much as it could. 'All I want to say is what the old folks say, "If you don't know, ask." But, don't let anybody make you do something you don't think is right. Your mother already raised you. Stay steady. And if that makes somebody mad, they can scratch their mad place and get glad.'

We laughed together. Our friendship was possible because Ivonne was wise without glitter, while I, too often, glittered without wisdom.

69

7

The costume store gave me the sense of being in a zoo of dead animals. Rusty bear skins hung on one corner rack; their heads flopped on deflated chests and their taloned paws dragged the floor. Ostrich feathers and peacock plumes in tall bottles were swept in a confined arc by each gust of wind. Tiger skins were pinned flat against the walls and lengths of black feather boa lay curled in a glass-topped counter.

I explained to a heavily made up quick-moving black man that I needed some G-strings and net bras and rhinestones. He flounced around the counter with a feather's grace and scanned my body as if I had offered to sell it and he was in the market.

'Who are you, dear?'

I wondered if it was against the store's policy to trade with just anybody.

'I'm Rita. I'm starting to work tomorrow night at the Casbah.'

'Oh no, dear. I mean what's your act? Who are you?'

There it was again. I thought of glamorous black women in history.

'I'm Cleopatra and . . . Sheba.'

He wiggled and grinned. 'Oh, goody. Two queens.'

'And Scheherazade.' If I felt distant from the first two, the last one fitted me like a pastie. She also was a teller of tall tales.

'Then you'll need three changes, Right?'

He had begun to jot notes on a pad. I thought of Ivonne's advice and decided that since I really didn't know what I was doing, I'd better ask somebody.

'Listen, excuse me. I've never danced in a strip joint and in fact, the owners don't even want me to strip. They just want me to wear brief costumes and dance.'

The man's jerky movements calmed, and when he spoke, some of the theatricality had disappeared from his voice.

'You're new?'

I hadn't thought of myself as new since I was seven years old.

'Well, I'm new in the sense that—'

'I mean, you have no act?'

'Yes. I have no act.'

His body took on a stillness as he looked at me. 'I will create your costumes. You will be gorgeous.'

He brought out beige net bras and G-strings and told me how to dye them the color of my skin by soaking them in coffee grounds. I was to sew brown shiny coq feathers on one set for the Sheba dance, red sequins on another for Scheherazade and gold lamé panels on a G-string for my Cleopatra number. He selected a stuffed cobra, which I was to

71

carry when I portrayed the Egyptian Queen, and ankle bells for Scheherazade. Sheba was to be danced with no frills – a brown doe upon the hills.

He seemed to know so much about show business, I asked if he used to dance.

'I was a female impersonator in New York for years, dear. Just years. When I came out here and found I had gotten older, I got this job, and now I sell pretty things to the pretty young boys.'

I paid for the purchases and was grateful that the man hadn't laced sadness in his sad story.

'If you need anything, come back or call me. Ask for Gerry.' He flipped away to another customer, then turned his head over his shoulder in my direction and said, 'Gerry with a "G".' His laughter snapped in the dusty air.

The first shows were anticlimactic. No crowds threw flowers at my bare feet, no deafening bravos exploded when I bowed after dancing for fifteen strenuous minutes. When I realized that I was the only person in the entire night club embarrassed by my near nudity, my embarrassment increased.

My body was all I had to offer and few of the serious-faced men in the audience seemed to notice. There had been scattered applause as the other dancers floated across the stage, flirting with their bodies and snuggling up to the soon-to-be-discarded bits of chiffon. My only applause for the first three performances were the desultory claps from Eddie, who, I decided, was programmed to automatically respond each time an orchestra beat out the closing chord.

The musicians encouraged me as I danced. 'Yeah, baby. That's right, shake it!' Their union had ruled that they must have fifteen minutes off each hour, and Eddie arranged for another pianist to come in and play for the acrobat.

Before the next show, Jack, the drummer, came to the dressing room. He had close-set eyes and a sharp countenance, as if his features had run away from his ears to gather at the center of his face.

'Rita, me and the rest of the cats dig you. Just tell us what you want. We can play anything, but all anybody asks for is "Tea for Two" and "Lady in Red" and "Blue Moon" and everything slow. I play so much draggy music, my butt is dragging. One thing I like about you is you don't drag your butt.' Then he smiled. His lips parted and a million white teeth gleamed. The abrupt change startled me away from my defenses. I stood watching that sparkling smile, unable to think of an appropriate response. His lips suddenly withdrew from the smile with the finality of a door being slammed.

'Here's the rundown. We'll do "Caravan" first. Then, "Night in Tunisia" and "Babalu." Then we go back to "Caravan." Okay?'

I managed an 'O.K.' and Jack left the dank dressing room. I had once fallen in desperate love at first sight when I was seventeen. He was a handsome, cocoa-bean-colored man, whose voice was as soft as mink. He had loved me in return and treated me gently. Now, again, there was a dull whirr in my ears and a tightness around my chest and the man wasn't even handsome, might be a brute or happily married and I didn't even know his last name. I only knew he was a drummer and that the sun rose when he smiled.

When Eddie announced my last turn, 'Here is Rita as the Arabian princess, Scheherazade,' and I went on stage, Jack became the blasé Sultan for whom I danced beautifully. When I finished, there was scattered applause. I turned first to Jack, but he was talking to the pianist. Hastily I remembered my manners, and spun around to bow to the audience. The solemn old men still leaned, hands occupied with diluted drinks. I looked over the audience and found Ivonne sitting alone at one of the tray-sized tables. She smiled and nodded. I smiled back and walked off the stage. Another patter of hands came from a table by the door. I saw two men at a table lighted yellow by the outside amber neons. One looked like a false eye-lashed mannequin; the other was Gerry – spelled with a 'G.'

For the first week after each show, I raced down the concrete stairs and put on my street clothes. Fully dressed, I tried to disregard the contemptuous looks of the strippers who clattered into the room, flung provocative garments over their naked bodies, then without sitting once, went back to the bar and the clients. I was afraid that I would be speechless if a customer spoke and mortified if he didn't. Furthermore, Jack, whose last name I still didn't know, continued to excite my imagination. I couldn't allow him to see me planted on a barstool guzzling down the fraudulent drinks. So when I danced I refused to look at the audience and kept my eyes half shut and my mind centered on Jack.

'Rita.' The bar was empty, except for the musicians packing down their instruments and the strippers waiting for their nightly take. 'Rita.' Eddie's voice caught me with my hand on the door. I turned.

'Come over here.'

I walked back to the bar, the air conditioner had stopped its hum and the room had settled in silence. The women seemed

74

to lean toward me in slow motion and the men on the stage might have been dolls handled by a drowsy puppeteer.

'Rita, we didn't pay your union dues for you to sit downstairs on your can. Do you think that's why we hired you?' He sounded like a teacher admonishing a mischievous child.

'I thought you hired me to dance.' My voice would not follow my urging and it came out nearly whining.

A woman snickered in the prurient dark.

'To dance? Dance?' His cough could have been a chuckle. 'This here's no concert hall. This ain't the San Francisco Ballet Company.'

The pianist laughed out loud. 'Lord, ain't that the truth.'

Eddie continued, 'You want the job?'

Yes. Desperately. I needed the money and I wanted to be near Jack and I loved to dance. I said nothing.

'Tomorrow night, you bring your fanny up here as soon as you change and sit at the bar. First joker that comes in here alone, you ask him for a drink. Or . . .' The unnamed threat hung in my ears. Teacher was brandishing his whipping cane.

'Tomorrow night. One more chance.' He began to count bills, thudding his hand on the bar. 'Okay, Kate. Here's yours.'

Last chance? He didn't know me. There was no chance, absolutely no chance that I'd be there the next night. I went to the door and fumbled at the lock.

'I'll help you, Rita.' I turned to see Jack's sharp face cutting through the gloom. My prince, my sultan.

'Thank you.'

He opened the door easily. The mustard light from the exterior neon sign robbed him of his own color. He slanted toward me and whispered, 'Wait for me. I'll just be a minute.'

Standing in the amber doorway, I decided I would call the sitter and tell her I'd be late. Jack would probably take me to breakfast at one of the popular after-hours places and we could talk softly over the loud music. He would smile his break-of-day smile and I would say how much he meant to me. The job was forgotten.

The musicians came out of the club together. Jack was the only one not surprised to find me at the entrance. He said, 'You cats go on. I'll meet you at the club. I'm going to walk Rita to a cab.' He took my elbow and steered me toward the corner.

'I understand you, Rita.' I knew he did. 'You think taking B drinks makes you cheap. Well, let me tell you it doesn't. These old guys come in strip joints because they want to look at pretty women. Pretty naked women. Some of them are married, but their wives are old and fat or young and mean. They're not trying to get you to go to bed or anything like that. If they wanted prostitutes, they'd go to whorehouses. They just want to see you and talk to you. Personally, I feel sorry for them. Don't you?' We stopped in front of another darkened night club. If he felt sorry for them, I pitied them to pieces. All I wanted from Jack was to know what he thought I ought to be thinking.

'My wife and I talk about them all the time. She's a waitress in a club like the Garden of Allah and every night she's got some story. I pick her up downtown and she right away starts talking about the guys she's waited on.'

A smile began to pull at his face. 'Philomena – pretty name, ain't it? She can tell a story that would break your heart. Or else she can make you split your sides. Anyway . . .' He forced his thoughts back to me. 'It's just life, Rita. Just life. Don't be afraid. You're in that joint to make money. So make

76

it.' He put his hand on my cheek. 'See you tomorrow night.' As he turned I caught a side glimpse of his smile. It was all for Philomena and not a wrinkle of it for me.

I spent the next day girding my mind for battle. I loved to dance and I needed to work. I could create steps and develop new choreographies. If men wanted to buy my drinks, I would accept and tell them that the drinks they were paying for were 7-Up or ginger ale. That, along with imaginative dancing, would erase the taint of criminality. Art would be my shield and honesty my spear, and to hell with Jack and his close-set eyes.

The next night Eddie's face moved slowly in surprise when I appeared at the bar. I gave a smile to encourage him.

'Rita. Well. Decided to join the gang, huh?'

I said, 'I want the job, Eddie.' And kept the grin easy.

'All right. You understand what I told you. Twenty-five cents off every drink and two dollars on a bottle of champagne. There's not many customers yet, but it's early. More'll be coming in soon. You stand a better chance sitting at the bar than at one of the tables. It's too dark for them to see you.'

I couldn't afford to ask if he was making a slur at my color. I grinned and waited.

'Want a little drink to warm you up?'

'No, thanks. I'll wait for a customer to buy me something.'

I looked around the club. A few men had come in, but the other dancers had already fanned out to sit at their tables. There was a dense romance to the room I hadn't noticed before. The white faces hovered like dully lighted globes and the gloom was fired by glinting rhinestone jewelry. The musicians' stands glittered under red, orange and blue revolving spotlights.

Eddie announced, 'And now the Garden of Allah proudly presents Rusty dancing "Salome and the Seven Veils."'

Rusty got up from her chair and shrugged off her filmy wrap. She draped it over the customer's lap and stepped up onstage. Her body angled stiffly across the floor in contradiction to the floating chiffon veils.

I hadn't watched any of the women perform since that first day of audition, and so I sat fascinated with Rusty's conception of what was erotically exciting. She glided and stopped, glided and stopped, while her long, lethargic hands draped to the cups of her bra, promising to remove it, then a better idea motivated them to float away and descend to the chiffon at her crotch where they arrived with the same intent. Miraculously a veil would drift off her figure and slowly onto the floor. Rusty's face seemed divorced from the actions of her body. It wore the resignation of a tired traveler on a cross-country bus ride. I knew that that wasn't carnal, but when I turned to get confirmation from the customers, their eyes were focused on the indifferent dancer. They were using her feinting body to erase their present and catapult themselves into a fantasy where sex-starved women lay submissive and split open like red, ripe watermelons.

If I was going to be a success, I had to elicit if not the quality then the same quantity of response.

I had heard all my life that white males, from boyhood to senility, dreamed of slipping into the slave cabin of young 'hot mommas' and 'ripping off a piece of black tail.' My arrogance and my hatred of slavery would not allow me to consciously batten on that image. I decided during Rusty's dance that I would interest the customers in my movements and hold them in the present, even as a tightrope walker hypnotizes an audience.

Eddie announced, 'Rita dancing Scheherazade.' I stepped upon the stage and into a thousand and one nights. The musicians were forgotten behind me as I moved to the edge of the stage. And the furtive men with their lonely longings became the sultans whom I had to entertain. I watched their faces come alive to me as I pointed and gyrated and swept my arms over my head and out and down to my sides as if I might fly offstage straight to a camel caravan waiting. I convinced myself that I was dancing to save my life, and without knowing why, the audience responded to my predicament. The amount of applause startled me, and even Eddie pursed his lips and nodded as I walked by the bar, headed for the stairs.

The dressing room was empty. I stood amid the costumes and wigs and hair rats considering my success and the next move. There was no time to waste. The men had liked my dance and surely one would buy me a drink. While I toweled my body I planned my strategy. Unlike the other dancers, I would not sit around the bar with kimono or peignoir thrown over my costume. I put on street clothes and went up to the bar.

Eddie showed his pleasure at seeing me by introducing a customer. 'Rita, here is Tom. He wants to buy you a drink.'

The first conversation was repeated so often, all customers might have been handed questions on slips of paper at the door and been forced to memorize the questions.

'Where'd you learn to dance like that?'

'In school.'

'Did you ever make love to a white man?'

'No.'

'Would you like to?'

'No. No, I don't think so.' Leave room for them to hope. Leave space for me to ask for another drink. 'May I have another drink?'

'Sure. Where're you from?'

'N.Y.' N.O.Y.B. None of Your Business.

'Long way from home. Don't you get lonely?'

'This drink is called a champagne cocktail and I get twenty-five cents for every one you buy, but really it's only 7-Up. If you buy a bottle of champagne, it'll cost you eight dollars and I'll get two of that. But at least it'll be real champagne and I can sit with you as long as it lasts.'

The ploy worked, but my interest was never aroused. The men awoke no curiosity in me. I did not follow them in my mind to their hotel rooms or their loveless homes. They were like markers on a highway, to be used without gratitude and to be forgotten without guilt.

The other dancers did not warm to me, nor I to them. They chatted to each other and kept their conversations and their glances to themselves. They had not forgiven me for that first week when I sat haughtily in the dressing room as they hustled around the bar soliciting drinks. And since they had the toughness without the tenderness I had found in Babe, I ignored them completely. Success at cadging drinks changed my public personality. I became sassy to the customers. Quick, brittle words skipped off my tongue like happy children in a game of tag. Some men liked the flippancy and began to come back to the club not only to watch me dance but to buy drinks, listen to me and talk.

8

Two months after I began working in the Garden of Allah the composition of the patronage changed. The lonely men whose hands played with their pocketed dreams slowly gave way to a few laughing open-faced couples who simply came in to watch the show.

Occasionally I would be invited to join a table of admirers. They had been told a good dancer was working in a strip joint. I answered their overused question by telling the truth. 'I'm here because I have to work and because I love to dance.' I also explained about the drinks.

Being so close to the tawdry atmosphere titillated the square couples. I decided they were the fifties version of whites slumming in Harlem's Cotton Club during Prohibition, and while their compliments pleased me, I was not flattered.

Away from the bar my days were cheerful. I was making real money. Enough to buy smart, understated clothes for myself and matching ensembles for Clyde. We spent Saturday afternoons at horror movies, which I loathed. He adored the blood and popping eyes of 'the Wolf Man,' the screams of 'vampire victims' and the menacing camel walk of Frankenstein's monster. He yelled and jumped and hid behind my arm or peeked through his fingers at the grisly scenes.

I asked him why he liked the fearful stories if they frightened him. His reply was a non sequitur. 'Well, Mom, after all, I'm only eight years old.'

Three months passed and I freely spent my salary and commissions in dining at good restaurants, buying new furniture and putting a small portion away for a trip – Ivonne and I had discussed taking our children on a vacation to Hawaii or New York or New Orleans.

I was young, in good health, and my son was happy and growing more beautiful daily.

One night Eddie paid off the other girls first, saying he wanted to talk to me. After they left, he bellyed up to the bar and cast his glance on the bandstand where the musicians were stowing away their instruments. When he didn't look at me, I knew it had to be serious.

'Rita, you're making more money than the other girls.'

I hoped so.

' . . . and they say they have a complaint.'

'What's the complaint, Eddie?'

'They say you must be promising to sleep with the clients. Otherwise why do you end up every night with four or five bottles of champagne and ten dollars or more in cocktails?'

'Eddie, I don't care whether they like it or not. I haven't promised anybody anything. I've just made more money. Let's leave it at that, O.K.?'

'It's not O.K., Rita. They can bring you up on charges with

the union, or even get the club in Dutch. You must be doing something. No new girl makes this kind of money.' His hand covered some dollars on the bar.

My protested innocence was forceful but without explanation. I could not reveal to him that I told all my customers about the ginger ale and that they knew the percentage I made from the champagne.

'Please believe me, Eddie. When I leave here, I go straight to my house and let the baby-sitter take my cab so she can go home. I have a child at home.'

'Rita, it's not me. Far as I'm concerned, you're a straight shooter. Good people. But these other broads. They, uh, what I mean is they can give us a bad time. If they want to make real trouble all they have to do is hint to the right people that girls here accept B drinks.' He wiped at a long-dried spill on the bar and my ears began to burn. 'The State Board of Equalization suspended our license once before.'

I had ignored the fact that officers from the Board visited the club in plain clothes. I told each man who offered me a drink the composition of the drinks and the percentage I would receive. So I had been dense before, but if I thought fast I could recover.

'Eddie, if they do that – I mean, tell the wrong person – they'll lose their jobs, too.'

He found another spot to rub. 'They don't care, not if they get mad enough. They'll just go to work down the street or around the corner. These joints are always looking for experienced girls. And that's what I want to tell you. I'm putting you on notice. Two weeks. You start looking for another place. I'll tell the girls tomorrow night that you're on notice. That ought to make them happy. If you haven't found something in two weeks, I'll try to keep you on a week at a time, but you won't have no trouble finding another job.'

Shock made me patient. I stood silent and sheeplike as he counted out my night's money. In the taxi I gathered his words together and poked at them dully. Two weeks' notice. Fourteen days before the good life faded and my son and I would be cut loose to scud again without anchor. The dancers didn't like me and the disaffection was mutual. If they envied the money I made, I was jealous of the whiteness of their skin that allowed them to belong anywhere they chose to go. They could pick up their tassels and pack up their G-strings and go to another job without hesitation, but I remembered Babe. She was as white as they, but just because she slept side by side with her black husband, she was banned from the street. And what about me? I was black all over. No – the strippers felt nothing for me that I didn't feel for them.

I was always tired after the six shows, but this night sleep did not rush to float me out of exhaustion.

The next evening the dressing room was filled with electricity. The women were costumed, but had not made their customary dash upstairs. When I entered, they all turned to look at me. Sour little grins played on their faces. Rusty said, 'So, you're leaving, huh, Rita?'

I gaped, surprised for a second. Eddie had told them already. I offered them my most gracious smile, looking into each woman's eyes.

'Good evening, ladies. Jody' – turn – 'Kate' – turn – 'Rusty.'

Jody said, 'Lovely evening, isn't it?'

My grandmother would have been proud of me. She had

purred into my ears since babyhood, 'Three things no person worth a hill of beans won't do. One is eat in the street and another is cry in the street. And never let a stranger get your goat.' If they were going to lick their chops over my distress, they would find their tongues stuck to a cake of salt.

Upstairs I greeted Eddie as if he was simply a bartender. I looked away from him quickly and around the club. A few women sat at the tables with male companions. Their two-piece knit dresses and bouffant hairdos were strikingly out of place in the musty club.

I sucked in my breath and followed the opening bars of my music to the stage. Since I was on notice, I could forget the audience and go for myself.

Three fashionably dressed men and a young Marlene Dietrich-looking woman huddled over a table in the center of the room. The woman had a shock of sunlight-yellow hair and brooded over a cigarette holder. The red-haired man had been in before, but had not spoken. Now the four sat watching me as if they were French couturiers and I was wearing the latest creation from Jacques Fath. The more I tried to ignore them, the more they intruded into my mind. Who were they? Some slumming socialites looking for thrills? I tried to give myself to the music, but the group stared so intently that for once the music wouldn't have me, and I stumbled around the floor creating no continuity in my movement and no story in my dance. It occurred to me that they might be talent scouts and maybe I was going to be discovered. I threw that silly thought out of my mind before it could take hold. Lana Turner and Rita Hayworth got discovered, black girls got uncovered.

I changed downstairs in the empty dressing room and half

expected, half wished that the quartet would be gone when I went back upstairs.

'Hello, I'm Don.' The redhead grinned and a map of freckles wiggled across his face. 'This is Barry.'

Barry was a tall, graying man whose smile was distant and distinguished. Don, obviously the major-domo of the group, waved his hand toward a pretty young man whose eyes were beautifully deep.

'This is Fred Kuh, and this' – he gestured like a circus announcer who had saved the lion tamer for the last – 'this is Jorie!'

She shook her head and her hair fell back from her face, heavily as if in slow motion. She spoke in a low, theatrical voice.

'Hello. My dear, you dance divinely. Just divine.'

Not Marlene Dietrich, I was wrong; she was Veronica Lake with substance, a young Tallulah Bankhead. 'And you're so refreshingly young.' Her perfume was thick, like the air in Catholic churches.

I said, 'I'm twenty-one.'

Barry asked if I would have a drink with them and I began my spiel about the B drinks, the percentages and the bad champagne.

Jorie said, 'It's true. My Gawd, it's true. You're right on cue. We were told that you'd say that.'

'What?'

'You're kind of famous, you know.'

Don grinned, 'You must be the only open-faced B-girl on the Barbary Coast.'

'In San Francisco,' said Barry.

86

Jorie corrected: 'In captivity.'

They approved of me and I warmed to them. I allowed myself their flattery. It was easy to suppose they liked me because I was honest. I did not want to pry into their acceptance for fear that what I found would be unacceptable to me. Suppose they thought me a clown?

Barry explained that Jorie was a chanteuse, currently starring at the Purple Onion, a nearby night club. He managed the place and was the emcee. Don Curry and Fred Kuh were bartenders and I was welcome anytime I could get away.

These beautiful people and their friends began dropping in each evening and I awaited their arrival. I danced indifferently until I caught a glimpse of their party near the back of the room, then I offered them the best steps I had and as soon as the dance was finished I hurried over. There was no need to butter up the manager or hustle the customers. It gave me a delicious sense of luxury to be sitting with such well-dressed, obviously discriminating people, while the strippers roamed among the tables looking for the odd drink and the lone man.

9

One evening I was invited to a wine party at Jorie's apartment after closing time. The house sat on a hilly street. A stranger opened the door and took no more notice of me, so I entered and sat on a floor pillow and watched the guests spin around one another in minuet patterns. There were glamorous young men with dyed hair who rustled like old cellophane. Older men had airs of sophistication and cold grace, giving the impression that if they were not so terribly tired they would go to places (known only to a select few) where the conversation was more scintillating and the congregation more interesting.

There were young women who had the exotic sheen of recently fed forest animals. Although they moved their fine heads languorously this way and that, nothing in the room excited their appetites. Unfashionable red lips cut across their white faces, and the crimson fingernails, as pointed as surgical instruments, heightened the predatory effect. Older, sadder women were more interesting to me. Voluminous skirts and imported shawls did not hide their heavy bodies, nor was their unattractiveness shielded by the clanks of chains and ribbons of beads, or by pale pink lips and heavily drawn doe eyes. Their presence among the pretty people enchanted me. It was like seeing frogs buzzed by iridescent dragonflies. The young men, whose names were Alfie, Reggie and Roddy and Fran, hovered around these fat women, teasing them, tickling them, offering to share a portion of their svelte beauty. None of the company spoke to me. That I was one of the three Negroes in the room, the only Negro woman and a stranger as well, was not a sufficiently exotic reason to attract attention.

I sipped the wine and listened to the concert of gossip and bon mots, repartee and non sequiturs.

Don stooped beside me and asked if I was all right and had I met everyone. I told him I was and I had, and added a sincere smile. His high pink color, green eyes and fire-red hair made him the prettiest person at the party, and he had a sense of humor I found missing in the other blades, despite their clacking laughter.

He looked into my eyes and found the lie. He stood and turned quickly. 'Everybody!' He spoke just below a shout. 'Everybody!' Voices quieted. When the room was still, he spread his arms and fanned his fingers away from his wrists and nodded toward me. 'Everybody, this is Rita. She's an artist, a truly tremendous dancer. She is absolutely the world's greatest. I thought you should know.'

People peered at me. Most found nothing remarkable about the announcement and, indeed, if at that moment I had executed a tour jeté from a sitting position, it would not have pried them away from their indifference. Only the plum-soft women marked the statement and cared. Each round face softened and smiled on me.

Don dropped his arms and said rather weakly, 'Well, I just thought you ought to know.' To me he said, 'Don't mind these people, Rita. They're only pretending to be blasé because they don't know what else to pretend to be. I'll get you some wine.'

One large woman came over to me carrying a pillow. She gracefully settled on the floor at my side, denying her bulk.

'I'm Marge.' Then she told me, 'And you're Rita.'

'That's right.'

'And what kind of dancing do you do, Rita?'

'Modern ballet and interpretive.' (I knew a shake dancer named L'Tanya who could quiver her hips so fast they disappeared in a blur and she called her performance interpretive.)

Marge's mouth made an O. One young boy who had been courting her wafted over to us. He folded down beside Marge and arched an arm over her round shoulders, his hand dropping on the rise of her breast.

'And what have we here, Mother dear?'

She nearly suppressed a giggle. 'Reggie, you're too naughty.'

He turned to me, holding his lips tight. 'How now, brown cow?'

I knew or should have known it would be a matter of time before some racial remark would be made. Here this chit was calling me a brown cow.

'Rita, this is Reggie. Isn't he a naughty boy? Naughty, naughty.' She nearly kitchy-kooed his chin.

I made my diction as prudish as the young man's was prissy. 'I haven't the faintest idea whether he's naughty or not. I do know that if he's your son, at least one of you has something to be ashamed of.'

Reggie blanched and tightened. 'You have a nasty mind to go with that nasty mouth.' His voice sharpened with indignation. 'What are you doing here, anyway? Who asked you?' He began to tremble.

Marge said, 'There's no reason to get excited, Reggie baby. Calm down, hear? Just consider the source.' She slipped out of his embrace and put both arms around his back and pulled him over into her lap. 'There now, baby, there, there.' She pressed chunky fingers on his hair and then looked up at me distraught.

I was thoroughly displeased with myself. I murmured 'Sorry' and rose to go, but a door opened behind me and I turned. Jorie stood in the doorway. She wore a long black dress and lights leaped in her hair.

'Well, darlings, aren't you kind. You started without me.' She laughed at her own good humor. I liked her more at that moment than I had before. She didn't appear to take herself too seriously. When she saw me she gave a little shriek of delight.

'How marvelous, Rita! You didn't forget. Has everyone met this most divine dancer?'

She came toward me as if she was going to take my hand like a referee and proclaim me champion. She stopped and patted my shoulder. 'Have you had wine? Are they treating you all right?'

I told her that they were and, satisfied, she walked on to meet the other guests.

I was in a quandary. Obviously I couldn't leave the moment

the hostess made her appearance, and just as obviously I couldn't sit back down on the floor near Marge and Reggie, who had finished ministering to each other's sorrow and were watching Jorie's movements keenly.

I wandered into the kitchen and claimed a drink. I had not drunk much dry wine before that night, but if white people could drink wine like Kool-aid, then there was no reason on God's green earth I could not do the same. The second glass went down smoother than the first and the third more swiftly than the second. Alone, seated in a strange house filled with strangers, I felt as if I were in dangerous waters, swimming badly and out of my depth. I was plankton in an ocean of whales. The image was so good I toasted it with another glass of wine. Loud laughter penetrated the closed door and I wondered how people became so poised, so at ease. Sophistication was not an inherent trait, nor was it the exclusive property of whites. My mother's snappy-fingered, head-tossing elegance would have put every person in the room to shame. If she walked in the house uninvited, even unexpected, in seconds she would have the party clustered around her, filling her glass, listening to her stories and currying for one of her brilliant smiles. My mother was more elegant than Kay Francis and Greer Garson put together, prettier than Claudette Colbert (who I secretly thought was the prettiest white woman in the world) and funnier than Paulette Goddard. Oh, yes. I drank a glass of wine to my mother.

When I found the door leading from the kitchen, I walked back into a near-empty living room. I would have sworn that I had spent no more than fifteen minutes over the wine, but it would have been impossible for the room to clear in that time.

Jorie, Don, Barry and Fred sat in easy chairs listening intently to a record. Gertrude Lawrence or Bea Lillie sang shakily in a reedy voice.

I interrupted, 'Oh, hello.'

They jumped up, startled into speaking all at once.

'Where have you been?'

'I thought you had gone.'

'What were you doing?'

'Where have you been?'

I told them I'd been in the kitchen drinking wine.

Jorie collected herself. 'Well, my dear, it's awfully late, but do come and sit a minute.'

My progress across the room was not as steady as I wanted, but I proceeded in what I hoped was a dignified manner.

Don got up and led me to a chair.

Barry said, 'We're listening to some songs for Jorie's act. She's going to open in New York at the Blue Angel.'

Jorie shook out her hair. 'My God, I've got to make New Yorkers laugh. That's what I call a challenge. What have New Yorkers got to laugh about?'

I said, 'But I thought you were a singer.'

Don said, 'She's a singer-comedienne. And' – he became protective – 'she's bloody brilliant.'

Jorie touched Don lightly and smiled, 'You don't need to defend me. She didn't say I wasn't bloody brilliant.'

Don caught her affectionate tone. 'Sorry, Rita, but of course you've never seen Jorie perform, have you?'

Barry said, 'And she won't, either. Her working hours, remember? Jorie leaves in three weeks.'

At that moment I thought about my job and covered my

fear by blurting out, 'I'll be able to see you next week. I'm on notice at the club.'

'You mean you've been fired?' Disbelief raised Don's voice and widened his eyes.

Jorie said, 'But, darling, you're the only talent they've got. I mean. Surely they don't think people come there to see those awful strippers in their awful sequins. I mean.'

I explained why I was fired, putting the blame on jealousy.

Barry asked what I'd do next and I could not answer. Only a small savings account stood between me and poverty.

'It's a pity you don't sing,' Barry said in his clipped accent. 'The Purple Onion needs someone to take Jorie's place.'

I had not told them I could sing.

'What about folk songs?' Jorie said. 'My dear, everyone, but every single soul today, knows at least one folk song. Of course, it has one thousand verses and lasts for two hours without intermission. I mean.'

Everyone laughed and I joined in. Not because I agreed, but because I was pleased to be in such clever company.

I said, 'I know a calypso song.'

The men exchanged knowing looks with Jorie, then turned to me, straight-faced for a minute, and broke into a mean laughter.

'That's a good one. Oh, Rita, you're good.'

They were laughing at me and I was expected to join them. Only the secure can bear the weight of a joke and only the very secure can share in the laughter.

'Do you think calypso music isn't folk music? Folks sing it. Or do you believe because the folks are Negroes their music does-n't count, or that because they're Negroes they aren't folks?'

It was obvious that my anger was unexpected. A pale shock registered on their features. Don's eyebrows rose, making him look like a leprechaun tricked out of his burrow. Barry, having found my loss of control distasteful, averted his eyes. Jorie blinked and winked her false eyelashes. Fred Kuh, who had said little, quietly offered: 'No one meant to hurt your feelings, Rita. Jorie has a passion against calypso. That's all there is to it.'

'What's wrong with calypso?' I had so strongly pulled anger to me as a defense that I could not shoo it away merely because it was no longer needed.

Fred said, 'I think it's because the singers rely more on the beat than on storytelling. And Jorie's concerns are just the opposite.'

'Oh, my dear' – Jorie was back with us – 'It's the god-awful thump, thump, thump. It's the "de man," "de girl," "de boat." My God, haven't we got beyond "dis" and "dat"? Really.'

It was a question of how I was to show that I was mollified without seeming to surrender my advantage.

'When you or any white person says "dis" or "dat," it is certain that you intend to ridicule. When a black person says it, it is because that's the way he speaks. There's a difference.' There was a delicious silence. For the moment, I had them and their uneasiness in the palm of my hand. The sense of power was intoxicating.

'You say you dislike calypso and that the songs have no story line. Do you know "Run Joe" by Louis Jordan?'

Their heads shook, which showed they were not totally immobilized.

'It goes like this.' I stood.

95

'Moe and Joe ran a candy store
Telling fortunes behind the door
The police came in and as Joe ran out
Brother Moe, he began to shout
    Run Joe
        Hey, the man at the do'
    Run Joe
        The man he won't let me go
    Run Joe
        Run as fast as you can
    Run Joe
        The police holding me hand.'

I had played Louis Jordan's record until it was gun-metal gray, so I knew every rest and attack of the song. I stretched my arms and waved my hands and body in a modified hula, indicating how fast Joe made his getaway. I tugged away from an imaginary policeman showing the extent of restraint imposed on Moe. I spun in place in the small area, kneeled and bowed and swayed and swung, always in rhythm.

When I finished the song, which seemed to consist of fifty verses, the assembly applauded loudly and their smiles were brilliant.

Jorie lifted a handful of hair and said, 'But I mean, pet, you can sing. Have you ever sung before?'

Don said, 'It's obvious you have. But professionally?'

When I was growing up in Stamps, Arkansas, Momma used to take me to some church service every day of the week. At each gathering we sang. So I knew I could sing. I did not know how well. Our church was bare because the parishioners

96

were poor and our only musical instruments were tambourines and our voices. I had never sung to piano accompaniment, and although my sense of rhythm was adequate, I had not the shadow of an understanding of meter.

Jorie said, 'But, my dear, if you can sing like that you should take my place at the Purple Onion. You'll be a smashing success. I mean they will simply adore you.'

'How many songs like that do you know?'

'How many musicians will you need?'

'What about gowns?'

'Can you have an act together in three weeks?'

My God. My world was spinning off its axis, and there was nothing to hold on to. Anger and haughtiness, pride and prejudice, my old back-up team would not serve me in this new predicament. These whites were treating me as an equal, as if I could do whatever they could do. They did not consider that race, height, or gender or lack of education might have crippled me and that I should be regarded as someone invalided.

The old habits of withdrawing into righteous indignation or lashing out furiously against insults were not applicable in this circumstance.

Oh, the holiness of always being the injured party. The historically oppressed can find not only sanctity but safety in the state of victimization. When access to a better life has been denied often enough, and successfully enough, one can use the rejection as an excuse to cease all efforts. After all, one reckons, 'they' don't want me, 'they' accept their own mediocrity and refuse my best, 'they' don't deserve me. And, finally, *I* am better, kinder, truer than 'they,' even if I behave badly and act shamefully. And if I do nothing, I have every right to my idleness, for, after all, haven't I tried?

Jorie said, 'Of course you won't get the mint or probably half of what you're making now. But, my dear, if you're not working after next week, you may as well take this on. For the time being.'

They began to make me up. I had to change my name. And wouldn't it be super duper if I had another origin? Something more exotic than tired old Southern Negro. People were tired of the moss hanging from the magnolia trees and the corn pone and the lynchings and all that old stuff. Anyway, I couldn't compete with Josh White, or Odetta, who I thought was the greatest singer of American Negro folk songs, and who worked nearby.

Couldn't we come up with something gayer, less guilt-awakening?

Jorie, Don and Barrie, along with quick assists from Fred, poked around in their imaginations as I sat watching. It was three o'clock in the morning and they were like children amusing themselves with play dough on a rainy day.

Because I was tall, I should be very grand, possibly from a long line of African kings. And could I speak any African?

I had studied African dance with Pearl Primus, but I had never met an African face-to-face. In fact, in the Negro community of 1953 the phrase used to describe a loud and uncaring person was 'as uncouth as an African.' I had lost a job in a leading dance school in Cleveland because I promised to teach 'African primitive dance' to the children of the black middle class.

No, I did not know any African. But I did speak Spanish.

Jorie announced that she had an idea: I could be Cuban. That was it. I could be a Cuban who spoke little English, although I sang in the language. I should be torrid and passionate onstage, but haughty and distant offstage: 'Rita, the Cuban Bombshell,' the Latin señorita whose father was a Watusi chieftain sold in Cuba.

They were casting me as the star in a drama and I had no real desire to refuse the role. I feebly wondered aloud what would happen if I was discovered a phony. Herb Caen, the acerbic columnist, was a Janus creature, who guarded the local past while guiding the locals' future. He liked Jorie and Stan Wilson and Mort Sahl. But, what if he found that I was a fraud? He could make me the laughingstock of San Francisco.

My new friends countered, 'Why should he care? If he did find out and mentioned it, San Franciscans would be amused.' People would laugh *with* me, rather than at me. After all, the city had more eccentrics than lights on the Golden Gate Bridge.

I not only agreed to the charade but began adding my own touches. My father, the Watusi chieftain, had not been a slave (ah, to rid myself of that stigma) but was the son of a chief who had sailed to Cuba to retrieve his sister, who had been stolen from Africa. Once there, he had fallen in love with a dark-eyed Spanish girl. He had won her after a bloody duel, married her and she had given birth to my father. They, my very well-to-do parents, had sent me to the United States so that I could see some of the world before I married and settled down in my own well-staffed hacienda.

My audience listened, mouths agape, as I reeled my story before them. Their imaginations had been good, but mine was better. They had been amusing themselves, but I was motivated by the desire to escape.

Ivonne sat watching me as I talked. She nodded to indicate not so much that she agreed with me but, rather, that she comprehended what I was saying.

'So I'm going to sing at the Purple Onion. I'll sing calypso songs. Jorie Remus, who is the star there now, and the manager and bartenders are fixing it all up.' I sipped the beer I had brought for a celebration. 'They're all white, but they're nice. Sort of like foreigners.'

She inclined her head.

'I mean they are Americans, but Jorie has lived in Paris. In France. And I guess that's why she's kind of different.'

Ivonne drank beer and waited. Our friendship had brought us so close, she sensed that I had something more to say and that what I was saving until last was the most pertinent of my news.

'They remind me of Hemingway and Gertrude Stein and that group that lived in France, you know?'

Because she had not read the books I had read, the names I mentioned did not bring to her visions of the Left Bank and Montmartre. She made no connections with a gay time when America's good white writers sat in places like the Deux Magots dreaming up a literature which would enthrall the world for decades.

My friend was at ease in her silence.

'So they suggested I change my name and . . .' What had been easy to accept in the company of strangers was almost unspeakable now in Ivonne's familiar living room.

I had thought only that an attempt to pass was an acceptance of that which was not true. As I searched for words, it occurred to me that what I was about to do was to deny that which *was* true.

'They suggested that I say I came from Cuba.'

Her black eyes and voice were equally cold and hard.

'Oh, Ivonne. For the romance. Just because it'll make me more exotic.'

'They want you to stop being Negro . . .'

'Oh no, come on.'

'And you say these people are free? Free of what? And free for what?'

'You don't understand.' I was exasperated with her. She and my mother had more in common than I had with either of them. 'And I'm going to sing. I'm going to have a new career.'

'You're going to sing Cuban songs? Like Carmen Miranda? With bananas on your head going "Chi chi boom boom?"' Sarcasm syruped in her voice.

'Listen, Vonne, I'm going to sing calypsos. And I'm going to be good.' I didn't relish having to defend myself. She was my friend. We shared secrets and woes and each other's money. We had keys to each other's houses and together watched our children grow.

'Just listen to this.' I got up and took a place in front of the coffee table.

> 'He's stone cold dead in de market
> Stone cold dead in de market
> Stone cold dead in de market
> I kill nobody but me husband.'

My voice faltered and fell. I lifted it into a shout. When it sharpened into a screech I softened it. I fled between and over the notes like a long-distance runner on a downhill patch. When it was all over, I had sung in about three keys and Ivonne leaned back on the nearly paid-for sofa. A small resigned smile played hide-and-seek on her face.

She said, 'I'll say this for you, Marguerite Johnson' – no one had called me by that name in years – 'You've got a lot of nerve.'

And she was right.

10

North Beach bubbled as noisily and colorfully as the main street in a boom town. Heavy drumbeats thudded out of the doors of burlesque houses. Italian restaurants perfumed the air for blocks while old white-shirted men loudly discussed their bocce games in Washington Square. Pagoda signs jutted from tenements in Chinatown and threatened the upturned faces of milling tourists. One block away on Columbus Avenue, Vesuvio's bar was an international center for intellectuals, artists and young beats who were busily inventing themselves. Next door, Allen Ginsberg and Lawrence Ferlinghetti read their new poetry at the City Lights Bookstore. Two hundred yards down Columbus, the Black Cat bar was a meeting place for very elegant homosexuals who draped themselves dramatically beside the bar and spoke loudly and familiarly of 'culture.'

The Purple Onion was a basement cabaret which Jorie called *la Boîte* (Don translated that into 'the sardine can'). Its walls were painted a murky purple, and although it was supposed to accommodate two hundred people, well over that number crowded into the room the first night I went to catch the show, and the air was claustrophobically close. Jorie in a simply cut, expensive black dress leaned her back against the curve of the piano. She partly sang and partly talked a torch song, waving a cigarette holder in one hand and languorously moving a long chiffon scarf in the other. Her voice scratched lightly over the notes.

> 'He's just my Bill
> An ordinary guy
>> you'd see him on the street
>>> [pause]
> And never notice him.'

She looked at the audience directly, shrugging her thin shoulders. Her look said that Bill really was quite awful and she had little understanding of why she herself had noticed Bill. Before our eyes she changed from the worldly-wise woman, disillusioned by a burnt-out love affair, into a 'regular' girl who was just one of the folks. The audience howled at the transformation, delighted by having been taken in.

I sat in the rear enthralled. It was hard to believe I was being asked to move into this brilliant woman's place, although my audition had gone well enough. The Rockwell family, led by the elder son, Keith, owned the club, and without much enthusiasm had signed a six-month contract with a three-month option for my services.

Jorie drooped over the piano dripping chiffon, and delivering accented witticisms. Or she would stand still, her shoulders down and her hands at ease and speak/sing a song that so moved her listeners that for a few seconds after she finished, people neither applauded nor looked at one another.

When I went to my first rehearsal, Jorie brought her drama coach to meet me. He was a tall, thin, black-haired man named Lloyd Clark, who spoke elegantly out of pursed lips and threw his fingers out as if he was constantly shooting his cuffs. He was accompanied by a handsome Dutch Amazon, whose blond hair was pulled back and hung in a two-foot ponytail. Her little girl's smile seemed incongruous on a face that could have modeled for a ship's prow.

And she spoke softly. 'I'm Marguerite Clark. I'm his wife.' There was so much pride in her statement that I would not have been surprised had she hooked her fingers in her armpits and stalked around the room. Lloyd took her adoration as his due and asked me if I had ever worked with a drama coach. I told him that I had not, but that I had studied drama and that I was a dancer.

'Well, first, my dear, you must sing for me.' He held a cigarette between his third and fourth fingers, reminding me of a European movie actor. He puffed fastidiously. There was a neatness about the man which showed most prominently in his diction.

'I can't know if I can help you until I have' – each beloved word chosen carefully and handed out graciously, like choice pieces of fruit – 'seen you perform.'

The piano player, who was white and experienced, intimidated me nearly as much as the drama coach. Earlier in the afternoon he had asked for my sheet music, and when I told him that the songs I intended to sing had hardly been published, he slammed the piano lid down and stood up.

'Do you mean I'm supposed to play without music? Just vamp till ready?'

I did not understand his indignation, nor the sarcasm in his last question. 'I've signed a contract and I'm supposed to open in two weeks. What can I do?' I had found that direct questions brought direct answers if they brought answers at all.

'Have some lead sheets written for you,' he said indifferently.

'Can you do it? May I pay you to write the lead sheets? Whatever they are.'

He gave me a thin smile and, partially pacified, said, 'If I can find the time.'

He sat again on the bench and opened the piano. 'What do you sing?'

I said, 'Calypso. "Stone Cold Dead in the Market." "Run Joe," "Babalu." Things like that.'

He asked, 'What key for "Stone Cold Dead"?' His fingers ran over the keyboard and I thought of my pervasive ignorance.

'I don't know.' The music stopped and the musician leaned his head on the piano. He was so dramatic I thought he should have been the star.

I said, 'I'm sorry to be a bother.' Usually when one throws oneself at another's feet, one should be prepared to do a fast roll to avoid being stepped on. 'But I'd appreciate your help – I'm new.'

The pianist rose to the occasion, which, given his sardonic expression earlier, might have come as a bigger surprise to him than to me.

'O.K.' He straightened away from the keyboard. 'Try this.' He started to play and I recognized the tune.

'Yes, that's it.'

'I know that's it,' he said dryly. 'Now how about singing so I can find your key.'

I listened carefully, squinting my eyes and tried to find where in all the notes he played I should insert my voice.

'Sing.' It was an order.

I started: 'He's stone cold dead in de market.'

'No, that's wrong. Listen.' He played, I listened. I started to sing.

He said, 'No, wrong again.'

Finally by chance I hit the right note. The pianist grudgingly nodded and I sang the song through.

He stood up and bounced a glance off me as he turned toward the bar. 'You need music. You really need it.'

I watched him order and then gulp down a drink greedily.

And here was Lloyd Clark, tended by his adoring Brünnhilde, telling me to repeat the awkward performance.

Whenever I had danced non-angelically on the point of a pin, I always knew I might slip and break my neck. It could be fatal, but at least all anxiety would cease. Because of that, I often rushed toward holocausts with an abandon that caused observers to think of me as courageous. The truth was, I simply wanted an end to uncertainty.

The pianist responded to my nod and with visible resignation sat at the piano and began to play the song we had tried earlier.

I looked beyond my audience and decided to ignore the musician and his snide attitude. I fastened my mind on the plot. A poor West Indian woman had been threatened by her brutal husband (my mother's father was Trinidadian, and although he was kind he was very severe) and she struck back in self-defense. My sympathies rested with the mistreated woman. So I told the story from her point of view.

Don said, 'Great, just great.'

Jorie asked Lloyd and the world at large, 'Didn't I say she's marvy?'

Lloyd rose smiling, he came toward me offering his hands. 'Fab, fab, darling, you're going to be fab. You're marvelously dramatic.' He turned to his wife, who was like a tall, white shadow following him. 'Isn't she, Marg? Just fab?'

Marguerite gave him a loving smile. 'Yes, Lloyd darling.' Then to me she said softly, 'You're good. So very good. And after you work with Lloyd . . . Oh, I can hardly wait.' Her voice belied impatience.

'Now, dear, do sit down. Come, we must do some serious talking.' Lloyd took my hands. He leaned around me and said to the musician who was beelining for the bar, 'Thank you, young man, thank you. And you did it without lead sheets. Brilliant!'

'Now, my dear, sit.' He pulled me along to Jorie's table. She patted my cheek and lowered one long-lashed eye slowly, meaning I was in, and hadn't she said so, and I had nothing to worry about and weren't we all so awfully smart. I winked back and grinned.

Marguerite sat so close to Lloyd she was nearly in his lap and Don made congratulatory little noises to me and to himself.

'First, dear, your name,' Lloyd said.

'Rita.'

'Is that your name? The name you were born with?' Disbelief was evident.

'No, my name is Marguerite.'

108

Marguerite Clark complimented us both. 'Oh, isn't that nice?'

'It's all right for you, Marguerite, but it doesn't do anything for her.' I had been named for my maternal grandmother, who would not have taken kindly to that statement.

'She needs something more exotic. More glamorous.' Lloyd turned to Jorie and Don. 'Don't you agree?'

They did indeed.

'A really good name,' Don said, 'is half the act.'

I thought about the popular entertainers who were mentioned in the newspapers weekly. I didn't know if their names were created for show business or if the entertainers had simply been lucky. I said nothing.

'Let's think. Think up some names.'

Don went to the bar and brought over a bottle of wine and some glasses.

Thaïs, Sappho, Nana, Lana, Bette, names of heroines from Greek history, world literature and Hollywood were bandied about, but none seemed to please my inventors.

I said, 'My brother has always called me Maya. For "Marguerite." He used to call me "My sister," then he called me "My," and finally, "Maya." Is that all right?'

Jorie said, 'Di-vine. Di-vine, darling.'

Don was ecstatic. 'It suits you, my dear, oh God, it suits you.'

Marguerite waited for Lloyd. He thought, looking at me pointedly, trying to find the name in my face. After a minute, he said, 'Yes, you're Maya,' as if he was christening me.

Marguerite said, 'Lloyd, you're right, darling. She *is* Maya.'

Don passed the wine around.

'Maya what?' Jorie looked at Lloyd. 'Do deliver us from performers with one name. Hildegarde, Liberace. No, she must have at least two names.'

I said, 'My married name is Angelos.'

Don chewed the words around, tasting them.

'Maya Angelos.' Jorie took the name over, weighing it on her tongue. 'That's not bad.'

Lloyd said, 'It sounds too Spanish. Or Italian. No, it won't do.' An idea broke his face wide open. 'I've got it. Drop the *s* and add a *u*. Maya Angelou.' He pronounced it Angeloo. 'Of course! That's it!'

Jorie said it was too divine. Don said it was perfection. Marguerite beamed her approval of Lloyd and then of the name.

We all drank wine to toast our success. I had a job, a drama coach, a pianist who was going to provide me with lead sheets, and I had a new name (I wondered if I'd ever feel it described the me myself of me).

We began to prepare for my debut. For three hours each day Lloyd coached me. His instructions included how to stand, how to walk, how to turn and offer my best profile to an audience. He worked over my act as busily as a couturier creating a wedding gown for royalty.

'My dear, but you *must* stand still. Glide out onstage like the *Queen Mary* slipping out of her berth, reach the piano and then stand absolutely, but absolutely, still. After a few seconds look around at your audience and then, only then, at your pianist. Nod your head to him and then you will begin your music. When he finishes his intro, then you will begin to sing.'

I found standing still the most difficult of all his instructions. During rehearsal when I was introduced my nerves

110

shivered and the swallows in my stomach did nose dives. I would hear '. . . and now Miss Maya Angelou,' and I would race from the dressing room, down the narrow aisle to the stage and, immediately, without waiting for the music, begin: 'Moe and Joe ran a candy store.'

'No, my dear. Still. Be totally still. Think of a deep pool.'

Again and again I tried until I was able to walk on stage, and, thinking of nothing at all – neither deep pools nor sailing ships – stand absolutely still.

Lloyd said I had to learn at least twelve songs before opening night. I plundered the memories of every acquaintance. Mornings found me in the sheet music shops and record stores, ferreting for material. By midday, I hurried to the pianist's apartment, where we practiced songs over and over until they began to have less meaning than words in a children's game. Afternoons I worked with Lloyd in my house. When he left, I selected some songs to practice in front of Clyde. Although I sang the cute, the humorous songs for his enjoyment and would prance around this way and that, he always watched me with a seriousness that would have impressed a judge. When I finished he would remove his horn-rimmed glasses and look at me speculatively and ask, 'Gee, Mom, how can you remember all those words?'

Clyde had become a talker. He talked to me, to the family, to strangers and had long, involved conversations with himself. His discourses ranged over the subjects of his life. He had become a voracious reader, consuming books whole at nearly one sitting, then reliving the plot in his conversations. He read science fiction (he loved Ray Bradbury) and western pulp, his Sunday School lessons, Paul Laurence Dunbar's poems and

111

animal stories and explained to all who would listen that he, Red Ryder and Fluke were going to ride their horses to the moon and talk to God, who was an old black man who played the guitar. Red Ryder was a Western character from books and Fluke was Clyde's invisible miscreant friend. Fluke made him laugh aloud with his mischievousness. He was able to do things Clyde could not do, and Fluke did them with impunity. If a lamp was overturned and broken, it was because Fluke was walking around on the lampshade. When the bathtub ran over and turned the tiled floor into a shallow pool, Fluke had gone to the bathroom after Clyde left and turned the spigot on.

Vainly I tried to explain the difference between lying and making up a story, but decided it was more important that Clyde keep his nonexistent buddy to lessen the loneliness of an only child. I liked to listen from the kitchen when he told Fluke good-night stories and when, in his morning bath, he laughed outright as he warned his friend against indulging in some troublemaking antic.

Francis, the dressmaker, took Gerry's (with a G) ideas and fashioned long, snug dresses out of bolts of raw silk and white corduroy. The gowns were slit on both sides from floor to hip, and underneath I wore one-legged pants of gay batik. When I stood still, the dress material fell gracefully, giving an impression of sober elegance, but when I moved the panels would fly up and it seemed as if one leg was bare and the other tattooed. I wore no shoes. The total effect was more sensational than attractive, but having no illusions about my ability to sing, I reasoned that if I could startle the audience with my costumes and my personality, they might be so diverted that they wouldn't notice.

Opening night, I longed for one of two things. To be dead – dead and forgotten – or to have my brother beside me. Life had made some strenuous demands on me, and although I had never ruled out suicide, no experience so far had shattered me enough to make me consider it seriously. And my brother, Bailey, who could make me laugh at terror or allow me the freedom to cry over sentimental things, was in New York State, grappling with his own bitter reality. So, despite my wishes, I was alive and I was alone.

I watched through a peephole as Barry Drew walked to the stage. He claimed that he was descended from two great theatrical families and had to live up to his heritage.

'And now, ladies and gentlemen' – he rubbed his hands together – 'this evening, making her debut at the Purple Onion' – he turned his best side to the light and opened his arms for the world – 'Miss Maya Angelou!'

There was some applause, not enough to hearten but not so little I could deny that people were waiting for me.

I counted three and walked slowly down the aisle and onto the stage. I stood still as I had at rehearsal, and a dead calm surrounded me. One second later fear plummeted to my stomach and made my knees weak. I realized that I could not see the people. No one had warned me that a combination of spotlights and nerves would cause blindness. The aisle down which I had walked still lay open and unobstructed. I looked at it once, longingly, then turned to the pianist and nodded. And although I did not know it, another career for me had begun.

Popularity was an intoxicant and I swayed drunkenly for months. Newspaper reporters began to ask for interviews and

I gave them in an ersatz accent, which was a mélange of the speech of Ricardo Montalban, Jorie Remus and Akim Tamiroff. I was invited to talk on radio and sing on television. Fans began to recognize me in the street and one well-to-do woman organized a ten-member Maya Angelou fan club.

Later I met people who said, 'I saw you dance at the Purple Onion.' I graciously withheld the information that in fact I was hired at the club as a singer, but the songs had many refrains and such complex rhythms that often I got lost in the plot and forgot the lyrics. So, when the words eluded me, I would admit my poor memory and add that if the audience would bear with me I would dance. The first few times I owned up to a weak memory, Lloyd Clark and Barry Drew frowned disapprovingly, but after the audiences applauded loudly Barry accepted it and Lloyd said, 'Wonderful, dear, wonderful. Keep it in. In fact, you should dance more.'

I shared the bill with a strange and talented couple. Jane Connell sang scatterbrained ditties, while her sober-side husband Gordon dryly played piano. Their patter was sharp and displayed their Berkeley university background. When they left to join Jorie in New York's Blue Angel, a frowzy blond housewife from Alameda auditioned and was accepted at the club. She brought a wardrobe of silly flowered hats and moth-eaten boas which she flung around her thin neck. Her laugh, which she shared often, was a cross between a donkey's braying and a foghorn. She said she would not change her name because when she became successful she wanted everyone to know it was, indeed, her herself. The name was painted in large white letters outside the club: Phyllis Diller.

114

11

Without a father in the house and no other male authority figure in his world, Clyde fell under the spell of uniforms. He began to adore policemen and daydream about becoming a bomber pilot.

'I'll zoom down like this, Mom, brrr and blow their heads off. Boom, boom, boom.' He marched and clumped around the house in a poor parody of Gestapo goose-stepping. He saluted walls and chairs and ordered doors to be 'at rest, Sergeant Door.' He had become enamored of the Air Force and every evening at bedtime he waited in his room for me to hear his prayers and then to sing (he would join in):

> 'Off we go into the wild blue yonder
> Singing songs into the blue . . .'

Each evening as I left for work, the baby-sitter would say, 'Our little soldier is bedded down in his bunk, huh?' I wished I could have cashiered her out of my service with dishonorable discharge.

115

I was dismayed, but I left him alone until I could decide on the best way to counter his sudden affection for violence. I hoped for divine intercession and bided my time. As his birthday approached he began spending time after school in the local five-and-dime store. He wanted a machine gun or a tank or a pistol that shot real plastic bullets or a BB gun. I took him to the local S.P.C.A. pound and told him he could have an animal. A small dog or any cat he wanted. He wandered around the cages, choosing one dog and then rejecting it when he saw a lonelier-looking cat. He finally settled on a small black kitten with rheumy eyes and a dull, dusty coat. I asked the attendant if the cat was healthy. He said it was, but that it had been taken from its mother too early and abandoned. It needed personal care or the pound would have to destroy it. Clyde was shocked. I could barely get him and his ragged cat out of the building before rage broke through. 'Mom, did he mean he would have to kill my cat?'

He was clutching the small animal so tightly I thought he himself might put an end to its miserable life.

'Yes, if no one wanted it, they'd do away with it.'

'But Mom, isn't that place called a place for the protection of animals?'

'Yes.'

'Well.' He thought for a few minutes. 'Wow! What sort of person would have a job like that? Going around killing animals all the time.'

I saw my opening. 'Of course, some people have jobs that order them to go around killing human beings.'

The earlier shock was nothing to the sensation that caught

and held him. He nearly squeezed the breath out of the kitten. 'What? Who? Who kills human beings?'

'Oh, soldiers, sailors. Pilots who use machine guns and bombs. You know. That's mainly what they're hired for.'

He leaned back in the car, stroking the kitten. Silent, thinking.

I never mentioned killing again and he never asked for another weapon.

Leonard Sillman's Broadway hit *New Faces of 1953* came West in 1954. San Francisco, already the home of irreverent comedians, political folk singers, expensively dressed female impersonators, beat poets and popular cabaret singers, took the witty revue to its heart. Don Curry and I attended an early matinée. When Eartha Kitt sang 'Monotonous' in her throaty vibrato and threw her sleek body on a sleek chaise longue, the audiences loved her. Alice Ghostly, with 'Boston Beguine,' created a picture of a hilarious seduction scene in a seedy hotel lobby where 'even the palms seemed to be potted.' Paul Lynde, as a missionary newly returned from a three-day tour of the African continent, and Robert Clary, as the cup-sized Frenchman rolling his saucer eyes, turned farce into a force that was irresistible. Ronnie Graham shared the writing and performed in skits with June Carrol.

I left the theater nearly numb. The quality of talent and quantity of energy had drained me of responses.

My family made plans to come to the Onion for an early show. Mother was coming with Aunt Lottie, and they were bringing a few old-time gamblers from the Fillmore district who never left the Negro neighborhood except to buy expensive suits from white tailors. Ivonne was bringing her

117

daughter, Joyce, and Clyde. I reserved front-row seats and then spent a nervous thirty minutes waiting for them to arrive.

The adults had a loud, happy reunion in the front row. A stranger could easily have deduced that they had not seen each other in months or more probably years.

Mother's friends examined Clyde and complimented him on growing so fast. He beamed and threw back his already wide shoulders. Lottie praised Joyce for 'turning into a fine young lady' and the conservatively dressed men who generally dealt the poker at the legally illegal gambling houses smiled at everyone and politely ordered drinks for the party. Ketty Lester, a great beauty who hailed from a small Arkansas town thirty miles north of my home, always opened the show. She sang good songs and sang them well. Phyllis Diller followed her and spread her aura of madness over the stage and onto the audience, and then I closed the round's entertainment. The older people were transfixed by Ketty's singing. She sang 'Little Girl from Little Rock' and the black people who all had Southern roots acted as if the song had been written expressly for Ketty to sing to them. From the rear of the club, I watched as they smiled and nodded to one another and didn't have to be in hearing distance to know they were exchanging 'That's right' and 'Sure is' and 'Ain't that the truth?'

There was only a minute between the last notes of her encore and Phyllis Diller's introduction. Curiosity kept me standing against the back wall, for I wanted to see how my family would take to the frumpy comedienne. Black people rarely forgave whites for being ragged, unkempt and uncaring. There was a saying which explained the disapproval: 'You

118

been white all your life. Ain't got no further along than this? What ails you?'

When Phyllis came out onstage, Clyde almost fell off the chair and Joyce started giggling so she nearly knocked over her Shirley Temple. The comedienne, dressed outrageously and guffawing like a hiccoughing horse and a bell clapper, chose to play to the two children (she had four of her own). They were charmed and so convulsed with laughter they gasped for breath, but being well-brought-up Negro youngsters who were told nice children do not laugh loudly, they put their hands over their mouths.

I slipped into the dressing room, pleased that at last there was something in the show for everyone. Only Ivonne had appeared less than enchanted with the two acts. But then I knew she was waiting for me to sing.

I walked down the aisle to the stage, registering the applause and hoping that my family was not so busy clapping their hands that they were unable to note that other people were applauding as well. I stood quietly, looking out into the audience (I had enlarged on Lloyd's coaching and now took the time to select faces in the pale light). My breath caught audibly as I recognized Alice Ghostly and Paul Lynde at a table midway in the room. Their presence exhilarated me.

I nodded to the three musicians and began my song.

> 'I put the peas in the pot to cook
> I got the paper and started to look
> My horse . . .'

I heard the 'shush' and 'hush' from somewhere around my kneecaps, but kept on singing.

119

> '. . . was running at twenty to one
> So me peas and me rice
> They get . . .'

The 'tsk's' and the 'sh's' were coming from my family. I looked down and saw everyone leaning in toward Clyde. His mouth was open and smiling, and then I heard his voice and knew why everyone was admonishing him. He was singing with me – after all, he had heard every song rehearsed a hundred times at home and now he decided to show me that he, too, could memorize the words. It might have been ignored if he had kept up with me, but his words lagged behind mine by at least one beat.

> 'I put . . .'
> *'I'*
> '. . . the peas in . . .'
> *'. . . put the . . .'*
> The pot to cook . . .'
> *'peas in . . .'*

Absolutely the first time I had a chance to sing for big-time stars and my son was messing it up. I looked at him, hard this time, and he laughed openly. His eyes nearly shut as his face gave way to his own private joke. He acted as if we were playing a game, like twenty questions or top this, and he was enjoying himself so much that I had to forget about the audience and settle for entertaining my son. I tried to slow down my delivery until he could catch up.

When we finished, still a beat apart, I thanked the audience and added that I had had some unexpected but very welcome help. I introduced my son, Mr. Clyde Bailey Johnson. He stood, turned to the audience and bowed, straight-faced, as he had seen his favorite Bud Abbott do in so many films. I gave Clyde a look that in parent/offspring language meant 'That was nice, but now we've stopped playing.' He translated aptly and was quiet through the rest of my performance.

In the dressing room my family clutched around me, talking in low voices, commending me, relieved that at least I was good enough to spare them embarrassment. They saved their compliments for Ketty and Phyllis, paganly believing that too much praise attracted the gods' attention and might summon their powerful jealousy. They also thought I just might get a swelled head if given too many compliments, so instead they gave me sly looks and furtive pats and when no one was looking the slick old men encouraged me to 'keep up the good work.' They whispered that Ketty and I were the best on the bill but we had 'better be careful' and 'take it easy, 'cause white folks get jealous when they see Negroes gettin' ahead.'

They left the club, taking with them the familiar nuances and I was somewhat relieved when they had gone. Insecurity can make us spurn the persons and traditions we most enjoy. I had always loved the gamblers when they sat in Mother's kitchen telling tales of the Texas Panhandle and reliving the excitement of boom towns in Oklahoma. But downtown, where educated whites might overhear the Negro grammar and think less of me because of it, I was uncomfortable.

Alice and Paul came to the dressing room and invited me out for a drink. I accepted immediately. We exchanged compliments and during the intermission we sat in an easy

121

friendliness until the next show began. A few nights later Alice brought other members of the company down to catch my show. One singer told me that Eartha was leaving and Leonard Sillman and Ronnie Graham were auditioning dancer/singers to replace her. She had been bound by a contract which had run out at last and was going to open in one of the big-paying Las Vegas hotels. And would I like to try for the part? Naturally I wanted to audition and just as naturally I was petrified.

The theater stage jutted out aggressively into an empty darkness. Sillman sat erect on a straight-backed chair, apart from, yet fearfully a part of, the proceedings.

I was shivering in the wings, thinking of the excitement Eartha brought to her music when a stage manager asked me if I was going to sing 'Monotonous.' The play on words occurred to me and I did not find it funny. I said yes, but did not add that I would not be singing it like Eartha Kitt. She was overtly sexy and famously sensual. I was friendly, gangly and more the big-sister type. No, I would have no chance if I tried imitating the brown velvet kitten.

When I was called I went out onto the stage and put my hands on my hips and a foot on the chaise longue. I sang a few bars, then swirled around and put the other foot on the chaise longue. I sang and danced, skimming over the stage (a dance teacher had told me when I was fourteen years old that a good dancer 'occupies space consciously'), always ending back at the seat with an attitude of haughty boredom. My plan was to capture attention by displaying absolute contradiction. Hot dance and cool indifference.

I waited an interminable two days for Leonard Sillman's 'reaction.' The phone call came and my heart jumped against my breastbone. I had the job. The famous show-business break had come. Ivonne's friend Calvin bought champagne and we celebrated at her house. I also bought champagne (although I did not care very much for it) and went to Mr. Hot Dogs, where Mom and Lottie and the counter customers helped me to celebrate. I told them that I would join the company for the rest of its tour, then settle down in New York City. My only hesitation was caused by the question of what to do about Clyde. Mom and Lottie said they would take care of him. He could have his breakfast at home as usual and come directly to the restaurant after school, by which time one of them would be going home on the split shift. I accepted that solution, knowing that when I 'made it,' as I was sure to do, I would rent a large Manhattan apartment and hire a governess for my son. And when I traveled I would take him along with the governess and possibly a tutor.

My life was arranging itself as neatly as a marble staircase and I was climbing to the stars.

Barry Drew met my announcement with an apoplectic explosion. 'Oh no, you're not. What? You can't close. What? We have you under contract, you can't walk out on a contract.'

I countered that I had already accepted the role, that he had the Kingston Trio and Rod McKuen opening at the club and they were as good or better than I. 'I will never have another chance like this again. I don't want to spend my life at the Purple Onion.'

He was firm. 'You didn't think that when we brought you in here. You're lucky we didn't offer you a year's contract. You'd have signed your life away to get a job like this.'

I cried and begged and hated myself for doing so. He remained unmoved. I ranted about his cruelty, throwing curse words at him like blobs of hot tar, hoping at least to smear his surface.

Barry said coolly, 'Sillman not only will not, but cannot, hire you if you break your contract. The union will have you up on charges and you will be blackballed.'

He acted as if he himself had founded the union and written its bylaws just to keep restless and irresponsible singers in their places. His contempt was impenetrable. My anger calmed enough for me to see my predicament. I was totally hemmed in and I left the club and headed home, glowering at every passerby and wrapped up close in sullenness.

I expected sympathy from the rest of my family and received it in generous portions. My mother said she was shocked at Barry's behavior, but then as she always said, 'The smallest insect makes the most noise,' and I should keep that in mind. Aunt Lottie stroked me, gave me tea and as if I were sick, offered to make a nice pot of soup. Ivonne told me on the telephone that I was right to be angry, but to consider that the role in the play simply was not for me and as the saying goes, 'You can't miss something you never had.'

My pain yielded to the well-worn adages and soft consoling voices. In the absence of anguish I was able to think. It became clear that the roles had been exchanged. Once I had had a need of the Purple Onion facilities and now the Purple Onion had need of my services. The thought that irritated me and planted a seed of disdain was that the managers of the club had not noticed the reversal and had not the grace to appeal to my sense of 'Turnabout is fair play.'

I had heard the statement made by wistful whites (and had also made it in my youth myself, hoping to prove worthy of acceptance): 'There's nothing as loyal as a Negro. Once you make a friend of one, you have a friend for life.' Like making a pet of a grizzly bear.

My attitude at the club proved either that the statement was fallacious or that I was not a Negro. I withdrew my affection and kept only the shell of cool courtesy.

12

'Hello, Mrs. Angelos?'

The telephone had rung on a bleary morning. It was a woman's voice.

'Yes?'

'This is Tennessee Kent at Golden Gate School.'

'Yes?' I suppose the wonder in my voice carried over the wires.

'Your son, Clyde, is a student here.'

My son's name brought me immediately clear of sleep. 'Yes, I know that.' Suddenly a clear-headed, responsible mother.

'I think possibly you'd like to come to school and discuss something Clyde has said.'

'Is he all right?'

'Oh, yes, don't worry about him.'

I did just that as I dressed.

Since our brief period of estrangement, I had worked very hard impressing Clyde that I was reliable, that in any conflict I was on his side. I had not forgotten the importance of my brother's impartial love during my own lonely childhood, and

126

since my son had no sibling, I had to make him know he had support.

I went to the school and found Clyde sitting forlornly on a straight chair in the corridor. I patted his shoulder and stooped to ask what had happened. His eyes were liquid with unshed tears.

He whispered, 'I don't know, Mom. They said I said something bad.'

'Did you?' He had learned some profanity at a day camp the year before and had been quite proud of it for a few weeks.

'I don't know,' he still whispered.

The two women remained seated when I led Clyde into the office.

'Good morning, Mrs. Angelos,' Miss Kent said. 'This is Clyde's teacher, Miss Blum.' A stout, middle-aged woman nodded to me seriously. Miss Kent went on, 'And maybe it's better to let Clyde sit outside in the corridor while we . . .'

'No' – I still had my hand on his shoulder – 'this concerns him. I want him to hear the discussion.'

The teachers exchanged looks. I directed Clyde to a chair and sat beside him.

'Well, maybe Miss Blum will tell you what happened,' Miss Kent said.

Clyde's little body was trembling. I patted his knee.

Miss Blum said, 'Yesterday was Armed Forces Day and I asked all the children what branch of the service they admired. Some said Navy, others Air Force, others Seabees, but Clyde stood up on his turn and said he'd go to jail first.' She looked at him with such venom I wanted to put my body between her look and my son.

Miss Kent said soothingly, 'Now, Mrs. Angelos, we know Clyde didn't get that at home. So, we wanted you to know that somewhere, maybe among his friends, he's picking up dangerous thoughts.'

I thought immediately about Joseph McCarthy. The witch hunt was in full stride and newspapers carried items about blacklists and jobs being jeopardized. Reputations had been ruined and some people imprisoned because they were suspected of harboring dangerous and treacherous thoughts. My own background was not without incident. When I was nineteen, I had enlisted in the Army and been given a date for induction, but had been summarily rejected because it was discovered that during my fourteenth and fifteenth years I had gone to a school which was on the list of un-American activities.

They said they knew he didn't pick up such thoughts at home.

'Yes, he got that at home, Miss Kent.' Oh Lord, my career. What would the Rockwell family do if I was accused of Communist leanings?

'Oh, is that your religious belief?' She was being nice-nasty, giving me a cowardly way out. My son sat beside me, waiting. He had stopped trembling and was holding himself tight, listening to the exchange.

'If you mean do I believe in it religiously, I do.'

'Oh, then Clyde was voicing your political views that you hold religiously?'

There was nothing for it but to agree. I said, 'That's right.'

And that was all Clyde had been waiting for. He bounced up out of his chair, arms stretched and flailing.

'Mom, isn't it true that just because U.S. Steel wants to sell more steel, I shouldn't go and kill some baby Koreans who never did anything to me?'

'Yes, that's true.'

'And, Mom, isn't it true that capitalists just make the poor people go and bomb other poor people till they're all dead and live on dead people's money?'

I did not recognize that line, but I said 'Yes.'

He lifted his arms like a conductor asking a full orchestra for the last chord. 'Well, that's all I said.'

The teachers sat silent as I stood up.

'Miss Kent, and Miss Blum, I think the session has been emotionally very tiring for Clyde. I'll take him home now and he'll come back to school tomorrow.'

They did nothing to hinder our departure.

That afternoon Clyde and I went to a movie that showed ten Disney shorts.

13

George Hitchcock was a playwright whose play *Princess Chan Chan* was being performed by the Interplayers at a little theater near North Beach. A tall, shambling man with large hands and a staccato laugh, he doubled as an aging character actor. His hair was always dusty because he did not effectively rinse out the white powder.

He watched my show and afterwards asked if he could see me home. I wanted to accept, but wondered what he would think of my living arrangements. I was a glamorous night-club singer, or at least wanted to be considered glamorous, but I still lived at home with my mother. Late evenings I would find her sitting at the dining room table drinking beer and playing solitaire, and definitely not waiting up for me. I was a grown woman and had better know how to look after myself. Just to make sure, she played solitaire until I came home. Her voice would greet the sound of the opening front door. 'Hi, baby, I'm in here.'

I would say, 'Good evening, Mom.' And when she lifted her face for a kiss, she'd ask, 'How'd it go this evening?' and I'd say, 'O.K., Mom.' That was what she wanted to hear, and all she wanted to know. Vivian Baxter could and would deal with grand schemes and large plots, but please, pray God, spare her the details.

I invited George home, and on the way, told him about my mother and my son. If he was surprised he didn't show it.

I countered Mom's 'Hi, baby. I'm in here' with 'I brought a friend home.'

George would have had to know my mother to have recognized how startled she was when he walked in. She stopped her laying out of red and black and said, 'Welcome,' then 'How are you tonight?' As if she knew how he had fared the night before.

George seemed at ease.

Mother looked at his worn tweed jacket, rumpled trousers and not quite clean hair and asked, 'How long have you known my daughter?'

I knew where she was heading. I said, 'We've just met tonight, Mom. George is a writer.' That information held her steady for a while.

'He asked me out for a coffee and I thought maybe you'd have a pot on.' Coffee was drunk by the potful at breakfast, but never served in my mother's house after morning. 'But, of course, we can go down the street to the Booker T. Washington Hotel.'

She bounced out of her chair. 'Only takes a minute. How about some breakfast?'

I knew the idea of her daughter going into the then swankiest Negro hotel in town, escorted by a raggedy-looking white man would cause hospitality to flow like water.

131

She invited us into the kitchen.

'What about a little omelette and some bacon?' She turned on the oven and I held out my hand. Whenever she baked biscuits she removed her large diamond rings and put them on my fingers. 'And just a few hot biscuits?'

She began the arrangement of bowls and pans and I excused myself and left George to his fate.

When I returned, changed out of evening clothes, the meal was nearly ready and she ordered me to set the table for two, and asked, 'So, did you know that George makes a living as a gardener?'

'No, how do you know? Did George tell you that?'

George said, 'Yes.'

Mom was moving round the kitchen talking, cooking, singing little wisps of songs, the diamond earrings twinkling.

He was hypnotized.

'Put some butter on the table, Maya, please, and did you know he's unmarried and not thinking about getting married in the foreseeable future? Will the strawberry preserves be all right? Get that platter out of the cupboard, will you? Hum, hum . . .' She whipped up the eggs with a whisk.

'George, how did you come to tell my mother so much of your business?'

He shrugged his shoulders helplessly. 'She asked me.'

Mother said later that since he was white that was enough to make him unsuitable, but he was also much too old for me. Still I found his company easy and his intelligence exciting. He understood loving poetry, and although I would not show him my own poems, I recited Shakespearean sonnets and Paul Laurence Dunbar late at night in his house in Sausalito.

We shared long walks in Golden Gate Park and picnicked in John Muir woods. His mother was a well-known San Francisco journalist and he told me endless stories of the area and its colorful characters.

A gentle affection, devoid of romance, grew up between us and I enjoyed watching from his window as night faded over the Golden Gate Bridge. I was always back home before day-break because Clyde expected me at the breakfast table while he chatted about his dreams or Fluke's misdoings.

I answered the telephone.

'Meez Angeloo?'

'Yes.'

The voice was male and rich and the accent thick and poetic.

'My name is Yanko Varda. I am a painter.' He was a well-known figure in San Francisco art circles.

'Yes, Mr. Varda.' Why was he calling me?

'No, pleez – Yanko. Just Yanko.'

'Yes, Yanko?' Yes, but why was he calling me?

'Meez Angeloo, I have heard so much about you, about your beauty and your talent and your grace. I have decided I must meet this wonderful woman with whom all the men are in love.'

I could not think of a soul who was in love with me, but who can resist the suggestion that one has secret admirers?

'How nice of you to say that.'

'Not atall. No, not atall. I have decided that I must give a dinner for you so that I myself may see this phenomenon: a beautiful woman with a great mind.'

I knew I did not fit his description, but I would have torn my tongue out before I would have denied it.

He set Monday night for dinner and said he lived on a houseboat in Sausalito.

'George Hitchcock will bring you to my boat, which is called the *Vallejo*. I shall prepare, as only I can prepare, an ambrosia fit for a princess, but if you are in fact a queen, as I suspect, I hope you will condescend to take a sip from these humble hands. George will bring you to me. *Au revoir*.'

He sounded like a character in a Russian novel. The embroidery of his language, complex and passionate, enchanted me.

What did one wear to an ambrosial dinner on a houseboat? I selected and rejected every outfit in my closet and finally settled on a flowered dress that belonged to my mother. It was gay but not frivolous, chic but not formal.

George and I drove across the Golden Gate Bridge through a swirling fog and he stopped the car near the water. I stepped out onto wet mud. He rushed around and took my hand. 'Follow me, walk on the planks.'

Thick boards extended to a small rickety bridge. Lights shone dimly in the mists, but I had to keep my attention on the walkway or I might fall into the sullen-looking water below.

There were turns and steps and more turns. Then George stopped, turned and moved around me in the short space. 'Here's where I get off. You go on up these three steps and knock at the door.'

I tried to see his face in the overcast night. 'What are you talking about?' His features were indistinct.

'I'm not invited tonight. This dinner is just for you.'

'Well, wait a minute, I'm not going to . . .' I reached for him.

He backed away, laughing, it seemed to me, sardonically. 'I'll be back to pick you up at eleven. *Bon appétit!*'

During our short relationship, I had projected an air of independence, kindly but assured, and I could not scream at him or race down the flimsy walkway to clutch his retreating back.

I stood until George melted in the mist, then I turned and looked around. The shape of a large boat seemed to shiver in and out of a dark, misty sky, its windows beaming happily like lights in a giant jack-o'-lantern.

I walked up the remaining stairs wondering if I had been set up for an orgy – or perhaps I was to be an innocent participator in devil worship. I knew you could never tell about white people. Negroes had survived centuries of inhuman treatment and retained their humanity by hoping for the best from their pale-skinned oppressors but at the same time being prepared for the worst.

I looked through the porch door window at a short sturdy man quickly lighting candles in wine bottles, which he put on a long wooden table. No one else was visible, and although he looked strong, I decided I could probably take care of myself if he tried to take advantage of me.

I knocked sharply on the windowpane. The man looked up toward the door and smiled. His face was nearly as brown as mine and a sheaf of gray hair trembled when he moved. He came directly to the door, his smile broadening with each step.

'Rima,' I thought I heard him say through the closed door. He pulled the door open and in the same movement stepped away from it and admired me.

'Ah, Rima, it ees you.' He could not have been happier.

135

'No. Uh. My name is Maya.'

He was expecting someone else. I quickly traced the days. This was Monday. Had I misunderstood him because of his accent or my excitement? But then, George must have made a mistake too.

'Don't stand there, my dear. Come in. Let me take your coat. Come in.'

I walked into the warm kitchen, whose air was dense with the odor of cooking herbs. I looked at my host as he closed the door and hung my coat on a wall peg. His arms were thick and muscled and his neck broad and weather-roughened.

He turned. 'Now, Rima, at last you've come to me. Let us drink wine to this meeting.'

He seemed so happy, I was truly sorry to disappoint him. 'I'm sorry, but I'm Maya Angelou. I'm the singer.'

'My dear, I have known since I was a small boy on a hill in Greece that when I met you, you'd never tell me who you were, you would give another name. Equally beautiful and equally mystical. But I would know you by the music in your voice and the shadow of the forest on your beautiful face.'

I was completely undone.

Over goblets of wine, he re-created his own version of the Rima legend for me. A creature, half girl and half bird, came periodically to earth assuming full womanly form, singing lilting birdlike melodies and lightening human hearts. Her stays were brief, then she became a bird and flew away to her beloved forest where she was happiest and free. While we ate a thick meat soup, he told me of W. H. Hudson's *Green Mansions* and the heroine, Rima, and said he would lend me the book, since its story was based on my magic.

'I shall address you as Maya in both public and private, for I fear if I continue calling you Rima, you may become annoyed and fly away. But you shall always know that in a small place in my heart I am thanking you for your visit.'

The walls were adorned with delicately tinted pastels, and he guided me to each one, explaining, 'In this collage I have tried to show a Carthaginian ship, swathed in grace moving from the harbor on its route to pillage another civilization. And here we have the King and Queen of Patagonia before the Feast of Stars.' He talked about the beauty of Greece and the excitement of Paris. He was a close friend of Henry Miller and an acquaintance of Pablo Picasso. The time sped by as we ate fruit and cheese and I listened to the stories told in English as ornate as a Greek Orthodox ritual.

'I have a set of young friends who will be embellished by your presence. I beg you to be kind enough to come back to the *Vallejo* on a Sunday afternoon and meet them. We form a party each week and drink wine, eat soup and feast upon the riches of each other's thoughts. Please come – the men will surely worship you and the women will adore you.'

George returned for me, and after a ceremonial glass of wine and an embrace from Yanko's leathery arms, he took me back to his house and patiently listened to my story of the evening. He stopped me: 'Maya, I believe you're infatuated with Yanko.'

'I most certainly am not.'

'Many women find him irresistible.'

'Probably.' And I added without thinking, 'but he is old and white.'

George got up and turned on the record player.

*

137

One night at the Purple Onion I bowed to a full house and as I raised my head I heard 'Bravo,' 'Bis,' 'Bravo.' A group of people were standing in the middle of the room applauding, their hands over their heads like flamenco dancers. I bowed again and blew kisses as I had seen it done in movies. They continued applauding and shouting 'More!' until the other patrons rose and, joining the group, implored me for another song. I always planned for at least two encores, so it was not the requests that embarrassed me but, rather, the overt display of appreciation which I had never received before. I sang another song and retreated to my dressing room. A waiter brought me a note which informed me: 'We are friends. Please join us. Mitch.'

I went to the table reluctantly, fearing they might be drunks, out for an evening's hilarity at anyone's expense.

As I approached, the group stood again and began applauding. I was ready to flee to the safety of my dressing room.

A large, dark-haired man offered me his hand.

'Maya, I am Mitch Lifton.' He indicated the others individually. I shook hands with Victor Di Suvero and Henrietta, Francis and Bob Anshen, and Annette and Cyril March. 'We are friends of Yanko and he suggested that we come to see you. You are absolutely wonderful.'

We sat drinking wine and they gave me their particulars. Mitch Lifton's parents were Russian Jews, he was born in Paris, grew up in Mexico and was interested in film. Victor Di Suvero was a descendant of an Italian family that still had businesses in Italy and he was seriously courting the breathtaking Henrietta. Cyril March was a dermatologist from France, and architect Robert Anshen was a Frank Lloyd

Wright devotee, whose wife, Frances Ney, gave great parties, kept a wonderful house and her own name. Annette March was an American who spoke French and was a blond, vibrating beauty. I took their cues and told them the things about myself that I thought it wise for them to know.

After my last performance they again stood and shouted their bravos and applauded as if Billie Holiday accompanied by Duke Ellington had just finished singing 'I Cover the Waterfront.' They left together after reminding me that we all had a date on Sunday, and because I was used to BYOB parties, I asked what I should bring.

'Imagine you're coming to Corfu,' Victor said, 'and remember that cheese and fruit have never been rejected in the Mediterranean.'

Gaily colored pennants floated on posts attached to the boat. Cut-glass windows, oddly shaped, broke the monotony of weathered wood. Large pieces of sculpture stood sentinel in the area leading to the bridge in the sunlight. The boat looked like a happy child's dream castle.

Yanko greeted me warmly, but without surprise, allowing me to feel not only welcome but expected. Mitch came forward smiling, followed by Victor. They both embraced me and complimented George on his good luck. The three men fell into a private exchange and I wandered away to observe the gathering.

The party was in lingual swing. European classical music provided a background for tidbits of conversation that drifted clear from the general noise. In one corner Annette and Cyril spoke French to a wild-haired woman who never allowed one sentence to end before she interrupted. A thin, professorial man stroked his goatee and spoke to Yanko in Greek. Bob Anshen waved me over and I stayed awhile listening to him discourse on the merits of solar heating systems. Victor joined the group who warbled in Italian as melodious as a concerto.

Other languages I could not recognize spattered and rattled around the room. One handsome Negro was talking to a group around the long table. When he saw me his face spread in a broad smile and he stood up. If he had started speaking to me in an African language, I would not have been surprised.

'Hello there. How are you?' Straight, university, Urban League, colored, NAACP middle-class Negro accent.

'Fine, thank you.'

'My name is Jim, join us.'

I had never been found attractive by middle-class Negro men, since I was neither pretty nor fair-skinned, well-off or educated, and since most were firmly struggling up Striver's Row they needed women who could either actually help them or at least improve their visual image.

I sat down and found myself in the middle of a discussion on the recent Supreme Court ruling in *Brown* vs. *Board of Education* that had banned racial segregation in education. Jim and I and a pretty blond woman on the other side of the table argued that not only was the ruling just, it was very late in coming. Our opponents contended for the legitimacy of states' rights. As voices were raised and the selection of words became keener, I noticed that I was less angry than interested. I knew many whites were displeased by the ruling, but I had never heard them discuss it.

One debater was called away; another, bored with the

display of passion, said, 'You people are too serious,' and left to kibbitz a chess game.

Jim impressed me. Hearing his formal accent, I had not expected such resolve. 'Where do you live?' Maybe I could invite him to Mother's for dinner.

'We live in Mill Valley. What about you?'

I heard the 'we' and restrained myself from a new examination of the room. The place was so crowded I must have overlooked his wife.

'I live in San Francisco.'

The blonde who had been on our side in the argument and had made perceptive points in the controversy edged forward on the bench. She leaned toward me.

'San Francisco's not far from Mill Valley. Why don't you come over for dinner?'

Jim said, 'And meet our kids.' He laughed a little self-consciously. 'Jenny is learning how to cook greens and she bakes a mean pan of cornbread.'

Jenny blushed prettily.

I said, 'Thank you, but I work nights.' I had not quite accepted that white women were as serious in interracial marriages as white men.

A statement that had great currency in the Negro neighborhood warned: 'Be careful of white women with colored men. They might marry and bear children, but when they get what they want out of the men, they leave their children and go back to their own people.' We are all so cruelly and comprehensively educated by our tribal myths that it did not occur to me to question what it was that white women wanted out of the men. Since few Negro men in the interracial marriages I had seen had a substantial amount of money, and since the women could have had the sex without the marriage, and since mothers leave their children so rarely that an incident of child abandonment is cause for a newspaper story, it followed that the logic of the warning did not hold.

I excused myself from the table and went to stand on the deck. The small exclusive town of Tiburon glistened across the green-blue water and I thought about my personal history. Of Stamps, Arkansas, and its one paved street, of the segregated Negro school and the bitter poverty that causes children to become bald from malnutrition. Of the blind solitude of unwed motherhood and the humiliation of prostitution. Waves slapped at the brightly painted catamaran tied up below me and I pursued my past to a tardy marriage which was hastily broken. And the inviting doors to newer and richer worlds, where the sounds of happiness drifted through closed panels and the doorknobs came off in my hands.

Guests began to leave, waving at Yanko, who stood beside me at the rail: 'À tout à l'heure,' 'Adiós,' 'Ciao,' 'Adieu,' 'Au revoir,' 'Good-bye,' 'Ta.' Yanko put his hand on my elbow and guided me back inside.

We had become a crowd of intimates around the table. Annette ladled the soup into large bowls and they all talked about sailing plans for next Sunday. If the weather was nice we would leave early so that we could have a full sail in before the Sunday crowd came for open house. Cyril wondered if I would like him and Annette to pick me up, since they also lived in San Francisco. Mitch said he wanted to talk to me about a short film he was going to do. Possibly I would like to narrate it. Victor said he and Henrietta were going to the Matador on Saturday for lunch and I should join them.

They did not question whether I wanted acceptance into their circle. I was chosen and my being a part of the group was a fact; the burden of choice was removed from me and I was relieved.

I told them I had a young son, and before I could ask, Yanko said, 'Bring him. The sea is a female. And females desire young and masculine life. Bring him and we shall pacify the mother of us all. Bring him.'

One morning we sailed out on a smooth sea. Cyril was at the helm and Victor was regaling us with a gallant tale of medieval conquest. A young Scandinavian was on board, and when Victor was finished he, in turn, told a Viking story of heroic deeds and exploration.

Yanko slapped his forehead and said, 'Ah, yes. Now I know what we must do. We must all plan to go abroad and civilize Europe. We must get a large ship and sail down the Thames and cultivate Britain first because they need it most. Then we cross the Channel and bring culture to France. Cyril, you shall be the first mate because you have by nature and training the mechanical mind. Mitch, you shall be the boatswain because of your "Samson strength"; Maya, you shall be the *cantante*, sitting in the prow singing us to victory. Victor, you shall be second mate because your talent is to organize. Annette, you shall be our figurehead, for your beauty will stun the commoners and enchant the aristocracy. I shall be captain and do absolutely nothing. *Allons, enfants!*'

Yanko allowed me to enter a world strange and fanciful. Although I had to cope daily with real and mundane matters, I found that some of the magic of his world stayed around my shoulders.

14

If *New Faces of 1953* excited the pulses of San Franciscans, *Porgy and Bess* set their hearts afire. Reviewers and columnists raved about Leontyne Price and William Warfield in the title roles and praised the entire company. The troupe had already successfully toured other parts of the United States, Europe and South America.

The Purple Onion contract bound me inextricably, but it also held the management to the letter of the law – I could not be fired except after having committed the most flagrant abuses.

On *Porgy and Bess*'s second night I called Barry and said, 'I'm off tonight. You may say I'm ill.'

'Are you ill?'

'You may say so.' And hung up.

I had matured into using a ploy of not quite telling the truth but not quite telling a lie. I experienced no guilt at all and it was clear that the appearance of innocence lay mostly in a complexity of implication.

I went to the theater ready to be entertained, but not expecting a riot of emotion. Price and Warfield sang; they threaded their voices with music and spellbound the audience with their wizardry. Even the chorus performed with such verve that a viewer could easily believe each singer was competing for a leading part.

By intermission I had been totally consumed. I had laughed and cried, exulted and mourned, and expected the second act to produce no new emotions. I returned to my seat prepared for a repetition of great music.

The curtain rose on a picnic in progress. The revelers were church members led by a pious old woman who forbade dancing, drinking and even laughing. Cab Calloway as Sportin' Life pranced out in a cream-colored suit and tried to paganize the Christians.

He sang 'It Ain't Necessarily So,' strutting as if he was speaking ex cathedra.

The audience applauded loudly, interrupting the stage action. Then a young woman broke away from a group of singers near the wings. She raced to the center of the stage and began to dance.

The sopranos sang a contrapuntal high-toned encouragement and the baritones urged the young woman on. The old lady tried to catch her, to stop the idolatrous dance, but the dancer moved out of her reach, flinging her legs high, carrying the music in her body as if it were a private thing, given into her care and protection. I nearly screamed with delight and envy. I wanted to be with her on the stage letting the music fly through my body. Her torso seemed to lose solidity and float, defying gravity. I wanted to be with her. No, I wanted to *be* her.

In the second act, Warfield, as the crippled Porgy, dragged the audience into his despair. Even kneeling, he was a large man, broad and thick-chested. His physical size made his affliction and his loss of Bess even sadder. The resonant voice straddled the music and rode it, controlling it.

I remained in my seat after the curtain fell and allowed people to climb over my knees to reach the aisle. I was stunned. *Porgy and Bess* had shown me the greatest array of Negro talent I had ever seen.

I took Clyde to the first matinée and he liked the dancing and 'the little goat that pulled Porgy off the stage' at the end of the opera.

The Purple Onion had picked up my three-month option and I decided to develop my own material. I began making up music for poems I had written years before and writing new songs that fit the calypso form.

One night the club was filled and more people were waiting outside for the room to clear. I lifted my head from a bow and standing before me was a beautiful black woman holding a long-stemmed rose. I bowed to her and she returned the bow, continuing to bend until she laid the flower at my feet. She blew a kiss and walked down the aisle to her table. Her friends began applauding again. I was not sure whether it was for me or for her, so I nodded to the musicians and started another encore. Halfway through I recognized the woman. She was the soprano who sang the 'Strawberry Song' in *Porgy and Bess*. I almost bit my song in two; all the people at that table were probably from *Porgy and Bess*.

I went directly from the stage to the table and took the rose along.

The group stood and applauded again. I laid the flower on the table and applauded them. The audience, infected, began to applaud us.

'These are the great singers from *Porgy and Bess*,' I shouted over the noise. People stood up to look, and soon the whole audience was standing and we were applauding ourselves for our good taste to be alive and in the right place at the right time.

We went to Pete's Pool Room, a large rambling restaurant on Broadway where the beats and artists and big-eyed tourists and burlesque queens went for a breakfast of hard rolls and maybe a game of pool. I wanted to call the whole room to order and present to them the singers from *Porgy and Bess*. We found seats and I heard the names again.

Ned Wright, a tall muscular man of about thirty, said I was excellent and 'Don't run yourself down, darling, there are plenty of people in the world who will do that for you.'

Lillian Hayman, the dramatic soprano, who was as plump as a pillow and biscuit-brown, laughed often, trilling like a bird and showing perfect white teeth. Chief Bey, the drummer, mumbled in a deep voice that seemed to shake his wiry black frame. Joseph Attles, a tenor, was at forty the oldest of the group. He was tall and very delicately made. A lemon-yellow man, he was understudy for Cab Calloway, who was Sportin' Life, and Joseph James, who sang the role of Jake.

And, of course, Martha Flowers, a great soprano and at that time a Bess understudy. Martha said, 'My dear, you stand like an African queen holding off a horde of marauders. All alone.' She was short, but as she talked and gestured, body erect, she grew tall before my eyes. I told them how their singing had

147

affected me, and when the opportunity arose, I asked about the dancer.

Martha said, 'Leesa Foster, Elizabeth Foster. She is also a soprano and I hear she is going to be one of our Besses.' They promised to bring her to the club the next evening.

Martha bettered her promise by bringing not only Leesa Foster but even more people the next night. The voice teacher, Frederick Wilkerson, and two or three other cast members sat with the original group at two tables pushed together. Again they all said they enjoyed my singing, again I demurred, saying that I was really a dancer. Leesa was instantly interested and we spoke of dance schools, teachers and styles. Again we went to Pete's for breakfast. Wilkie, as the voice teacher was called, leaned forward and boomed, 'You are singing totally wrong. Totally wrong. If you keep it up you'll lose your voice in five years.' He leaned back in his chair and added, 'Maybe three years, yes, yes. Maybe three.'

His pronouncement pinched my budding confidence. I looked around the table, but no one seemed perturbed by his warning. I asked him what I could do to prevent disaster. He nodded and said in sonorous tones, 'You are intelligent, yes I see that. You are intelligent. Get to a voice teacher, a good voice teacher. And study very hard. Apply yourself. That's all.' He smacked his lips as if he had just tasted a favorite sweet.

'How can I find a good teacher?'

The singers were as curious about his answer as I. They looked at him.

'Now that's another intelligent question,' his voice boomed. 'As a matter of fact, I plan to leave *Porgy and Bess* and relocate myself in San Francisco. I am willing to take you as a student if, and only if, you work hard and listen to me. I don't have time for any more students; however, I want to help you. If you don't get help, you not only won't be able to sing, you'll hardly be able to talk.'

Robert Breen, *Porgy and Bess*'s good-looking and balding producer, came to the Purple Onion the next evening accompanied by his wife, Wilva, a pleasant little blond woman; the business manager, Robert Dustin; and an attractive, well-built woman who was introduced to me as Ella Gerber, company drama coach. When we shook hands, her dark-lashed eyes studied me.

Breen said he had heard I was a professional dancer. I admitted that.

'We may have an opening soon for a dancer who sings. Would you come to the theater and audition for us?'

I thought about my contract. I would not be free to take the job for nearly three months. Should I tell them? It would be honest and fair to leave the job open for another dancer. I told myself that I loved honesty and openness, not so much for its own sake but for its simplicity – I would be free from apologies, recriminations and accusations. Then I thought of Leesa Foster dancing to the sound of great voices, tossing herself into music and movement as if within that marriage lay all human bliss.

'Would I have to audition to a record or could I work with the company?'

Breen turned his pink, baby-skinned face to Dustin.

'We have a full rehearsal scheduled,' Dustin said, 'and if you want Maya to try out, that could be arranged.'

They looked at me, Ella Gerber's eyes computing the

length of my legs, the size of my brain and the amount of my talent.

Breen suggested a date and I agreed. We drank a cold white wine to the audition and they left.

I went to the bar and told Ned about the conversation I had had with Breen. 'Dance, darling.' He raised his hands to eye level and snapped his fingers. 'Dance until they see Nijinsky in a duet with Katherine Dunham.' Snap!

All the singers were in street clothes, as if they had stopped by the theater en route for something more important. Some stood on the empty stage, others stood in the wings or lounged in the front row of the theater.

Billy Johnson, assistant conductor, waited while the musicians warmed up and tuned their instruments in the orchestra pit. Trills and arpeggios of voices came from backstage.

The stage manager, Walter Riemer, had a flashy smile and was as elegant as John Gielgud, whom he resembled. He took a position just off the stage. 'Watch me, dear, when I do this' – he waved his hand like a flag in a high wind – 'that's your cue.' And he left me.

I sneaked around the curtain and watched as Billy lifted his arms as if he was trying to pull the orchestra out of the pit by invisible strings. The music began to swell, the singers poised.

At a casual indication from Johnson's right hand the voices exploded, ripping shreds in the air.

When Riemer's hand floated my cue, I was laughing and crying at the wonder of it all. I ran on stage, stepping lightly between the singers' notes. If I was supposed to portray a woman carried away by music, blinded and benumbed by her surroundings, enchanted so by the rhythm and melody that she fancied herself a large, gloriously colored bird free to fly rainbows and light up the winds, then I was she.

Three days later, Bob Dustin offered me the job.

I said, as if newly indignant, that the Purple Onion would not let me out of my contract. Dustin commiserated with me and added, 'We'll be auditioning people for the next two months. We have to have a lead dancer before we go back to Europe.'

Even my imagination had never dared to include me in Europe. Whenever I envisioned foreign countries, I saw them through other people's words or other people's pictures. London to me was as Dickens saw it, a folk song in a cockney accent, Churchill V-ing his fingers, saying, 'We shall fight on the beaches,' and so forth. Paris, in my mind, rang with the hoofbeats of horse-drawn carriages from the age of Guy de Maupassant. Germany was Hitler and concentration-camp horror or beery burghers in stiff white shirts sitting on benches photographed by Cartier-Bresson. Italy was the hungry streets of *Open City* or curly-haired people singing and eating pasta.

The images had been provided by movies, books and Pathé News, and none included a six-foot-tall black woman hovering either in the back or in the foreground.

15

When *Porgy and Bess* left San Francisco I resigned myself to the night-club routine, and the burden of life was lightened only by twice-weekly sessions with Wilkie and Lloyd and the romping growth of Clyde.

Three days before my contract ran out I received a telephone call from Saint Subber, the Broadway producer, inviting me to come to New York City to try out for a new show called *House of Flowers*. He said Pearl Bailey would be starring and he had heard I was a great deal like her. If I satisfied him and got the role he had in mind, I would play opposite Miss Bailey.

New Yorkers may love their hometown loyally, but San Franciscans believe that when good angels die they stay in northern California and hover over the Golden Gate Bridge. I appreciated the chance to try out for a Broadway show, but the invitation did not make me ecstatic. It meant leaving San Francisco, without the prospect of Europe with *Porgy and Bess*.

Mom and Lottie and Wilkie encouraged me to go. The

voice teacher and my mother had found that they had much in common and Mother invited him to move into our house. He came bringing his piano, students, huge rumbling voice and his religious positivism. He could cook nearly as well as the two women and the kitchen rang and reeked with the attempts of three chefs to outtalk and outcook one another.

They would take care of Clyde until I found an apartment and then he could fly to me. Of course I was going to get the part. There was no question of that.

I arrived in New York and went to a midtown hotel which Willkie had suggested. The congested traffic and raucous voices, the milling crowds and towering buildings, made me think of my tiny fourth-floor room at the end of a dark corridor a sanctuary.

I telephoned Saint Subber, who said I must come to his apartment. I wriggled around his invitation, not wishing to face the street again so soon and hesitant about going to a strange man's apartment – especially a New York producer's apartment. Hollywood films had taught me that breed was dangerous: each one was fat, smoked large smelly cigars and all said, 'All right, girlie, ya got talent, now lemme see ya legs.'

'Mr. Saint Subber' – or was one supposed to call him Mr. Subber? – 'I need to have my hair done. May I see you tomorrow?'

He blasted my excuse. 'No, no matter, I won't be looking at your hair.'

See, my legs. Just as I thought.

'I want to see what you look like.' He gave me his address and hung up.

I had come three thousand miles, so surely I had the courage to go a few more blocks.

A uniformed doorman in front of a neat East Side apartment house raised his brows when I told him my destination, but he walked me into the lobby and reluctantly handed me over to a uniformed elevator operator. The operator pulled his face down as if to say 'So, hot stuff, huh?' but he said 'Penthouse,' and we began our smooth ascent. When we stopped he rang a bell and the door opened.

A beautiful blond young man offered me his hand. 'Miss Angelou?' He did not look as if my legs would interest him.

'Yes. Mr. Subber?'

The elevator door closed and we were in a beautifully furnished living room.

'No, I'm not Saint. My name is Tom. I'm helping on the production. Please have a seat.' He led me to a sofa. 'Saint will be with you in a few minutes. What can I get you to drink?'

While he was away I looked at the room and wondered about the tenant. Paintings adorned the walls and flowers were fresh and gay on little tables. A man's voice in argument came through a louvered door.

Tom returned with a gin and tonic in a very tall, extraordinarily thin glass. He asked about my trip and tried to reassure me when I told him I was nervous.

A man rushed through the shuttered door; he was small and thin and his dark hair was cut in a 'Quo Vadis.'

'Well, that's over. Oh, my God!' He threw himself on a chaise longue and gingerly put both hands to his head. 'Oh, God! What do they want? Oh, my head. Virginia!'

A large Negro woman came through another door. She

wore the kind of apron I had not seen since I had left the small country town in Arkansas. It was white, bibbed, starched and voluminous. She went directly to the man and began to massage his temples.

'That's all right, Saint honey, that's all right, you hear. Now don't think about it, honey. Everything's going to be all right.'

I could not believe it.

Neither had taken notice of me and I was so enthralled I frankly stared, recording the scene.

Tom and I could have been an audience while two actors performed a scene in experimental theater.

It was decidedly too new, too strange. I started laughing.

The man sat bolt upright. 'Who are you?'

'I?' I held the laughter. 'I'm Maya Angelou.'

'You can't be.' He was still sitting straight.

'But I am, I am Maya Angelou.' I was willing to swear to it.

'Well, my God, how tall are you?'

'I'm six feet.'

'But you can't be!' He seemed sure.

'I am, I am too.'

'Stand up. I don't believe it.'

I stood up, hoping I had not shrunk in the plane or in the taxi or in the elevator.

'My God, it's true, you're six feet tall.'

I laughed because I was happy that at least my height had not betrayed me and because he was funny.

'And a great laugh, too. Oh, my God, I know, you're a black Carol Channing.'

That made me laugh again. He stood up and came to me.

155

'We'll do your hair red. Will that be all right? Red or blond?'

I said, 'I don't think so.'

'Oh, you wouldn't like that?' It was a sincere question.

'Noooo.' I pictured myself with hair as red as Gwen Verdon's and started laughing again. 'No, I don't think it would work.'

'All right.' He chuckled, too. 'We'll think of something else.'

I was still laughing.

'What's so funny?'

When I could catch my breath I told him. 'I expected you to smoke a cigar and pinch my cheeks, to roll your eyes at me and make some lewd proposition. I've been dreading that all the way from California, and I get here' – the funny bone was struck again – 'I get here and . . . Tom and you and Virginia and my red hair.' He, too, began to laugh at the absurd situation. Tom joined in.

Saint Subber said impulsively, 'Stay for dinner. Virginia, we'll be another for dinner.' For all his theatrics, or maybe because of them, I knew he was a strong man. I had always been more comfortable around strong people.

After a dinner of frogs' legs (I had never eaten them before and had to ask if they were eaten with a knife and fork or with the fingers like spare ribs), he told me to come to the theater the next morning and not to sing any special material, because Truman Capote was going to be at the theater and 'Truman hates special material.'

I thanked them both for their hospitality and went back to the hotel to telephone Mom. 'Do your best tomorrow' she

156

said, 'and don't worry. Remember, you've got a home to come back to.' I spoke to Clyde, who sounded fine, and hung up and went to bed.

The Alvin Theater was on Broadway and I had been asked to go to the stage door around the corner. I walked quite cheerfully among the crowds on the sidewalk. I had stopped at a music store and bought a copy of 'Love for Sale,' for no reason except that it had been on display and I had heard it sung so often. If Truman Capote did not like special material, I would sing a standard for him. I noticed only after I had turned the corner at the theater that a line of Negro people stretched around the block headed in the direction I was taking. I exchanged smiles with some of the young standees and gave good mornings to some of the older women with pleasant faces. The line stopped at the stage door. I had never auditioned in New York and thought maybe all Broadway shows had their tryouts in the same theater.

I knocked at the door and Tom opened it. I would not have been surprised if I had been given a number and told to take my place in line. Instead, he said, 'Oh, Miss Angelou. Please come in. I'll tell Saint you're here.'

He led me to a corner and excused himself. The blurred forms inside the theater became more visible. There were over a hundred Negro people lined up along the backstage wall, waiting, alert.

Tom waved me over and whispered, 'Saint will hear you now. Have you your music?'

I said, 'Yes.'

'Give it to me,' he said, 'I'll take it to the pianist. Do you want to run over it with her?'

I did not think so – after all, it was only 'Love for Sale.'

'Just a minute and I'll call your name. Walk right through here.' He showed me to the wings and an entrance stage left. 'The pianist is in the pit. You nod to her and she'll begin.' Just like the old Purple Onion days.

'And there's nothing to worry about.' He added, 'Truman Capote is out there and Saint and Yip Harburg and Peter Hall. Do your best.'

I waited, trying not to think about trying out and thinking about New York. The Apple. I would make it and send for Clyde, then we would spend afternoons in Central Park, perhaps not as nice as Golden Gate Park, but then . . . I would find a lover, too; among all those millions of people there had to be a man who had been waiting for me to come along and cheer up his life. I would not think about trying out. Just wait until my name was called and then go out and sing.

'Miss Angelou, Maya Angelou.'

I walked out in front of the velvet curtain. The lights were bright and hard and white, and the theater seats, only dimly lighted near the stage, darkened into oblivion. I saw a small clump of figures in the distance. On the right side of the orchestra pit a woman sat patiently at a grand piano.

I took my position, thinking of Lloyd Clark: 'Stand still, stand perfectly still, darling, still.' I stood. Wilkie's teaching ran in my thoughts: 'Drop your jaw. Don't try to look pretty by grinning when you sing. Drop your jaw.' I dropped my jaw, and then nodded to the pianist, moving nothing but my head.

She stroked out the first notes of my song and I began.

'Love for sale, appetizing young love—'

She stopped.

'Uh, no, uh, I'm playing the verse. If you don't want the verse I'll go right to the refrain.'

I had read the verse when I bought the music, but I had never heard it sung.

'Just the "love for sale" part, please.' I thought I heard a titter from backstage, but I could not be sure. She played the first three notes and I began to sing. 'Love for sale, appetizing young love for sale.' I imagined I was a girl in a trench coat and a beret, standing under a streetlight in old Chinatown in a light rain. Men passed me by after looking me over and I continued my plaintive offer.

I was so engrossed in telling the story that I did not know when the music and I had parted company, or quite how we could get back together. I only knew I was in one key and the piano in another. I looked at the pianist. She began to strike the keys harder, and in a vain attempt to settle correctly I began to sing louder. She lifted her hands and pounded on the piano. I raised my voice and screamed, 'If you want to buy my wares' a mile away from what she was playing.

She half rose, crouched over the keyboard. There was a frantic determination in the position of her body, in the bend of her neck. She would get me back on pitch or there would just be splinters left on the piano.

Plunk plunk – she was as loud as I – and I heard a low vocal grumble as she sought to overwhelm my voice into submission. I shouted, 'Follow me and climb the stairs.' A thin but definite screech slid through my nose. I dropped my jaw to try to force the sound down into the back of my mouth where I could control it. The pianist was standing. Her brow was knit and her teeth bared. She was about to attack the piano for the final chord. I barged in, overtook her and in a second outdistanced her as I yelled 'Love for sale.'

She flopped on the piano stool exhausted and in defeat.

I was just a little proud that I had gotten all the way through the song. Then I heard the sounds. There were gurgles and giggles from the theater and the muffled bubbling of outright disorderly laughter from backstage.

The flush of heat crawled up my face and spread through my body the instant I realized that I was the object of derision. But I was, I told myself, the person who'd had flowers put at her feet. And I was the entertainer asked to take Eartha Kitt's role in *New Faces*. I was the dancer *Porgy and Bess* wanted to follow the fabulous Lizabeth Foster. And I was being laughed away just because I could not sing 'Love for Sale.' Well, they need not.

'Excuse me,' I said, and looked over the rows of seats toward the indistinct shadows. 'I understand that Mr. Capote doesn't like special material. And you've asked me to come out here to show you what I do. I am willing to sing calypso for you or I'd be just as happy to go home.'

Indeed, it would be nicer to go back to California. To my mother's big house and good food. To my son, who needed me, and Aunt Lottie, who loved me. Back to the wonderful Purple Onion where my friends would welcome me. The period between becoming a great Broadway star setting New York on its ear and returning to the family's bosom was shorter than the first intervals between the overheard laughter.

There was little sound from the audience. They clapped as if they were wearing furry gloves.

'Yes, Miss Angelou, sing whatever you like.'

160

I said, 'I'm going to sing "Run Joe," and since I was discouraged from bringing my sheet music, I'll have to sing it a cappella.' Wilkie had told me that music sung without accompaniment was called 'a cappella.'

If I was going home, I had to show them what they were missing, and that I had some place to go.

I gave them the special Saturday-night standing-room-only encore version. The one where I spun around, my body taut. The one where I yelped small noises and sighed like breaking ocean waves.

When I finished, the first applause came from the pianist. She was smiling and clapping so energetically that I surmised that I had rescued her recently endangered belief in the human voice. There was more applause from the audience, and this time it sounded fresh and sincere. I did not know what I was expected to do next. I stood still for a moment, then bowed and rather stiffly turned away.

'Will you wait backstage, Miss Angelou?' Tom's voice sprang through the void.

'Yes, thank you.'

Whenever I was embarrassed or felt myself endangered, I relied on my body's training to deliver me. Grandmother Henderson and Grandmother Baxter had drilled my brother and me in the posture of 'shoulders back, head up, look the future in the eye,' and years of dance classes had compounded the education. I turned and walked to the wings like Cleopatra walking to the throne room (meanwhile clasping the asp in her bodice).

Backstage a few of the hopeful contenders tapped their hands together or snapped their fingers when they saw me.

161

They grinned saucy compliments to me, probably as much for my own sassiness in standing up and talking back as for what they heard of my second song.

Saint Subber, Tom and Truman Capote came backstage and walked over to me.

Saint Subber said, 'You've got a certain quality.'

Tom's praise was as generous as his manner.

Truman Capote spoke, and I thought for a desperate moment that he was pulling my leg. He said in a faint falsetto, 'Miss Angelou, honey, ah love yoah work.' He sounded just like a rich old Southern white woman. He reminded me of a Countee Cullen poem:

> She even thinks that up in heaven
> Her class lies late and snores
> While poor Black cherubs rise at seven
> To do celestial chores.

Yet I could not detect a shread of superciliousness on his face or in his soft yielding manner. I thanked him. Tom said he would be in touch with me and I shook hands with the men and left the theater.

Outside I passed the line of people still waiting. They scanned my features intently, trying to read the outcome of my ordeal and thereby prophesy their own. If I was triumphant it meant that success was in the air and might come to them. On the other hand, it could mean that I had just filled the vacancy that they themselves might have taken.

Theirs was a grievous lot. Ten or twenty jobs for two thousand or more trained, talented and anxious aspirants. Another

Countee Cullen poem stated that God, should he choose, could explain why he gave the turtle such a strange yet lovely shell, why the spring follows winter, why the snake doffs its skin, 'yet,' said the poet, 'do I marvel at this curious thing, to make a poet Black and bid him sing.' And of all things, to bid him sing in New York City.

I thought of *Porgy and Bess*. Of the sixty people who sang and laughed and lived together, the camaraderie and the pride they had in one another's genius. Although I had not heard from the company administrators for three months, I had received cards from Martha Flowers and from Ned Wright. I waited around in my small hotel room and prowled my dingy lobby. I called Mother, who ordered me to keep my chin up, and Clyde, who missed me and gave me news of Fluke's latest adventures. Wilkie reminded me that 'In God I live and have my being.'

On a Thursday morning I received a note which read: 'Miss Angelou, the *House of Flowers* company is happy to inform you that you have been chosen for the part in our production. Please come to the office Thursday afternoon at three to sign your contract.'

I shared the news with my family immediately, and when I hung up, the telephone rang again. I thought it was probably Saint Subber calling to congratulate me.

It was Breen's Everyman's Opera Company. Bob Dustin said, 'Maya Angelou?'

'Yes.'

'This is *Porgy and Bess*. We called your San Francisco number and were told you were in New York.'

'Yes.'

163

'We want you for the role of Ruby.'

How could there be so much of a good thing?

'But I've just got a part in a new show opening on Broadway.'

'Really? Oh, that's too bad. The company is in Montreal now and we leave for Italy in four days.'

There really was no contest. I wanted to travel, to try to speak other languages, to see the cities I had read about all my life, but most important, I wanted to be with a large, friendly group of black people who sang so gloriously and lived with such passion.

'I don't have a passport.'

'We are being sponsored by the State Department.'

I thought about the school I had attended which was on the House Un-American Activities Committee list.

He said, 'Don't worry about your passport. We can get a special dispensation. Do you want to join *Porgy and Bess*?'

'Yes, yes.' Yes, indeed.

'Then come to the office and we'll get you straightened out. You'll leave tomorrow afternoon for Montreal.'

I telephoned Saint Subber and explained that I had been offered another job. He asked me if I would give up a new Broadway show for a chorus part in a touring company.

I said 'Yes.'

16

My mind turned over and over like a flipped coin: Paris, then Clyde's motherless birthday party, Rome and my son's evening prayers said to Fluke, Madrid and Clyde struggling alone with his schoolwork.

I telephoned home again. Mother was pleased and gave me a load of phrases to live by. 'Treat everybody right, remember life is a two-way street. You might meet the same people on your way down that you met going up.' And 'Look to the hills from whence cometh your help.' Lottie said she was proud of me and that I had it in me to become great. Wilkie told me to hum a lot, place my voice in the mask and always drop my jaw. And to keep in my heart the knowledge that there was no place where God was not.

I asked to speak with Clyde. Using a tack I loathed, I talked to him as if he was a small child with faulty English. He asked when I was coming home and when was I sending for him. His voice became faint after I said I was not coming the next week but soon. Very soon.

165

Yes, he'd be a good boy. Yes, he would mind Grandmother and Aunt Lottie. And yes, he knew I loved him. He hung up first.

When I called Ivonne she told me to stop crying, that Clyde had no father, so it was up to me to make a place for both of us, and that that was what I was doing. She said she would go over to the house as usual and see him and take him out. After all, he was not with strangers but with his grandmother – why did I worry?

The past revisited. My mother had left me with my grandmother for years and I knew the pain of parting. My mother, like me, had had her motivations, her needs. I did not relish visiting the same anguish on my son, and she, years later, had told me how painful our separation was to her. But I had to work and I would be good. I would make it up to my son and one day would take him to all the places I was going to see.

I had been given a précis of the DuBose Heyward book on which George and Ira Gershwin had based their opera:

Porgy, a crippled beggar, lives in the Negro hamlet of Catfish Row, North Carolina. He is loved by the town's inhabitants, who eke out their meager living by fishing and selling local produce.

When Crown, a tough stevedore, kills Robbin, Serena's husband, in a crap game, the white police descend upon the hamlet to find the culprit. Sportin' Life, who runs the gambling and other nefarious money-making schemes, escapes into Ruby's house, but Bess, Crown's beautiful and worldly woman, is rejected by the community's women and is nearly captured in the raid. Just as the police dragnet is about to close in on her, Porgy opens the door of his hut and Bess finds

166

safety. Porgy falls in love with Bess and she accepts his love and protection, swearing that she will stay with him forever. Crown escapes from jail and comes to claim Bess at a picnic which Porgy does not attend. Bess is sexually attracted to her old lover and goes away with him for three days. Porgy goes to look for her. When she returns to Catfish Row, Porgy is away and the local women scorn her. Sportin' Life courts her, gives her cocaine and begs her to leave the small town and accompany him to New York, where 'I'll give you the finest diamonds on upper Fifth Avenue.'

> 'And through Harlem we'll go a struttin'
>> We'll go a struttin' and there'll be nuttin'
>> Too good for you.'

She cannot resist his entreaty, his style and the drugs. She leaves with him.

Porgy returns and is told of Bess's journey, and against the pleas of his neighbors, calls for his goat, hitches the cart to the animal and sets out to travel to New York to find his Bess.

The naïve story is given dramatic pace by the birth of a longed-for child, a hurricane in which a member of the community is killed and a picnic where Sportin' Life tries to tempt the religious people away from their beliefs.

On Friday, breathless, excited and afraid, I arrived at dusk in Montreal.

I was met at the airport, and although it was too early for the cast to assemble, taken directly to the theater. Backstage, men shouted to one another in French and English and hustled around, pulling ropes and adjusting pieces of scenery. When I walked onto the empty set, all the shards of the last two days' tensions fell away. I was suddenly in the papier-mâché world of great love, passion and poignancy.

I was examining Porgy's cabin and the house where Robbin's widow, Serena, sings her mournful aria when the singers began to trickle into the back of the theater.

Ella Gerber saw me slouching upstage in the shadows.

'Oh, Maya, you've arrived!' She came forward. 'Here's your script, your hotel and room number. A schedule for rehearsals. I suggest you watch this performance carefully and study your script tonight. You'll be rehearsing tomorrow.'

She said I had no dressing room because I would not be performing until we arrived in Italy, but she would tell the cast that I had arrived.

My fears that I had been forgotten turned out to be base-less. When Ella led me down the dressing room corridor, she called out, 'Maya's here!'

Martha Flowers ran out into the hall. *'La première danseuse, elle est ici!'*

Lillian Hayman followed smiling, saying 'Welcome.'

Barbara Ann Webb grinned, spread her arms and made 'Hey, girl' sound like 'Where have you been so long?' and 'Why weren't you here sooner?'

The three women shared a cluttered dressing room and I sat amid the costumes and the disarray of make-up, watching them prepare for the show. Martha was as delicately made as a Stradivarius. Her complexion was the rich brown of polished mahogany and her hands fine and small. She had large bright eyes. Her lips, full and open, revealed even white teeth in the dark face. She called herself, and was called by her friends, 'Miss Fine Thing.' Rightly.

If Martha was a violin, Lillian Hayman was a cello. She was a medium-brown woman of heavy curves and deep arches. Her dignified posture caused her to be regarded as stout rather than fat, and she moved lightly as if her weight might be only in the eye of the beholder. She had a handsome face softened by a ready warm smile. She was a dramatic soprano and the description was apt.

Barbara Ann Webb, a lyric soprano, was the innocent when I joined the company, and so she remained until I left. She was nearly as large as Lillian, but her curves were younger and more conventionally arranged. A Texan, she had an openness that reminded me of sunshine in movies by Technicolor. Her skin was a shade lighter than a ripe peach, and had she been white, she could have been a stand-in for Linda Darnell. Throughout ten countries and fifteen cities, those three women became and remained my closest friends.

That first night the chatter in the dressing room wound down and there was a knock at the door.

'Fifteen minutes.'

'O.K.,' Lillian shouted.

I had heard the announcement of 'Half-hour' earlier, but none of the women responded. Now Martha turned away from the mirror and her eyes glazed, began to sing 'Do re me fa sol la ti do.' I didn't know whether I was expected to say something, then Lillian also dropped her interest in our conversation and an unseeing look came into her eyes, she stretched her lips in a taut, false smile and holding her teeth closed, yelped 'Ye, ya, yo, you.' Barbara Ann stood and began

169

to sway slowly from side to side. She started to lower and raise her jaw and then sang 'Woooo Wooooo.'

They took no notice of me, but I couldn't do the same with them. I had never been so close to trained singers and the reverberations shook in my ears. I left the room and walked down the corridor to find my place in the wings. Sounds came out of each door I passed. One baritone roared like a wounded moose, another wailed like a freight train on a stormy night. The tenors yelped in high screeches. There were whines and growls and the siren of an engine on its way to a four-alarm fire. Grunts overlapped the high-pitched 'ha ha ho ho's' and the total cacophony tickled me; I could have laughed outright. These exquisite singers who would soon stand on the stage delivering the most lovely and liquid tones had first to creak like rusty scissors and wail like banshees. I remembered that before I could lift my torso and allow my arms to wave as if suspended in water, I had to bend up and down, sticking my behind in the air, plié and relevé until my muscles ached, arch-roll and contract and release until my body begged for deliverance. The singers were not funny. They were working. Preparation is rarely easy and never beautiful. That was the first of many lessons *Porgy and Bess* taught me.

I sat on a stool in the wings and watched the singers respond to the stage manager's shouted 'Places, please. Places.' They moved directly to their positions in *Porgy*'s world. There were a few whispers as the lights began their slow descent to black.

There was applause from in front of the curtain and the lively overture of Gershwin's opera swelled onto the stage. The curtain began sliding open and pastel lights illuminated the set. A group of men, downstage left, were involved in a crap game; some knelt, others mimed throwing dice. Then Ned Wright, as Robbins, threw the dice and sang 'Nine to Make, Come Nine.' The pure tenor line lifted and held in the air for a second, and in a rush the pageant began.

The sopranos and tenors, bassos and baritones, acted as if they were indeed the poverty-stricken Southern Negroes whose lives revolved around the dirt road encampment of Catfish Row. They sang and listened, then harmonized with each other's tones so closely that the stage became a wall of music without a single opening unfilled.

Their self-hypnotism affected the audience and over-whelmed me. I cried for Robbin's poor widow, Serena, who sang the mournful aria 'My Man's Gone Now.' Helen Thigpen, a neat little quail of a woman, sang the role with a conviction that burdened the soul. Irene Williams sang Bess, sassily tossing her hips as effortlessly as she flung the notes into the music of the orchestra. Leslie Scott, handsome and as private as an African mask, sang Porgy and in a full, rich baritone. When the first act was over, the audience applauded long and loudly, and I found myself drenched with perspiration and exhausted.

The singers, on the other hand, seemed to step out of the roles as easily as one kicks off too large slippers. They passed me in the wings on their way to the dressing rooms chattering about packing and whether they ought to buy more clothes in Montreal for the European trip.

I didn't like their frivolity. It seemed as if they were being disloyal to the great emotions they had sung about and aroused in me. It wasn't pleasant to discover they were only playing parts. I wanted them to walk offstage wrapped in drama, trailing wisps of tragedy. Instead, Martha came through a parting in the backdrop curtain. Her dark face split in a smile.

'Hey, girl. How do you like it?'

She would not have understood had I said I loved the singing but felt betrayed by the singers.

I said, 'I love it.'

'Is this the first time you've watched an opera from backstage?'

I told her it was.

The final act was more astounding than the first. I knew now that the actors were not wholly involved in their roles because I had seen the alacrity with which they shuffled off their characters, and yet they caught me again and wove me deftly into the pattern of the play.

The audience jumped to their feet, shouting 'Bravo' and clapping their hands, and the company bowed ensemble. Then the chorus members began to peel off the long double lines, leaving a neat arrangement of principal actors, and the audience thundered its approval.

Backstage after the final curtain, singers, stage hands, administrators acted as if the play had never been. The moods they had created, the tears they had wept so copiously and the joy they had reveled in were forgotten.

I wondered if I would make any real friendships or, to be more precise, I doubted that people who could be so emotionally casual had the ability, desire or need to make friendships.

Billy Johnson told me I was expected at the theater the

next afternoon for rehearsal. He asked if I could sight-sing and I answered no. Wilkie had encouraged me to study solfeggio so that I would be able to pick up a piece of sheet music and read it as naturally as one reads a newspaper, but I hadn't had the time. Johnson, a prematurely balding white man from Oklahoma, said we'd work it out. That I didn't really have much to learn.

I was assigned to the hotel where Martha and Lillian stayed and we sat late into the night telling our life stories. Martha was the daughter of a preacher in North Carolina. Lillian was choir director of a large church in Jamaica, Long Island. My grandmother had been Mother of the C.M.E. Church in Stamps, Arkansas, so we shared a common religious background.

Rehearsal wasn't as frightening as I had expected. Once Billy Johnson was convinced that the company administrators had actually hired a singer who couldn't read music, he took the situation in hand.

He sat at the piano and with one hand played my part. Having been surrounded by the group of highly trained, talented singers, it would be understandable if he had come to believe that not only could all Negroes sing, but they could all sing opera and had perfect pitch. He barely covered his shock at finding that I didn't have a good ear.

His accent was Southern and as refined as oil of wintergreen.

'Well, no, Maya, that's not quite it. Close, but not quite.' He played the air again, his fingers stroking the keys daintily. 'It's more like this.'

After an hour, during which I sang the same tune over and over again, he surrendered gracefully.

'I think you're going to have to put in some work on this before you open with us in Venice.'

In the dance sequence I was all right. The rhythm was complex, but I seemed to hear it easily and I danced it freely. Robert Breen had explained that he didn't want the piece to look choreographed. The dancer had to appear so bewitched by the music that she abandoned herself in a glory of dance. I surrendered to the music and allowed it to fashion my performance.

17

For three days I rehearsed in the afternoons and observed the company from the wings at night. But mornings I spent walking the clean streets of Montreal and listening to the foreign accents and looking at the people.

Among the many perversities in American race relations is the fact that blacks do not relish looking closely at whites. After hundreds of years of being the invisible people ourselves, as soon as many of us have achieved economic security we try to force whites into nonexistence by ignoring them.

Montreal provided me with my first experience of looking freely at whites. The underground railroad had had Canada as its final destination, and slaves had created a powerful liturgy praising Canada which was sung all over the world. Spirituals abounded with references to the Biblical body of water, the river Jordan. I had been told that Jordan, in our music, meant the Mississippi or the Arkansas or the Ohio River and the stated aim to get to Canaan land was the slave's way of saying he longed to go to Canada, and freedom.

Therefore, Canadians were exempt from many blacks' rejection of whites. They were another people. I observed their clean streets and the fact that their faces did not tighten when they saw me. The atmosphere was comfortable enough to allow me to try my recently learned French words. Sometimes I was understood.

The hotel lobby looked like a train station. Two children, sixty adults with their suitcases, coats, umbrellas, hats and other paraphernalia were trying to check out and board the two buses that were to take them to the airport.

A scene was played out which I was to see repeated in the capitals of Europe and North Africa. Remaining hotel guests were astounded by the horde of colorful people queuing up to windows, shouting across lines to each other, laughing at the joy of travel and the promise of Europe.

The stars of the company sparkled and attracted. Earl Jackson, our second Sportin' Life, had just joined the troupe when I arrived in Montreal. His wardrobe was as new to the old members as it was to me. He was not a trained singer and the gossip was that he had been hired from the streets of Chicago because he had firsthand information of the role he was to play. He wore a snappy, flashy suit and his hair was as black and slick as his pointy shoes. He knew he was handsome, and because he did not yet belong to any clique, he stood aloof and haughty, as if he were the absolute center of the universe and we were inconsequential people on the periphery.

Leslie Scott dressed expensively and behaved like a classic baritone. His fitted coat had a Persian lamb collar, which was accented by a cashmere scarf. He was a star and made no attempt to play it down.

The women who sang Bess were unfailingly and dramatically attractive. Martha was perfectly made-up and dressed in her dainty coat of many colors; Gloria Davy, tall and black, held her strangely Oriental beauty contained in distant impassivity. Irene Williams, golden and cheerful, looked as much like Bess in a hotel lobby as she did on the stage. John McCurry, who sang the role of Crown, was six foot six, two hundred and fifty pounds – a booming bass-baritone and the color of a ripe Satsuma plum. His wife was little and as white as he was black. She spoke softly and seldom. Because of the disparity in size, and color, they were called secretly Jack and Jane Sprat.

Most of the tenors who had visited Europe on an earlier tour and had the temperament of their vocal range, wore their coats over their shoulders with a studied indifference and carried walking sticks.

Eloise Uggams and Ruby Green were among the quiet, self-effacing women who looked and acted more like pillars of a religious order than singing members of a flamboyant opera company. Their male counterparts, Joe Jones, Merritt Smith, could have been church deacons, small business owners or solid insurance collectors. They not only didn't seem to belong to the dramatic group but appeared a little ill-at-ease with them in public. The sober members always managed to stand a little apart from the vociferous group as if they were waiting for another train going to a different destination.

The company descended on the airport like an invading horde of Goths on ancient Rome. Some people hummed little airs from *Madame Butterfly* or *Cavalleria Rusticana*. Others continued the conversations they had started on the buses in loud voices to override the general noise. At least five bags were lost, searched for, bemoaned and then found with cries of welcome. After processing about only twenty passports and fifty suitcases, looks passed between the Canadian officials as if they had rehearsed the scene: they raised their eyebrows, shrugged, looked in another direction and waved *Porgy and Bess* company through the turnstile and out of their sight.

The airplane stewardesses found that their aloof manner designed to keep obstreperous passengers in check did not work with their cargo of singers. The sopranos complained that the plane was too cold; the baritones were certain that the overheating was detrimental to their vocal cords; the tenors asked for rock and rye, and said generously they would settle for clover honey and fresh lemon juice. Panic increased among the stewardesses in direct relation to the requests made by their passengers.

When the pilot informed us we were passing over Newfoundland, which meant one hour from Montreal and eight whole hours from Milan, our final destination, the cabin attendants looked dazedly wild-eyed. They withdrew to the front of the plane and remained there, refusing to answer the persistent demands for attention.

Ruby Green was terrified of flying, so I had asked to be her seat companion. I knew that I was always at my best when I was near someone in a worse condition than I. When the plane took off she grabbed the seat arms, tensed her body and, by will alone, lifted the carrier safely in the air. I spoke to her of California, and thinking of Wilkie, reminded her (and myself) that 'there was no place God was not.' After a few hours she relaxed enough to join the conversation. She said

178

that she had no doubts about God but had no previous knowledge of the pilot, and that throughout three years of traveling with *Porgy and Bess* her serious misgivings about airplane captains had not diminished in the least.

The stewardesses appeared near the front seats. They began hauling out tablecloths and silverware from right to left as fast as possible. Once all our tray tables were down and dressed, they raced back to the minute kitchen stand and grabbed the meals. They handed them rapidly from right to left as quickly and deftly as a Las Vegas gambler deals a deck of cards. When we were all served they returned to their retreat without a single backward glance.

The Milan airport hustle differed only in language from the cacophonous noise of other airports I had known. I busied myself gathering my luggage and staying as close to my friends as possible without appearing to do exactly what I was doing – that is, clinging to their coattails for safety's sake.

The first part of the bus trip from Milan to Venice gave me and my colleagues no time to contemplate the Italian countryside. The driver was determined to show that not only did he know his vehicle and the roads, he was an artist at keeping the two in conjunction even under the most hair-raising circumstances. The bus – extra long and loaded with the entire company and all our baggage, and a guide who thought the language he spoke was English – skidded into curves, screeching like a stuck factory whistle; aimed itself at smaller vehicles as, growling, it leaped and bucked and swung around hills, holding onto the road by two wheels, one wheel, and then simply by sheer memory.

The guide shouted and gesticulated, held his upturned

hands away from his body and moved them up and down as if he were weighing two large grapefruit, his head rolling from side to side.

When the bus finally entered a small town, children and dogs became feathers blown out of its path; adults screamed at the driver, who, keeping his foot on the accelerator, turned his head and answered them shout for shout. We stopped at a square in the center of town and relief prevented us from cursing the driver, who stood by the open door, pride in his skill written on his face.

The guide led us to a restaurant and said, 'blah, blah, Verona, blah blah.' The word 'Verona' hit my ears like a clap of remembered thunder. Here was Verona, the home of Romeo and Juliet. The home of the Montagues and Capulets. I walked away from the crowd and looked at the buildings and up at the stone balconies. I placed Juliet above me, imagined her asking 'Romeo, Romeo! wherefore art thou, Romeo?' I put her lover in a shadow across the square and allowed him to praise Juliet's beauty and to wish: 'O that I were a glove upon that hand, that I might touch that cheek!'

I was really in Italy. Not Maya Angelou, the person of pretensions and ambitions, but me, Marguerite Johnson, who had read about Verona and the sad lovers while growing up in a dusty Southern village poorer and more tragic than the historic town in which I now stood.

I was so excited at the incredible turn of events which had brought me from a past of rejection, of slammed doors and blind alleys, of dead-end streets and culs-de-sac, into the bright sun of Italy, into a town made famous by one of the world's greatest writers. I ran to find Martha and Lillian.

They had saved a chair for me inside the café.

'Martha, did you know this is Verona?'

She looked up from the menu she was studying. 'Yes, and it's only twenty miles to Venice.'

Lillian said, 'My God, if we don't get a different driver, we may never get there.'

'Or if we keep this one we'll be there in five minutes.' Martha laughed.

I said, 'But I mean, this is Verona. Where the – This is the setting for Shakespeare's *Romeo and Juliet*.'

'We all heard it on the bus, Maya.' Lillian smiled at me as if I were an excited child. 'The guide told us. Weren't you listening?'

Martha pursed her lips, 'The Everyman Opera Company goes to the tremendous expense of hiring a guide who speaks an unheard-of language and moves his arms like a semaphore in a strong wind, and our prima ballerina doesn't even listen to him. Alas.' She went back to the menu.

Lillian looked at me and shook her head. 'Maya, in the next year you'll probably be in the place where Hamlet died, where Othello killed Desdemona or where Cleopatra did herself in with an asp. You're not going to get this excited each time, are you?'

Martha said, 'Dear, do let her have her day. After all, this is her first time in Europe.' They had both traveled with Gertrude Stein's *Four Saints in Three Acts*, and they acted as if they had chalets in Switzerland and villas in Spain where they took weekend visits. Martha continued, 'Let me help you with the menu.'

I decided that day never again to let them know how I

really felt. If they wanted to play it cool, then I'd show them how to play it cool. I asked for the menu and with my heart beating loud enough for them to hear it, gazed at the list of foods, written in Italian and in a script I'd never seen before. I recognized *uova* as eggs on the basis of my high school Latin and ordered. I knew that I must buy a dictionary the next day and start to teach myself Italian. I would speak the language of every country we visited; I would study nights and mornings until I spoke foreign languages, if not perfectly, at least coherently.

Neither books nor films had prepared me for Venice. I had seen *Blood and Sand,* the Tyrone Power movie, and felt I could walk easily among bullfighters and the beautiful señoritas of Spain. *The Bicycle Thief* and *Open City* gave clear if painful images of Italy after World War II. The Ali Baba and Aladdin's lamp stories, although portrayed by actors with heavy Central European accents, gave me some sense of the Moslem world. But Venice was a fantasia I had not experienced even secondhand. Our bus drove through narrow streets walled by tall buildings. Erratically we burst away from enclosures and saw open water where gondoliers plied their boats with as much élan as our driver conducted his vehicle. Balconies thrust above our heads; vegetable stalls and small shops jutted out beyond the pavement.

Across the square we stopped in a small plaza where there was a hotel. Tables sat out in front of a restaurant. As the company piled out of the bus and began the routine of sorting themselves and their baggage into individual lots, I stood looking at the black-coated waiters who were covering the tables with red checkered cloths.

A few had seen and heard the singers identifying their belongings in loud voices and they had rushed to the restaurant door to call to their fellow workers and Venetian customers. Men and women flowed out of the restaurant and onto the square, their eyes on the crowd of colorful Negroes who hadn't the time or the inclination to give them the slightest thought.

The ogling crowd who waved their hands in a kind of balletic concert were the first large group of native Italians I observed carefully. In Verona I had been too busy coping with my memories and the ancient romance and my own image to really look at the waiters or the other customers. But now, as I stood apart and had the opportunity to take in the whole scene, the Italian faces were contorted with what I took to be revulsion; I concluded that they had never seen so many black people before and were frightened and repelled.

A tall, tub-chested man in a white coat, who had been standing with the gawkers, said something which brought laughter from the crowd and walked toward the bus. I headed back to where the guide was ineffectually standing guard over a raggle-taggle mound of suitcases and offering his arms and head and torso and garbled tongue as a sacrifice to the god who reclaimed lost luggage. The white-coated man searched among the teeming, shouting singers and settled on John McCurry, who was bent double talking to his wife.

The man stood as if at attention. He spoke to John in Italian, then shot his hand out from waist level. Understandably, John, who had grown up in New York, jumped. The man began to wave his arms, and John, like most of the group who knew Italian from singing Puccini, Rossini,

Verdi and Bellini answered him in the poetic language of opera. The man beamed. He turned to the people who waited in the doorway of the restaurant and shouted. They clapped their hands and started toward the bus, talking loudly.

In general, black Americans do not take kindly to being rushed by a crowd of strange white men. John McCurry was still talking to the man who had acted as scout, but the other singers saw the crowd advancing across the square, and we reacted as if choreographed. We drew in closer to each other, our bags and the bus. The movement was subtle, but it was made with a fair amount of haste. The two small children stood nearer their fathers, who began talking earnestly with their wives. Ned Wright and Joe Attles chose that time to put their arms into the coats which they had always thrown cape-like over their shoulders.

As the group of Italians neared us, their smiles became evident; they were welcoming us to Venice. Our tight group relaxed and the old breezy attitudes returned. We mingled and mixed with the Italians, laughing and shaking hands.

They crowded around John McCurry and shouted, thinking he was the star of the opera. Leslie Scott and Laverne Hutchinson, who alternated in the lead role, were not pleased. John kept saying, 'No, no, io sono Crown.' But because of his size, his wide smile, large bass-baritone voice and probably his impeccable Italian accent, the new fans were certain they were admiring the right person.

Rose Tobias, who handled public relations for Porgy and Bess, stepped in to clear up the matter. She was a bright, young New Yorker, confident and pretty. She took Leslie and Laverne by the arms and pulled them into the center of the fray. The Italians were pumping John's hand as if they were priming a well.

Rose, still holding on to her stars, wedged herself between the Italians and John. She shook her head rapidly, causing her heavy blond hair to swirl in the men's faces. She pointed her finger at Laverne and then at Leslie, saying loudly, 'Porgy, Porgy.' She repeated the action until she was sure that credit went where it was due. She was happy because she had accomplished the task set before her. Rose Tobias was a success as our publicist, even in Italy. It hardly mattered that she didn't speak a word of Italian.

18

After I registered at the hotel, handed over my passport to the desk clerk and was shown my room, I decided to see Venice on my own. The company manager advanced each singer a portion of salary in lira. I bought a map, a cheap guide to Italian which contained useful phrases and a small Italian-English dictionary, and began my exploration.

The ancient buildings sat closed and remote, holding dead glories within their walls. The canals fanned in every direction from the pavement edge, while red and black gondolas slid along on the water's surface like toy boats sailing on ice. The gondoliers whose crafts were empty sang to amuse themselves or to attract customers. They chanted bits of arias and popular music and their voices pranced over the water, young and irresistible. I wandered, following the map, to the Grand Canal, which in the dusk looked black and oily, and with the lighted gondolas skimming along, it could have been the San Francisco Bay burdened with an array of Chinese junks.

I found the Piazza San Marco, and sat at a small table

facing the square. I ordered coffee in my tourist-book Italian and sat watching the people in the grand square and the lights playing on the façade of the Basilica of Saint Mark and dreaming of the age of the doges and the city states of Italy which I had read about. The table I had chosen was in a fairly empty area of the restaurant, but the space was filled rapidly. Voices, suddenly closer, burst through my reverie. I looked around and discovered myself hemmed in by strange faces. I was the focus of at least thirty pairs of eyes. They all seemed to be searching my face – my mouth and nose, hairline and ears – for something precious that had been lost. There was a bizarre sense of being caught in a nightmare dreamed by a stranger.

I looked at my book for the necessary phrase. The waiter came over. 'I would like more coffee.' He chattered something back to me and nodded toward a group of men among the crowd staring at me. I repeated my request and he may have repeated his answer, because he nodded again toward the men. This time I followed his nod and saw three glasses lifted and smiles directed to me. They were toasting me. Surprise did not prevent me from returning their smile with a cool, restrained one of my own. I inclined my head and the crowd burst into laughter.

One woman asked, '"St. Louis Blues"?'

One man sitting near me stood up and came very near my table. His black eyes were shining.

'*Americano?*' He leaned toward me unnecessarily – his voice carried around the restaurant and out into the plaza.

I answered as quietly as my grandmother would have replied if she was trying to show a loudmouth how to behave. 'Yes.'

His smile widened. 'Harlem?'

I nodded again, because I knew what he meant.

He bent his knees and put up his hands in a professional boxer's pose. He jabbed at the air. Everybody laughed. The man withdrew from the position, and looking at me again, asked, 'Joe Louis?'

I didn't know how to tell him I knew who Joe Louis was but I didn't know him personally. He repeated, 'Joe Louis?'

I put both hands together and raised them over my head in a winner's gesture, and the crowd laughed and raised their glasses again.

It was amazing that the people were all so handsome. Those at one table motioned that I should join them. I only thought about it a second, then went over and sat down in a chair that had been pulled out for me.

Again there was a general noise of approval. As soon as I sat down, men and women at other tables pulled up their chairs. I put my booklet on the table, pointed to it and smiled. A waiter brought a glass and I had a sweet and bitter Campari, which I'd never tasted before. When I grimaced the people wagged their heads and clucked. I looked through the dictionary for the word 'bitter'; it wasn't there. A man took the book and began to look for something, but his search was in vain. A woman held her hand out for the book, and when it was passed to her she riffled through the pages and also failed to find what she was looking for. I was given another Campari. As the book traveled from hand to hand we all smiled at each other and the customers talked among themselves. I was having a lovely time and didn't understand a word that was said except 'Americano' and 'bellissima.'

188

It was time to go. I smiled and stood up. About thirty people rose and smiled. I shook hands with the people at my table and said 'Grazie.' The others leaned forward, offering their hands and their beaming faces. I shook hands with each one, and walked out onto the square. When I looked back at the lighted café the people were still waving.

The year was 1954, only a decade since their country had been defeated by my country in a war fought for racial reasons as well as economic ones. And, after all, Joe Louis, whom the man seemed so proud to mention, had beaten an Italian, Primo Carnera. I thought my acceptance in the restaurant had been a telling show of the great heart of the Italian people. I hadn't been in Europe long enough to know that Europeans often made as clear a distinction between black and white Americans as did the most confirmed Southern bigot. The difference, I was to discover, was that more often than not, blacks were liked, whereas white Americans were not.

I prepared for bed after examining each object in the small bedroom and bath next door. Touching the washstand, the walls and the fine cotton curtains assured me that I was indeed out of the United States. I slept a fitful sleep, longing for my son and feeling nervous because the next evening I would debut in the role of Ruby.

19

The interior of the Teatro la Fenice was as rococo as the most opulent imagination could have wished. The walls were paneled in rich red velvet interrupted by slabs of white marble and gold mosaic. Heavy crystal chandeliers hung on golden chains. The rounded seats were covered in the same velvet and the wide aisles were carpeted with a deeper red wool.

The dressing rooms had been designed and built by people who possessed a great appreciation for singers and actors. They were large and comfortable to the point of being luxurious. The smaller rooms were furnished with a small sofa, dressing tables and wide lighted mirror and a washstand. And the stars' quarters could have easily passed for superior suites in a first-class hotel.

Irene Williams and Laverne Hutchinson had not been seen all day. In the manner of operatic stars they had been in seclusion. However, singers of the less strenuous roles had walked along the canals and shopped in the small stores. Ned Wright had met a gondolier and arranged a late-night boat ride on the

Grand Canal for a few friends. He invited me. I had seen posters of John McCurry and me posted around the city, and as I walked alone in the streets, small boys followed me chanting *'La prima ballerina,' 'La prima ballerina.'* The children's pale-gold complexions and their joyful spirits reminded me of Clyde.

The stars materialized and dress rehearsal began. I was in costume and in place. There was a marked difference between observing the play – carefully scrutinizing each move, paying the closest attention to every note – and being a part of it and having some responsibility for the drama. The poignancy of Porgy's love for Bess and the tragedy of his fate brought tears to my eyes and clogged my throat, so that I could barely push notes out of my mouth. I was certain that in the course of time the play would become stale to me and I would become partially indifferent to its pathos. Over the next year, however, I found myself more touched by the tale and more and more impressed by the singers and actors who told it. The actual performance put dress rehearsal in the shade. The singers sang with fresh enthusiasm as if they had been called upon to create the music on the spot and were equal to the challenge. When Dolores Swann sang 'Summertime,' the audience was as hushed as the plastic doll that lay in her arms, and when she crooned the last top note the theater exploded with the sound of applause. Serena's lament and the love duet brought the audience to its feet. In the second half, when I finished my dance, the audience cheered again; as I followed the singers to the wings I received kisses and hugs and pats on the back.

Martha caught my hand and said, 'Oh, Pavlova, I knew you were the one.'

Lillian gave me a grin and said, 'You danced your tail off, girl.'

The curtain opened and revealed the theatergoers standing in the brightly lit auditorium. They clapped their hands and shouted up a pandemonium: 'Bravo,' 'Bravo.' During rehearsal the theater had been like a large inverted rococo snuffbox, but now, filled with beautifully dressed people screaming their appreciation, it was warm and rich and nearly too gorgeous to behold.

The curtains opened and closed and opened and closed and the audience refused to release the stars. Flowers were brought to the stage. I watched from the wings as Irene received bouquets gracefully in her arms until they piled up, threatening to obscure her face. Laverne bowed and smiled, holding on to her hand, then left her alone to take the kudos. When the curtain closed again, they exchanged places and he stood in the center accepting the applause. When the curtain closed for the last time, we hugged each other and danced with ecstasy.

The opening night of our European tour was a smash hit. The Italians were the most difficult audiences to sing for. They knew and loved music; operas, which were mainly for the elite in other countries, were folk music and children's songs in Italy. They loved us, we loved them. We loved ourselves. It was a certainty: if Italy declared us acceptable we could have the rest of Europe for a song.

We stayed in Venice for one sold-out week. During that time the stars were feted by city officials and the well-to-do, while the chorus was adored by the ordinary folk. We were hailed in the streets like conquering heroes and given free rides on the canals by gondoliers, who sang strains from *Porgy and Bess*. One owner of a glass-blowing factory presented us with delicate figurines, which we stowed in layers of cotton for our imminent trip to Paris.

I bought a French-English dictionary and packed it with the Italian-English phrase book and other belongings and had them taken to the bus which waited in the square. Fans crowded around us, offering cheeks to be kissed, hands to be shaken and flowers. We exchanged hugs and some tears with people who hadn't known of our existence only seven days before.

When the bus drove toward the station where we were to take a train to Paris, I thought of the city as a larger replica of some of its museums. Venice was itself an object of art, and its citizens the artists who had created it and were constantly re-creating it. I waved my hands, wagged my head and made sorry, sad faces to the well-wishers, as if I was being carried off against my will. Loving Venice and Venetians nearly made me Italian.

The Blue Train sped through Italy. I sat in a compartment with Lillian, Martha and Barbara Ann, listening to them talk about recital salons, and concert halls. Lillian mentioned a voice teacher whom someone in New York had recommended. Martha drew herself up and said the greatest voice teacher in the world was her teacher, in New York, and she wouldn't stand for anyone else messing with her voice. (Operatic singers are fiercely loyal to their teachers.) Lillian told her that was stupid: 'Your teacher couldn't be the best vocal teacher in the world because I've heard some terrible stories about her.' An argument grew and thrashed around the small space between us. I had nothing to add, since Wilkie was the only voice teacher I'd ever met, and I didn't want to mention his name in case I'd be obliged to defend him. I kept quiet. Barbara Ann said conciliatingly, 'Well, you know, it's hard to say who is the best voice teacher in the world. That is until you've heard everyone. There are teachers in Texas no one has ever heard of who are very good.' That was for Martha. She turned to Lillian and said, 'Just because a person is gossiped about doesn't necessarily mean that the person is guilty.' She looked at me for confirmation and added, 'I mean, look how they talked about Jesus Christ. Am I right or wrong?'

I said I didn't know, and all three singers turned to me, their questions pouncing on my ears.

'What do you mean you don't know about Jesus?'

'They talked about him like a dog.'

'Don't you remember about the Philistines and the Pharisees?'

'Your grandmother would have been ashamed of you.'

'What about the money lenders in the temple?'

Martha said, 'What about 'buked and scorned?' and then she began to sing: 'I been 'buked and I been scorned.' Her voice was the most perfect I had ever heard in my life. It was like hot silver being poured from a high place.

Lillian laid her full contralto under the glistening sound:

> 'I been 'buked
> And I been scorned
> I been talked about
> Sure as you're born.'

Barbara Ann wedged her clear soprano between the other voices, embracing first one tone then the other, getting so near the other trills that her sound almost melted into theirs. The music written hundreds of years before soared in the Italian train, erasing the dispute, and placing us all somewhere between the agony of Christ and the ecstasy of Art.

As the train pulled into the Gare du Nord I heard my name shouted above the clamor of luggage carts and the calls of porters: 'Maya Angelou,' '*Où est* Mademoiselle Maya Angelou?' I knew I shouldn't have left my son. There was a telegram waiting for me to say he had been hurt somehow. Or had run away from home. Or had caught an awful disease. The train ground to a halt and I forced the conductor aside and opened the door.

Five feet away stood the handsome and rugged Yanko Varda and Annette March, as svelte as a model. They were searching the train and yelling, 'Maya Angelou,' 'Mademoiselle Maya Angelou.'

I felt weak with relief. 'Yanko, Annette, *je suis ici.*'

We caressed one another like lovers. Annette handed me a basket that held cheese and fruit, a bottle of wine and a loaf of bread. They motioned to me to look back along the track. Victor Di Suvero, Mitch Lifton and Cyril March were handing out similar baskets to some of the singers as they detrained. They said, 'Welcome to Paris. This is in honor of Maya Angelou. This is in honor of Maya Angelou. Welcome to Paris.'

Yanko called to them, and when they saw me they ran over. Mitch and Victor hugged me and grinned. Cyril, who was always more reserved, gave me the European embrace.

I asked what they were doing in Paris, and they asked me to go with them for a glass of wine. They would explain everything.

I went to Bob Dustin to get the name and address of my hotel and an advance in francs. He agreed to send my baggage along, and my San Francisco friends took me to a sidewalk café.

They had not come to Paris together. Yanko was returning from a trip to Greece.

'Maya, I have found the only beautiful brunette in the world,' Victor said. 'She is a sculptor, a Greek, a goddess. You will meet her here. She will come to Sausalito. She will light up San Francisco with her black eyes and the men will fall at her feet like Turks. She is Aphrodite.'

Victor was en route to Italy on family business. Mitch was on a visit, and the Marches had moved to Paris, where Cyril was practicing medicine. San Francisco papers had run a notice that I had joined *Porgy and Bess*. My friends in Paris had read the company's advance publicity and found when and where we were due to arrive.

I described the fabulous success in Venice, giving myself a little more credit than I deserved. We drank wine, talked about San Francisco and they promised to attend opening night.

20

Paris loved *Porgy and Bess*. We were originally supposed to stay at the Théâtre Wagram for three weeks, but were held over for months. After the first week I discovered that I couldn't afford to stay in the hotel that had been assigned to me. The policy of the company was to pay the singers half their salary in the currency of the country we were in and the other half in dollars. I sent my dollars home to pay for Clyde's keep and to assuage my guilt at being away from him.

I moved into a small pension near the Place des Ternes, which provided a Continental breakfast with my tiny room. There was a cot-sized bed and just space for me and my suit-case. The family who owned the place and my fellow roomers spoke no English, so perforce my French improved.

One evening after the theater a group of black American entertainers who lived in Paris came backstage. They enchanted me with their airs and accents. Their sentences were mixed with Yeah Man's and Oo la la's. They fluttered their hands and raised their eyebrows in typically Gallic fashion, but walked swinging their shoulders like Saturday-night people at a party in Harlem.

Bernard Hassel, a tall nut-brown dancer, worked at the Folies-Bergères, and Nancy Holloway, whose prettiness brought to mind a young untroubled Billie Holiday, sang at the Colisée. Bernard invited me to see the night life of Paris.

'*Alors*, something groovy, you know?'

We went to the Left Bank, and he showed me where F. Scott Fitzgerald and Hemingway did some flamboyant talking and serious drinking. The bareness of the bar surprised me. I expected a more luxurious room with swatches of velvet, deep and comfortable chairs and at least a doorman. The café's wide windows were bare of curtains and the floor uncarpeted. It could have been the Coffee Shop in San Francisco's North Beach. High up over the façade hung a canvas awning on which was stenciled the romantic name DEUX MAGOTS.

L'Abbaye was a bar owned by Gordon Heath, a black American who provided his own entertainment. He sang in a weak but compelling voice and projected an air of mystery. After each song the audience showed their appreciation by snapping their fingers. Heath did not allow hand-clapping.

The Rose Rouge on the Left Bank was closer to my idea of a Parisian night club. It had velour drapes and a uniformed doorman; the waiters were haughty and the customers well-dressed. Acrobats and pantomimists, magicians and pretty half-naked girls kept up a continuous diversion. Bernard introduced me to the handsome Algerian owner, who I immediately but privately named Pepe Le Moko. He said if I wanted to do an act in his club, he'd find a place for me. I said I'd keep it in mind.

Around three o'clock in the morning my escort took me to the Mars Club, which he pronounced 'Mairs Cloob' near the Champs-Élysées. It was owned by an oversized American man from New York and specialized in black entertainment. Bernard pointed out the names printed on the door of people who had worked in the smoky and close room. The only one I recognized was Eartha Kitt. Ben, the owner, repeated Pepe Le Moko's invitation. I said I was flattered and I'd think about it. I knew I wouldn't. Where would I find a musician in Paris who could play calypso accompaniment?

Ben asked, 'Why don't you give us a song now?'

I looked at the pianist, who was white and thin and had a long sorry face. He sat playing a quiet moody song. When he finished, Ben called him to the bar and introduced us. 'Bobby Dorrough, this is Maya Angelou, she's a singer.'

He smiled and his face was transformed. His cheeks bunched under sparkling eyes and his teeth were large and white and even. He said, 'Happy to know you, Maya,' and the drawl made my skin move along my arms. He couldn't have sounded more Southern white if he had exaggerated.

Ben went to the microphone and announced, 'Ladies and gentlemen, we have with us tonight one of the stars of *Porgy and Bess*.'

I was hardly that, but why correct him? I stood and bowed while the audience applauded fiercely.

The pianist said 'Welcome to Paris' in a molasses accent. For months I had been away from the sound that recalled lynchings, insults and hate. It was bizarre to find myself suddenly drenched with the distasteful memories in a Parisian *boîte*.

I made myself speak. 'Where are you from?'

'I'm from San Antonio.' At least he didn't say 'San Antone.' 'Where are you from?'

'San Francisco.' I said it so briskly I almost bit my lip.

'Would you like to sing something? I'd be happy to play for you.' The graciousness dripped honeysuckle all over the old plantation.

I said, 'No. I don't think you can play my music. It's not very ordinary.'

He asked, 'What do you sing? The blues?' I knew he would think I sang blues. 'I play the blues.' I was sure he'd say he played the blues.

'No, I sing calypso. Do you also play calypso?' That ought to hold him.

'Yes. I know some. How about "Stone Cold Dead in the Market"? Or "Rum and Coca-Cola"?'

I followed him to the piano in a mild state of shock. I told him my key and he was right. He played "Stone Cold Dead" better and with more humor than my accompanist did at the Purple Onion. The audience liked the song and Bobby applauded quietly. Everything about the man was serene except his piano playing and his smile.

'Want to sing another? How about "Run Joe"?'

Although that had been the song which started my career and I always used it to close a show or as a dramatic encore, it was not really well known. I was surprised that the pianist knew it. 'Yes. I'll sing one more.'

He took only a few bars to fall into the mood I was creating and then raced along with me and the story, never drowning my effects but always holding his own. When we finished I felt obliged to shake his hand over the loud applause.

'Aw, Maya, there was nothing to it. You're very good.'

Bernard and Ben met me back at the bar. They were still clapping as I approached.

'How about doing one spot a night for me, Maya?' Ben was grinning as he shook my hand. 'One show a night. You'll be a sensation in Paris.'

Bernard said, '*Chérie*, it'll knock them out.'

'But I don't get out of the theater until eleven-thirty.' It was nice to be begged to do what I liked to do.

'You could do a show here at twelve-thirty.'

I thought about the money. I would be able to move out of the grim little pension that had no luxuries and was minus certain things that I as an American considered necessities. I could afford a room with private bath again and a toilet that wouldn't be at the end of dark stairs. And I could continue sending the same amount of money home. Or, it occurred to me, I could stay where I was – the pension wasn't all that bad – and send more money home. Mom could buy something wonderful for Clyde every other week and tell him I'd sent it. Then perhaps he would forgive my absence.

I asked Ben, 'Could you pay me in dollars?'

Ben had been in Paris a long time. His large, round face became wise and hard. 'You've got a good connection for exchange?'

I knew some people in the company sold their dollars on the black market and received a higher percentage of francs than banks would give.

I said, 'No. I have a son at home. I have to send money for his keep.'

His expression softened a little. 'Of course, of course, kid, I

201

can give you dollars and you'll be paid every night. That's the way we do it in Paris. You want to talk it over with Bobby? He'll be playing for you.'

I waited until the pianist joined us at the bar. 'I'm going to start singing here. Ben has offered me a job.'

'Well, isn't that nice.'

Oh God, I didn't know how I could bear that accent. If he would only play the piano and never speak to me, we'd get along very well.

'When are you going to start?'

Ben asked, 'How about day after tomorrow. You could rehearse with Bobby tomorrow and next day and begin that night. How's that, kid?'

That was fine with me and the musician. Bernard bought drinks and we closed the deal by clinking glasses all around.

Bobby Dorrough had a pitch as fine as crystal. I sang snatches of songs to him in the empty bar and as if he were a music machine, the notes went into his ears and immediately his fingers pressed them out of the piano keys. In the first afternoon's rehearsal we ran over my entire repertoire and agreed to spend the next day polishing the numbers. It was nearly dusk when we walked out of the bar.

'Do you want me to get you a taxi, Maya?'

I said, 'No, I just live near the Place des Ternes.'

'All right then, I'll walk you to your hotel.'

'Oh no, thanks. I mean, I feel like walking slowly.'

'Well, I wasn't planning to race you down the streets.'

'I mean, I'd just as soon walk by myself.' I tried to tell him, without hurting his feelings, that I didn't really want to be with him. Suppose some of my friends from the opera met us.

I didn't know one person who would be surprised or offended if I was seen with a white man, but neither did I know one who wouldn't be shocked into uncomfortable recall by the Southern accent.

'Would you like to have lunch tomorrow? Before rehearsal?' He was very slow in getting the message.

I said, 'No, thank you.'

Rejection dawned on him and his pale face flushed with understanding. He said, 'All right then, Maya, I'll see you tomorrow.'

I walked away, heading toward the Arc de Triomphe.

Martha and Lillian said they'd come down with me to the club. Ned Wright and Joe Attles and Bey promised to drop by for the last show. The news that I had a second job did not displease the company's administration because any publicity I received was good for the opera.

After the midnight show I introduced my friends to the full audience. 'Ladies and gentlemen, some members of the *Porgy and Bess* company.'

The audience stood up to look at the suddenly modest singers, who refused to rise, but simply nodded grandly from their seats.

I knew what was wrong. I hadn't singled them out and made individual introductions giving their names and the roles they played. 'Ladies and gentlemen, I would like you to meet Miss Lillian Hayman, who sings Maria and Serena.' She was understudying the two roles. Lillian stood and graciously took the applause. She sat down gratified. 'Joseph Attles, Sportin' Life.' He stood, waved his long hands and blew kisses. 'Ned Wright, Robbins.' Ned stood and flashed a smile like a beacon around the room. 'And Miss Martha Flowers, Bess.' Martha stood up slowly and solemnly. She inclined her head, first to the right, then to the left, then to the audience directly in front. Only after she had bowed did she smile. Her sense of theater was never better – she began the smile slowly, keeping her mouth closed and simply pulling her lips taut. Then she allowed a few teeth to show and gradually a few more, and then more. When her lips were stretched as tight as possible and her teeth glimmering like a row of lights, she snapped her head back and laughed, the high sound tinkling like chimes.

The audience was bewitched. They began to shout, '*Chantez*, Bess. *Chantez, chantez*, Bess.'

Martha suddenly became demure, and shaking her head in refusal, draped her small body in her seat. Her action incited the crowd and their clamor rose in volume. At exactly the correct moment, Martha stood up and shyly went to the piano. She leaned and whispered to Bobby. He struck one note and took his hands from the keys.

> 'O they so fresh and fine
> And they right off'n the vine.'

She was singing the vendor's song a cappella and her voice floated free in the quiet room:

> 'Strawberries, strawberries!'

I looked around – everyone was beguiled, including our fellow singers. Martha ballooned her voice, then narrowed it, dipping down into a rough contralto, and then swung it high beyond the lyric soprano into the rarefied air that was usually the domain of divine coloraturas.

For a second after she finished there was no sound. Then people applauded her and began to crowd around her table. She coyly accepted the attention as if she hadn't worked hard for years to earn it.

One of the lessons I learned from *Porgy and Bess* was that jealousy is conceived only in insecurity and must be nourished in fear. Each individual in our cast had the certainty of excellence.

After the din over Martha's singing diminished, I asked Lillian to please sing.

She stood up without reluctance and sang,

> 'Go way from my window
> Go way from my door
> Go way, way, way from my bedside
> And bother me no more
>   And bother me no more.'

Her voice was as colorful as Martha's was pure, and the customers were again enchanted. Ned Wright sang a medley of popular songs, beginning with 'I Can't Give You Anything but Love,' which the French people recognized and loved. Joe Attles gave the audience 'St. James Infirmary' and they literally stood in the aisles.

Maya Angelou was a crazy success. A smash hit! The audience thought they had never been better entertained. Ben was certain I would improve business; the bartender and waiters smiled gratefully at me. If I hadn't memorized a story my grandmother told me when I was a knee-high child, I might have become conceited and begun to believe the compliments I did not totally deserve.

The old story came to mind:

Mrs. Scott, a woman well past middle age, fancied young men. She was a great churchgoer and used each religious gathering to search for the objects of her choice. All the young men in her town were aware of her predilections, and she was unsuccessful in snaring them.

One day a new man appeared at the meeting house. He was handsome and although he was adult, he was still young enough to be gullible.

The woman caught him directly after service and invited him to her home for late Sunday afternoon dinner. He accepted gratefully.

She rushed home, killed a chicken and put it on to fry. While the chicken cooked, Mrs. Scott took a small needle from her sewing kit, and putting on her bifocals, picked her way down the lane from her front door. When she reached a tree a hundred yards away, she stuck the needle in the bark and returned to the kitchen to finish preparing the meal.

When the young man arrived, they sat down to a tasty dinner (for Mrs. Scott was an excellent cook), and after they finished, Mrs. Scott invited the man to sit on the porch in the swing, to let his dinner digest. She brought out lemonade and sat with him. Dusk was falling and the shapes of things were blurred.

Mrs. Scott sat bolt upright and turned to the young man. 'What on earth is that I see sticking in that tree?' She pointed down the lane to the oak, which was barely a shadow in the darkness.

206

The young man asked, 'What tree, Mrs. Scott?'

'Why, that oak tree at the bottom of the lane.' She squinted and bent her neck. 'I do believe that's a pin.'

The young man, squinting, tried to pierce the gloom.

'Mrs. Scott, I can't hardly see the tree. And you can see something sticking in it?'

'Yes.' Mrs. Scott had relaxed her scrutiny. 'At first I thought it was a pin, but when I looked for the head it wasn't there – I saw instead a hole. So it's got to be a needle.'

The young man turned and looked at Mrs. Scott with admiration.

'You know, ma'am, when you left church this morning, some folks told me to be careful. That you were an old woman who loved young men. But I must say, if you can see the hole in a needle a hundred yards away after the sun has gone down, you're not nearly as old as they say you are.'

Mrs. Scott, proud of her compliments and forgetful of her subterfuge, said, 'Well, thank you for that. I'll just go and get the needle and show it to you.'

She flounced up out of the swing and stepped jauntily down the stairs. When she reached the bottom step she turned to smile at the appreciative young man, and then continuing, she walked two steps and tripped over a cow sitting in the lane.

Yes, I was a success in Paris at the Mars Club. I would have been a fool to have thought the praise was all mine. Ben liked me because I was good enough, but appreciated me because the members from *Porgy and Bess* were likely to drop in and sing for free. Bobby liked me because I was good enough, and he had a chance to play music for which he seldom received requests. The audience liked me because I was good enough, and I was different – not African, but nearly; not American, but nearly. And I liked myself because, simply, I was lucky.

I gave thanks to *Porgy and Bess*, my good fortune and to God. I wasn't about to trip over a cow.

21

Paris was changing the rhythm of that old gang of mine. Martha took a two-week leave from the company to give a Town Hall recital in New York City. Lillian had said to me often, 'I'm so glad I wasn't born here, because I'd never have learned to speak this language,' but she had found new French friends and I seldom saw her after the theater. Barbara Ann's husband flew from the United States to be with her, and since they were newly married, they could spare little time for anyone beyond their tight circle of romance. Ned Wright and Joe Attles were bent on a ferocious discovery of Paris. After the final bow they raced from the theater as if an emergency call awaited them. They unearthed little-known restaurants and bars in obscure corners of the city.

From my third-floor (which the French perversely called second-floor) room, I assayed my value to Paris and its promise for me. I had accepted the Rose Rouge offer and become a typical Parisian entertainer. I sang a midnight show at the Mars Club, threw a coat over my sparkly dress, hailed a cab and rode across the Seine to do a second show at the Rose Rouge. My songs were well enough received and fans were beginning to remember me. Some sent notes and occasionally flowers to my dressing room. A few expatriates and two Senegalese students I had met advised me to leave *Porgy and Bess* and make my mark in Paris. The Africans said that in France I would never hear of lynchings and riots. And I would not be refused service in any restaurant or hotel in the country. The people were civilized. And, anyway, the French people loved Negroes. Look at Sid Bechet. Lil Armstrong, a former wife of Satchmo played piano at the Le Jazz Hot and had an avid following. Bambi, a tall, deliciously thin model, could hardly walk the streets in Paris without men following her and raving over her black beauty. Nancy Holloway and Inez, who owned Chez Inez, sang American songs as well as popular French melodies and were welcomed with hyperbolic Gallic admiration. And, of course, Josephine Baker was a national institution.

I considered the advice seriously. I could find an apartment and send for Clyde. He was bright and would learn the language quickly. He would be freed from growing up under the cloud of racial prejudice that occasionally made every black childhood sunless. He would be obliged to be good for his own sake rather than to prove to a disbelieving society that he was not a brute. The French students wore short pants and blazers and caps, and I knew my son would look beautiful in his uniform. The prospect looked glorious.

A woman asked me to join her table after my show at the Rose Rouge. She welcomed me and introduced me to her friends.

Her voice was tiny but piercing, and a baby-doll smile

never left her pink-and-white face, and her eyelids fluttered only a little faster than her hands. She reminded me of Billie Burke and very small door chimes.

'Mademoiselle, do you know who is Pierre Mendès-France?' Smile, blink, rustle.

I said, 'Yes, madame. I read the papers.'

'I want an affair for him to give.' Her English was not broken, it was crippled.

I said in French, 'Madame, let us speak French.'

She bubbled and gurgled. '*Non. Non.* I love this English for practice to speak.'

Alors. She limped along verbally, explaining that she wanted me to sing at a reception which she planned to host. It would be a fund-raising event and they would gladly pay me for my services. I would be expected to sing two songs. Something plaintive that would move the heart, I thought, and loosen the purse strings.

'The blues.' Madame said, 'Oh, how the blues I love. Will you sing "St. Louie Blues"?' She started singing the first line: 'I hate to see, that evening sun go down.'

Her shoulders hunched up to her ear lobes and she made her eyes small and lascivious. Her lips pushed out and I saw the red underlining of her mouth.

'"I hate to see that evening sun go down."'

She shook herself and her breasts wobbled. She was imitating her idea of a *négresse.*

I stopped her. 'Madame, I know the song. I will sing it at the reception.'

She was not fazed by the interruption, but clapped her hands and told her friends to clap theirs. We agreed on a price, and she said, 'You are with *Porgy and Bess*. The great opera. If Bess or Porgy or your friends desire to come with you at the reception, they will not be made to pay.'

She smiled, laughed, waved her hands and generally jangled like a bunch of keys. I thanked her and left the table.

Since my friends in *Porgy and Bess* were otherwise engaged, I asked the two Senegalese men to escort me to the reception. They were pleased to do so and appeared at the theater's backstage door in tuxedos, starched shirts and highly polished shoes. Their general elegance put me in a party mood. I walked into the salon with a handsome, attentive man on each side, and as we stopped inside the door, I felt that the three of us must have made an arresting tableau.

Madame was informed of my arrival and she floated over in wisps of chiffon, smiling her cheeks into small pink balloons.

'Oh, mademoiselle. How it is kind of you to come.' She offered me her hand, but gave her eyes to my escorts. They bowed smartly. 'And your friends you brought. Who of you is the Porgy? I do love "Summertime."' She had wafted into singing '"And the living is easy."'

I said, 'No, madame.' It was hard to wrest her attention from the two men. 'No, madame, they are not with *Porgy and Bess*. These are friends from Africa.'

When the import of my statement struck her, the smile involuntarily slid off her face and she recovered her hand from my grasp.

'*D'Afrique? D'Afrique?*' Suddenly there were no bubbles in her voice.

M'Ba bowed formally and said in French, 'Yes, madame. We are from Senegal.'

212

She looked at me as if I had betrayed her. 'But, mademoi-selle—' She changed her mind and stood straight. She spoke in French, 'Please wait here. I will have someone take you to the musicians. *Bonsoir.*' She turned and left.

After I sang, a young woman gave me an envelope with my pay and thanked me warmly. I never saw Madame again.

Paris was not the place for me or my son. The French could entertain the idea of me because they were not immersed in guilt about a mutual history – just as white Americans found it easier to accept Africans, Cubans or South American blacks than the blacks who had lived with them foot to neck for two hundred years. I saw no benefit in exchanging one kind of prejudice for another. Also, I was only adequate as an enter-tainer, and I would never set Paris afire. Honesty made me admit that I was neither a new Josephine Baker or an old Eartha Kitt.

When the *Porgy and Bess* administration informed us that we were moving on to Yugoslavia, I found a woman to give me lessons in Serbo-Croatian and bought myself a dictionary.

Adieu, Paris.

22

In Zagreb the company was called together to be told that the Yugoslav government and the American State Department wished us to be discreet; we were, after all, guests of the country and the first American singers to be invited behind the iron curtain. We would be driven from the hotel to the theater and back again. We could walk only within a radius of four square blocks of the hotel. We were not to accept invitations from any Yugoslavians, nor were we to initiate fraternization.

The hotel corridors smelled of cabbage and the dust of ages. I found the maid on my floor and asked her in Serbo-Croatian if there was anything interesting to see near the hotel. I had little hope that she would understand me, but she readily answered, 'Yes, there's the railroad station.' I was elated that the money I had spent on language lessons had not been spent in vain.

I said excitedly, 'Madame, I can speak Serbo-Croatian.'

She looked at me without curiosity and said, 'Yes?' She waited for me to go on.

I repeated, 'I learned to speak Serbo-Croatian two weeks ago.'

She nodded and waited heavily. No smile warmed her features. I couldn't think of anything to add. We stood in the hall like characters from different plays by different authors suddenly thrust upon the same stage. I grinned. She didn't.

I said, 'Thank you.'

She said, 'You're welcome.'

I went to my room taking my confusion along. Why hadn't the woman been amazed to find an American Negro woman speaking Serbo-Croatian? Why hadn't she congratulated me? I knew we were the first blacks that had stayed in the hotel and possibly the first that had ever visited the town.

At first I concluded that because the maid had never been out of her country and everyone she knew spoke her language, she thought Yugoslavia was the world and the world Yugoslavia. Then I realized that the staff must have undergone intensive indoctrination before our arrival. In the lobby no one stared at us; obviously, we were being studiously and politely ignored. The desk clerks and porters, waiters and bartenders, acted as if the sixty black American opera singers roamed the halls and filled their lobby every other week. I was certain that we were the only authentic guests in the establishment. The others, who averted their eyes at our approach and buried their heads in their newspapers, seemed less innocent than Peter Lorre in an Eric Ambler movie.

Outside, however, it was a different story. Ordinary citizens crowded three deep to peer into the hotel windows. When one gawker could catch a glimpse of us, he or she nudged the persons nearby and all craned their necks, eyes bulging, and

215

then laughed uproariously, revealing stainless-steel teeth that looked ominous. They had to be talked to sharply like obstreperous children at a summer fair.

Martha, who had rejoined the company, and Ethel Ayler, the new and glamorous Bess, refused my invitation to go for a walk.

Martha leaned back and looked up at me. 'But Miss Thing, they think we're monkeys or something. Just look at them. No, my dear, I'm counting on Tito to keep his people outside and I swear Miss Fine Thing will stay inside.'

Ethel laughed and agreed with Martha. 'They think we're in a cage. I wouldn't be surprised if they threw peanuts at us.'

Ned warned me, 'I don't think that's the smartest thing you could do. Look at those silver teeth. Those people might start thinking you're a chocolate doll and eat you up. Stay here in the hotel. I'll play you some tonk and buy you a slivovitz.'

I hadn't taken Serbo-Croatian lessons just to try out the language on hotel staff who wouldn't even pass the time of day. I walked out of the hotel.

People crowded around me. Short, stocky peasants from the country wore pointed, knitted hats and had eyes that would have been at home in Oriental faces except for their blue color. I spoke to them. 'Good afternoon. Please excuse me. Thank you.'

It took a few seconds for those nearest me to realize that they could understand me, and then a hilarity exploded that would have been well received at a Fourth of July Shriners' picnic. They shouted and pushed in closer to me. A small surf of panic started to lap at my inner mind. I held it off. I couldn't afford terror to freeze me to the spot or force me to bolt.

Hands began to reach for me. They clutched at my sleeve, at my face. I stretched as tall as possible and shouted, 'Excuse me, I am going through.' I had followed Wilkie's teachings attentively, and if the quality of my singing did not show a marked improvement, the volume at least, had certainly increased.

I boomed again, 'Excuse me. I am going through.' The noise abated and the country people's mouths gaped. The crowd parted and I strode through their moment of fluster and down the street. I didn't dare turn to see if any had chosen to follow me. Mobs of any color terrified me, and had I seen the mass behind me, without a doubt I would have taken flight and been lost in a second.

When passersby saw me, they stiffened in their tracks as if I were a fairy queen or an evil witch who had the power to suspend their mobility.

I walked into a small store which sold musical instruments. The salesman took one look at me and rushed back to a draped doorway. He shouted, 'Come and see this!' Then, as if I had not heard and seen his action, he dressed his face in the universal sales-pitch smile and asked, 'How are you? Good morning. May I help you?' He jerked his face away and toward the door again. 'Come. Come now.' Then back to me with a courteous manner.

I said, 'I'd like to buy a mandolin.'

He interested me as much as I interested him. It was fantastic that he thought he ceased to exist for me when he removed his attention.

'A mandolin? Certainly.' His eyes fled toward the back room. I grabbed his attention: 'Here. How much is this one?'

While he removed a mandolin, beautifully inlaid with mother-of-pearl, children began to tumble through the rear door and into the store. They were followed by a heavy woman with a large, florid face. When they saw me they stopped as if they had rehearsed the scene.

The woman directed a question to the man. He looked at her and answered but I couldn't catch the language. They all began to talk at once, the children's voices stabbing in and out of the deeper sounds. I continued examining the mandolin, strumming on it, turning it over in my hands to appreciate its fine woodwork. I ignored them and said to the man that I would like to buy the instrument.

He interrupted the family dialogue and told me the price; I gave him the money. The family had advanced on me. The mother was holding back as many of the children as she could reach while she inched closer to me.

I spoke to her. 'Good morning, madame.'

She smiled tentatively, but the incredulous look on her face remained.

'Good morning, madame,' I repeated, looking directly in her eyes. If they thought I was a talking bear, then they would have to admit that at least I spoke Serbo-Croatian.

Her husband was wrapping my package, so I continued, 'How are you, madame?'

Finally, her lips relaxed and opened and I saw the bar of metal that substituted for teeth. She placed herself between me and the children, then said, 'Paul Robeson.'

It was my turn to be stunned. The familiar name did not belong in Byzantium. The woman repeated, 'Paul Robeson,' and then began one of the strangest scenes I had ever seen.

She began to sing 'Deep River.' Her husky voice was suddenly joined by the children's piping 'My home is over Jordan.' Then the husband teamed with his wife and offspring, 'Deep River, Lord.' They knew every word.

I stood in the dusty store and considered my people, our history and Mr. Paul Robeson. Somehow, the music fashioned by men and women out of an anguish they could describe only in dirges was to be a passport for me and their other descendants into far and strange lands and long unsure futures.

> 'Oh don't you want to go
> To that gospel feast?'

I added my voice to the melody:

> 'That promised land
> Where all is peace?'

I made no attempt to wipe away the tears. I could not claim a forefather who came to America on the *Mayflower*. Nor did any ancestor of mine amass riches to leave me free from toil. My great-grandparents were illiterate when their fellow men were signing the Declaration of Independence, and the first families of my people were bought separately and sold apart, nameless and without traces – yet there was this:

> 'Deep River
> My home is over Jordan.'

I had a heritage, rich and nearer than the tongue which gives it voice. My mind resounded with the words and my blood raced to the rhythms.

> 'Deep River
> I want to cross over into campground.'

The storekeeper and his wife embraced me. My Serbo-Croatian was too weak to carry what I wanted to say. I hugged them again and took up my mandolin and left the store.

Porgy and Bess received the expected kudos from sold-out houses in Zagreb, and after a few days we moved on to Belgrade. We had been told that Belgrade was a city that was reasonably cosmopolitan, and we were all eager for the bright lights.

The Moskva Hotel in Red Square was considered a large hotel but it could hardly accommodate our singers, administration and conductors. Bob Dustin, cheery as usual, announced that we would have to triple up, and that if we didn't want to be assigned bed space arbitrarily, we should choose roommates and let him know.

Martha, Ethel Ayler and I agreed to share one of the large high-ceilinged rooms. Ethel had made fast friends with Martha and was an excellent foil for Martha's always sharp, often acid comments. Ethel would smile calmly and say, 'Martha Flowers, you are a disgrace. Charming, talented, but a disgrace.' Martha would giggle and be coaxed out of her ill-humor.

We had expected three cots in our room, but found one

large lumpy bed, a very worn carpet and a single overhead light.

'You mean this is what these people got out of their revolution?' Martha daintily picked her way around the room. 'Someone should tell them that they're about due for another.' She wrinkled her pretty face in distaste.

Ethel said reprovingly, 'Martha, control yourself. Unless you want the NKVD to take you to Siberia. How could you sing with salt in your throat?'

Martha laughed, 'Miss Fine Thing can sing anywhere, darling. Even on the steppes of Byelorussia.'

Our bags were brought to the room by a porter who didn't raise his eyes. We tried to tip him, but he rushed away as if afraid.

Martha said, '*Regardez ça*. Maya, you speak his lingo, why didn't you tell him we wouldn't bite? Of course; only because he's not cute enough.' With the mention of men, Martha and Ethel and I fell into an old conversation which had never concluded and was interrupted only by sleep, performances and forced separation on journeys. The value of men. Their beauty. Their power. Their worth, excitement and attractiveness. Were American Negro men better than Africans? Better companions, better lovers? Yes. No. Whoever had a story to substantiate her point of view told it in detail. Were white American men sexier than French or Italian? Yes. No. We told secrets to each other on trains, ships, in hotel rooms and backstage. I was never loath to exaggerate a tale to make my point, and I'm certain that some of the accounts that were told to me were as fictitious as my own. We were all in our mid-twenties, and given that my two friends had spent ten years cloistered in vocal studios and secreted in institutes of music and I had had fewer romantic experiences than most college coeds, our imaginations got more exercise than our libidos.

Ethel slept in the middle and Martha beside the night table. She jumped when the telephone rang.

'Who on earth, what time is it?' The telephone and Martha's outrage awakened Ethel and me. Something must have happened and Bob Dustin or Ella Gerber wanted the company to gather at once.

Martha sweetened her voice. 'Good morning.' She sang the greeting.

'Mistress who?' We were all sitting upright in bed. 'Mistress Maya Angelou?' Her voice revealed her disbelief. 'And you are Mr. Julian? Hold on.'

She put her hand over the receiver. 'Mr. Julian wants to speak to Mistress Maya Angelou. At eight o'clock in the damned morning. Now, ain't that something?' The phone wire wouldn't extend across the bed. I had to get up in the cold and pad around to the other side.

'Hello?'

'Is this Mistress Maya Angelou?' The question was asked by a voice I had never heard.

'Yes. I am Maya Angelou.' I answered to a background of disgruntled noises and curious looks from my roommates.

'Mistress Maya, I am being Mr. Julian. It's that last night I am seeing you dance. I am watching you leap across the stage and looking at your legs jumping through the air and, Mistress Maya, I am loving you.' The words ran together like dyes, and it was difficult for me to separate them into comprehension.

222

'I beg your pardon?'

Martha groaned. 'Oh, my goodness, can't he call you after the sun rises? Or does the sun never rise in Yugoslavia?'

'It's I am loving you, Mistress Maya. It's that if you are hearing a man is throwing his body into the Danube today, and dying in the icy water, Mistress Maya, that man is being me. Drowning for the love of you. You and your lovely legs jumping.'

'Just a minute. Uh, what is your name?'

'I am being Mr. Julian, and I am loving you.'

'Yes, well, Mr. Julian, why do you want to drown? Why would loving me make you want to die? I don't think that's very nice.'

Ethel and Martha were both leaning on their elbows watching me.

Martha said, 'Would he promise to die before sundown? Do you think he'll do it in time for us to get a little sleep?'

Ethel said serenely, 'Now Maya sees what her saintly life-saving attitude has brought.'

'Look, mister.'

'It's being Mr. Julian.'

'Yes, well, Mr. Julian, thanks for the telephone call—'

'May I please be seeing you? May I please be taking you to one expensive café and watching your lovely lips drinking down coffee with cream?'

'No, thank you. I am sorry, but I have to hang up now.'

Martha grumbled, 'Hang up, or down. Just let me go back to sleep.'

'Miss Maya, if you're not seeing me, if you're not letting me see your lips drinking down coffee with cream, then today, I am sending you my heart.'

223

Oh, my God. The woman who gave me Serbo-Croatian lessons in Paris was a Yugoslavian émigré. After my last class she told me solemnly, 'Don't ever in the warmth of passion tell a Yugoslav that you can't live without him. You will find him, his trunks and his family at your door. Ready to move in and improve your life.' I had thought she was making a sarcastic joke, for she had said the best thing about Yugoslavia was that she couldn't return to it. When I chided her on exaggeration, she swore that what she said was absolute truth. That Slavs were passionate and so romantic they would gladly mutilate themselves to demonstrate their sincerity. And here this unknown man was threatening to send me his heart.

'Oh, no, Mr. Julian. Please. I beg you. Don't send me your heart.'

Martha said, 'Tell him to send you his tongue so he'll shut up.'

'Mistress Maya. It is that I am sending it to your theater, by hand, this morning. Good-bye, lovely legs leaping.' The line went dead.

Martha flopped back on the bed. 'Well, thank God for small favors.'

Ethel looked at me, waiting to see if I wanted to talk about the phone call.

I said, 'I'm going to take a bath.'

She said, 'O.K. See you,' and wiggled down under the heavy quilts.

I was tickled and frightened. 'It's I am being Mr. Julian,' indeed. He sounded old and rusty – like aged garden furniture, pushed around on concrete. 'It's that I'm loving you. I am sending you my heart.' Oh no, please.

I walked down the hall to the communal bathroom, thinking

224

about a gory heart wrapped in newspapers waiting in my dressing room.

I stood in the drafty tub sudsing myself and imagined the blood congealed, clotted around the aorta. I dried with the thin towel and assured myself that no one in the world, even in fiction, had ever cut out his own heart. Then I remembered hara-kiri, or the ritual Japanese samurai suicide where the protagonist arranges for friends to help him perform his self-murder. Were the Yugoslavs as dramatic? I prayed not.

Martha and Ethel woke as I was leaving to go downstairs for breakfast.

'Going to meet Mr. Julian, Maya? Going to bring back his heart?'

'I am going to breakfast, ladies. Just breakfast.'

'Don't eat braised heart on toast, girl.' I could have wrung Martha's silver throat. My appetite fled on the heels of her remark. Downstairs I forced down tea and continually pushed away the bloody pictures which assailed my mind. I couldn't go to the theater early because we were under the same restriction in Belgrade that had obtained in Zagreb. We could walk only in the prescribed four-block area, and buses took us to and from the theater.

I waited throughout the day. Drinking slivovitz and writing letters, forced happy letters, to my family.

Finally, the cast assembled in the lobby and we trooped onto the buses and were driven to the theater.

'Maya, there's something in the dressing room for you.'

He did it. The poor bastard. Actually cut out his heart and had it sent to me. I kept my face serene, but my body trembled and the muscles in my stomach were in revolt.

225

I opened the room door, half braced to see a bloody organ still thumping like a prop in the *Bride of Frankenstein*. A harmless-looking flat package wrapped in gay paper lay on my dressing table. If it was a heart, it had been sliced sliver-thin. I closed the door for privacy and picked up the box. It might have been a See's box of Valentine candies. The note read: 'Mistress Maya, here is my heart. I am loving you. I am wishing to see you. Goodbye, my lovely legs. Mr. Julian.'

He had to be alive. Otherwise how could he hope to see me? I unwrapped the paper carefully because I might need it again. I pulled the last layer away.

Mr. Julian's heart was a cake. An inedible concoction of flour dough, water and probably concrete. It was a quarter of an inch thick and a little tanner than uncooked biscuit dough. A wisp of paper warned in Serbo-Croatian and French, 'DO NOT EAT!' I inspected the thing and decided the warning was entirely unnecessary. Bits of plate glass and small squares of windows were punched down into the cake and there were shreds of paper doilies and tatters of lace which vied for space with dead leaves and dried flowers. The whole thing was sprinkled over with grains of rice, barley and wheat which were glued to the surface.

I swayed somewhere between relief and indignation. At least I didn't have the onus of trying to explain to the Yugoslavian government and the U.S. State Department how a Communist citizen's heart came to be found in my dressing room. On the other hand, what could I do with the putty heart? My luggage was already overweight. I had bought sweaters in Venice for myself and a few presents for my family in Paris. I wanted a few pieces of pottery in Greece and it had been hinted that we were going to Egypt. Certainly I'd find something there to take home. And here I was, saddled with something I did not want or could not give away. There wasn't a soul in the world I disliked enough to give the ugly thing. There was a small catch in the back of the heart which indicated it was meant to hang on the wall. I placed it under my dressing table behind the shoe rack. There would be time enough to deal with it when I had to pack to leave Yugoslavia.

Mr. Julian telephoned every morning at eight o'clock. When I spoke to him sharply, ordering him to cease and desist, he answered, 'It's that I'm loving you. It's that I am dying because of you. It's that I'm falling in front of a train.'

I asked the desk clerk to stop putting his calls through to our room. The clerk said, 'In Yugoslavia, we answer the telephone.' Martha refused to answer the ring any longer, for when she told him on the second morning that I was out, he responded with: 'In Belgrade? There is no place for her to go. Maybe she is going to the bathroom. I will telephone later.' Ten minutes later he said to her, 'This is being Mr. Julian. I am wanting to speaking with Mistress Maya Angelou.'

Ordinary courtesy bade me to exchange places with Martha so that I could at least answer the telephone.

'Mistress Maya, it's that I am dying.'

'All right, Mr. Julian. I can't help that. Only please, don't send me any other parts of your anatomy.'

Harsh words did not deter him, nor did kind words give him solace. I answered the telephone each morning and unemotionally, fuzzily and sleepily told him to get lost.

Other members in the cast reported similar conquests. Women fairly hung on the coattails of the bachelor singers,

227

and one evening when Martha was taken to a ballet by an admirer, I left Ethel in the room manicuring her nails and went down to the bath.

When I returned, she was sitting yoga fashion on the bed and a strange man was spread-eagled, face down, on the floor at the foot of her bed.

I stood in the door in mild shock.

Ethel said, 'Maya, I've been waiting for you. Help me to get this fool out of the room.'

I threw down my towel and soap.

'Mister, mister. Get up.' I turned to Ethel who had risen from her lotus position and was standing at the man's feet. 'Is he drunk?'

'No, girl, he's crazy.'

'O.K. Mister, we're going to put you out in the hall.'

His cheek was on the carpet and his eyes wide open. 'It is not that I am being drunk. It is that I am loving Mistress Ethel. It is that her love is killing me. It is burning in my heart like a fire.'

I said, 'O.K. I understand.'

Ethel said, 'Here, Maya, you take the left foot. I'll take the right. We'll drag him.'

The man made no resistance and allowed his body to be scudded across the room. I opened the door and we deposited him, still flat on his stomach, in the hall. Throughout the action, he had continued his litany.

'I am loving Mistress Ethel. I am dying out of love for Mistress Ethel.'

We closed the door.

'Ethel, how in the hell did he get in here?'

'There was a knock at the door, and I thought it was you. So I said "Come in," and in comes this fool. He takes one look at me and falls flat on the floor. I thought maybe he had died or something so I went around and bent over him. To take his pulse. That's when I saw his eyes were open and he started chanting, "Mistress Ethel, I am loving you. Dying! Killing myself." And all that stuff.'

'Why didn't you call the desk?'

'I figured you'd be back soon, and he seemed harmless.'

We were laughing when we heard Martha's voice at the door and a series of quick raps.

'Hey, open the door. Open up, will you?'

Ethel went to the door and opened it. She called, 'Maya, come quick.' I raced to Ethel and looked over her shoulder. Martha was trying to disentangle herself from her escort, whose arms were octopus-ing all over her body.

'Get this fool off me, will you?' Ethel and I grabbed the man and untwined his arms.

'Hey, mister. What do you think you're doing?'

He struggled to regain his hold on Martha. 'It's that I am loving Mistress Martha. Mistress Martha, I drink your eyes. I drink your nose.'

We freed our friend, and as we gained the security of our room and slammed the door we heard the man's muffled voice. 'Mistress Martha, I drink your ears, your nose, your fingers. Mistress Martha, it's that I'm loving you. I am dying.'

One evening near the end of our Yugoslavian run, I felt I had danced particularly well, and although I might not have sung the music as written by George Gershwin, my fellow singers had greeted my harmonies with raised eyebrows and approved.

A young couple was directed to my dressing room. The man was a photographer and the woman a dancer. They spoke excellent French and complimented me on my dance. The husband asked to photograph me and invited me to their home the next evening for a pre-Christmas party. They said they would pick me up at the theater and would return me to my hotel after the party.

I considered the invitation. We had been told to stay within the allotted areas and I didn't relish the idea of calling down the wrath of two governments on my head. However, I was myself. That is, I was Marguerite Johnson, from Stamps, Arkansas, from the General Merchandise Store and the C.M.E. Church. I was the too tall, unpretty colored girl who had been born to unhappy parents and raised in the dirt roads of Arkansas and I was for the only time in my life in Yugoslavia. I divined that if I ever became rich and famous, Yugoslavia was not a country I would visit again. Was I then to never see anything more than the selected monuments and to speak to no one other than the tour-guide spies who stuck so close to us that we could hardly breathe? No. I accepted the couple's invitation.

Martha and Ethel warned me at the hotel that I had better not contravene the official orders. I tried to explain my reasons, but they either would not or could not understand. Like all company information, the news that I was going to a private party was common knowledge by noon the next day. Friends stopped by my lunch table cautioning me to change my mind. I thanked them for their advice.

Others came by my dressing room that evening to add their counsel to the general consensus. I was amazed when Helen Ferguson said the couple had invited her too, and that she was going to come along. She was one of the youngest singers in the cast, pretty and so petite she looked like a child. I said, 'You know, we're not supposed to go away from the group.'

She said, 'Listen, I'll never come to Yugoslavia again in my life. I want to talk to some of the people here so I can have some real memories.'

We waited outside the stage door and were surprised when a strange young man approached us. 'Miss Ferguson? Miss Angelou?'

'Yes.'

'Please come with me. I am to take you to the Dovic party.'

We followed him around the corner to a flatbed truck which held about thirty people crowded together, laughing and talking. With their help, Helen and I climbed up and joined them. The man slammed the flap, ran around and started the engine, and we were off on our adventure.

The men and women were about our ages and they all spoke some French. They passed bottles of slivovitz around and we drank the fiery liquid and tried to talk over the motor's loud roar. Finally, the crowd began to sing. I couldn't follow the words, but the melodies sounded like Hungarian tziganes. They were heavy and touching. I was so busy listening that I was slow to realize that we had left the lights of Belgrade behind and the old truck was struggling along on a bumpy dirt road. The night was clear and cold, and in the bright moonlight the flat countryside looked familiar, as if I had seen it all before. I had to remind myself that I was behind the iron curtain, not taking an innocent ride in central California. The people could be taking us to Siberia. Helen and I caught each other's looks and laughed, for there was nothing else we could do. The engine began to slow down as we went over an even rougher lane when we finally stopped in front of a large gabled Charles Addams-type house. The crowd of people gave a loud shout and began to jump over the sides of the truck. Helen and I and some of the other women waited until the flap was released.

The Dovic couple came out to welcome us and lead us into an already crowded living room. Helen and I were introduced (the rest seemed to already know each other), and while we were welcomed heartily, no one stared at us as though we were apparitions from a nightmare. I soon felt at ease and got into a discussion on the future of art and its relative value to the masses.

In an adjoining dining room we were given festive foods and drink. My hostess told me she had some records I might like to hear and she called for quiet in the room. People sat down on the floor in groups, sharing bottles of wine and slivovitz. The host put the record on a wind-up record player and Lester Young's saxophone yowled out of the silence. My ears and brain were at extreme odds. I was in Yugoslavia and the ordinary people of the country had no freedom to travel. According to my language teacher in Paris, the common citizen found it impossible to obtain an exit visa or a travel document; they were prisoners in their own land. And outsiders seldom visited the iron curtain countries; few wished to come and fewer were allowed. But I was listening to Lester Young. Helen and I exchanged surprised glances. When the record was over, the host replaced it with a Billie Holiday song and then exchanged that for a Sarah Vaughan, then Charlie Parker.

The host saw my startled expression, and said, 'We love music. Everyone at this party is an artist. We are painters, sculptors, writers, singers, dancers, composers. Everything. And we find ways to stay aware of innovations in art everywhere in the world. Bebop was the most important movement in music since Johann Sebastian Bach. How did we get the records?' He smiled and said, 'Don't ask.' I didn't.

The party was slowing down and I had begun to think of the long, bumpy ride back to the hotel when an old woman emerged from a side door. She wore a chenille bathrobe and slippers to match. She shuffled through the thinning crowd, greeting each person informally and receiving embraces in return. She had to be the grandmother of the house. She had made her way to the center of the living room before she saw me. Her face was immediately struck with panic. She squawked and turned, nearly falling, and headed for the room she had just left.

The host, hostess and other guests came quickly and apologetically to me.

'Miss Angelou, please excuse her. She is eighty years old.'

'She is very old and ignorant.'

'She has never seen a black person before.'

'She does not mean to hurt your feelings.'

I said, 'I understand her. If I had lived that long and never seen a white person, the sight of one would give me a heart attack. I would be certain I was seeing a ghost.'

'Please. You shouldn't be bitter.'

233

It wasn't my intention to be sarcastic. I was sincere.

The hostess went to the door through which the old woman had disappeared and in a moment the two came out together. The hostess, draping her arm across the woman's frail shoulders, gently guided her toward me. When they were about four feet from where I was sitting, I said in Serbo-Croatian, 'Good evening, madame.'

She gave me a very faint 'Good evening, madame' in return.

I asked, 'Will you please sit with me?' The hostess removed her arm and the old woman inched slowly away from her fear and came to join me on the sofa.

I asked, 'How are you?'

She whispered, 'I am well,' and kept her gaze unwavering on my face. She raised a wrinkled hand and touched my cheek. I didn't move or smile. Her hand brushed my hair slightly, then the other cheek. Without shifting her look from me she called her granddaughter.

'Go and bring food and drink.'

'But Grandmother, she has already eaten.'

'Go.'

Mrs. Dovic brought a small meat pie and a shot of slivovitz with the accompanying apricot preserve. I took a bite of the savory and one small spoonful of preserves. Without hesitation I gulped down the jigger of brandy and followed it with another spoonful of preserves.

The old woman smiled and patted my cheek. She began to talk to me so fast I couldn't keep up with her. I laughed and she laughed, showing a full set of the regulation metal teeth. Only after the party relaxed and general conversation resumed did I realize how tense the atmosphere had been. The grandmother patted my cheek again and touched my knee, then she rose laboriously and headed for her room. I called, 'Good night, Grandmother,' but she didn't respond. The host said, 'She has already forgotten you. She is very old. Thank you for being so kind.'

We were collecting our coats when the door opened again and the old woman again emerged, but this time followed by an older man. He, too, wore a chenille robe and matching slippers, and sleep had not yet released his face. When I noticed that he did not look around the room for someone or something strange but began greeting the guests closest to him, I knew the old woman was playing a joke on him. He hobbled from one person to another and the old woman stayed close to his side. Suddenly he saw me and almost leaped out of his ninety-year-old antiquity. He screamed and turned as quickly as he could to escape, but the old woman caught his sleeve, and with words I couldn't understand, began to berate him for his ignorance and chide him for being rude.

She guided him to the sofa and made him sit on one side of me while she sat on the other.

'Go bring food and drink.'

Again I went through the ritual. When the old man saw I could both eat and drink and I could speak some Serbo-Croatian, he not only decided I was human, he declared me a Yugoslav. Just a very dark one.

'What is your name?'

'Maya.'

'A good name.'

'Who is your father?'

235

'Bailey Johnson.'

'What a strange name for a Croatian. But I am sure I know him. Who is his father?'

'William Johnson.'

'Vilyon? Vilyon? What does he do? I know everybody. I am ninety-three years old. Now tell me, was that Vilyon from Split or the one from Dubrovnik? Tell me.'

No one could convince the man that I belonged to a different race and country.

As we headed for the door he said, 'Tell Vilyon you have met me. Tell him to come after Christmas. We will talk of the old times.'

The desk clerk at the hotel had to unlock the door to let us in. He said, 'Miss Angelou. Miss Ferguson. Did you enjoy the party at the Dovic home? Did you enjoy the American records and the food? The old man and woman are very amusing, are they not?'

So much for our sense of freedom.

The next morning a clean-cut American asked to see me. I went to a room in the hotel and listened to a strange white man talk to me as if I were a child.

'You have been asked, Maya, not to wander around Belgrade. The Yugoslavs don't want it. They are a different people from us. They don't understand our ways. You are, after all, a guest in their country. Simple courtesy demands that you honor the wishes of your host.'

I said, 'I am not the one of the two of us who needs lessons in common courtesy. I did not say one thing last night that I didn't mean, nor that I would be reluctant to repeat. Good morning,' and I left.

If *Porgy and Bess* didn't like it, they could find another singer who could dance, or a dancer who could sing. I had already seen Venice, Paris and two towns in Yugoslavia. I could go home to my wonderful son and my night club career.

I never heard any more about the incident, nor did I ask Helen if she had been questioned on our return.

'Good morning, Mistress Maya. As you know this is being me, Mr. Julian.'

It was also the morning of our closing night in Belgrade.

'Yes, Mr. Julian.'

Nothing had deterred him. Neither strong words nor outright insults kept him from telephoning. Martha and Ethel became so used to the ring that it no longer awakened them.

'It's I am loving you yet. It's that when you are leaving tomorrow I am dying.'

'Yes, Mr. Julian.' The night before, I had joined Joe Jones, Martha, Ethel, Ned and Attles in a slivovitz-and-song fest at a local bar. I felt as if the harsh brandy had baked my brain, and if Mr. Julian could wait until the next morning to die I would best him by twenty-four hours.

'I am not drowning. It is being very difficult for me. Because I am being Yugoslavia's Olympic swimming champion.'

Swimming champion? Mr. Julian? Doggone it, I had slipped a bet. His voice had sounded ancient, as if it belonged to a body in the last stages of deterioration. I liked strong and muscular men. Had I known Mr. Julian was an athlete, I'd have seen him the first time he called.

'I am loving you and wanting to see you, oh . . .'

'Maybe I can see you tonight, Mr. Julian.' I couldn't make

up for the time wasted, but there was no reason I should lose another night.

'Is it true? You will let me take you to one expensive café? And watching you drinking down coffee with cream in your lovely lips?'

'Yes, Mr. Julian.' You bet. 'After the theater you come to the stage door.'

'Mistress Maya, there are always being so many people around your theater. Is it that you can be meeting me one block away?'

'Sure, yes. Of course.' It seemed a little late for him to show a shy side.

'One block away near the park. I will be standing. I will be wearing a green suit. I will be smiling. Oh, Mistress Maya, my heart is singing for you. Good-bye, my lovely.'

'Good-bye, Mr. Julian.'

I hung up the telephone as Martha and Ethel turned over and sat up.

'So, at last. My Lord, we'll get to see this damned Mr. Julian.' Martha was grinning and nodding her head.

Ethel said, 'Maya, you *are* cold-blooded. You know the man loves you. And you wait until the last night to see him.'

Martha added, 'It *is* cold – he wants to marry you so you can take him to the States. Now there's no time to get a license. You're just going to use that poor man and toss him away, like a sailor does a woman in a foreign port.' She was laughing. 'Ohh, you're mean.'

I told them both to go to hell and went back to sleep.

Ned met me at lunch. 'So you're finally going to see Mr. Julian?'

Annabelle Ross, the coloratura, asked, 'Tonight's the night, huh?'

Georgia Burke, the oldest member of the cast and veteran actress, said, 'I understand Mr. Julian's finally got lucky. Well, there's nothing like sticking to it, they say.'

Barbara Ann sat down at the table. 'What made you wait so long, Maya? And what made you change your mind?'

I told her I had thought that he was an ancient lech and I couldn't abide the idea of going out with an elderly stage-door Johnny who would slobber on my cheek and pinch my thighs, but that he had finally told me he was a swimming champion and now I was sorry I waited so long.

She understood and sympathized with me.

An hour later Bey appeared at my door. 'O.K., Maya. Got yourself a swimming champion, huh?'

On the way to the theater, a few wags in the back of the bus began to harmonize: 'I'd swim the deepest ocean . . .'

Among the cast no news was private and no affairs sacred.

The audience began applauding in the middle of the finale. They were on their feet, throwing roses and shouting before the curtain fell. We bowed and waved and repeated the bows unremembered times.

Backstage, Marilyn, the wardrobe mistress, was supervising the labeling and packing of costumes. Departures were always her busiest time. She had to tag the clothes that had been torn so they could be sewn or replaced before our next opening night, and to keep separate the pieces due for cleaning and the shoes needing repairs.

As I passed the wardrobe room the door was open on a havoc of disarranged clothes, hats, shoes, baskets and umbrellas.

She looked up from her counting. 'Going to meet Mr. Julian, huh, Maya?'

My only chance of escaping the curious eyes of my fellow singers was to leave the theater by the front entrance. I gathered my costumes and dropped them in the wardrobe room, as we were required to do. Marilyn's attention was on her work. I slipped past the stage hands who were breaking down the set and stacking scenery. I tiptoed across the stage and jumped from the apron to the theater floor. The lobby was empty and dark as I eased out the door. I had avoided everyone. As I walked to the intersection I looked down the street. I saw a crowd of well-wishers at the stage door; they would keep the company occupied for a least a half-hour. Mr. Julian, I am coming and coming alone. You'll never know what a remarkable feat I have accomplished.

I approached the designated corner, searching for a tall well-built man in a dark-green suit, possibly a tweedy affair. He might be smoking a pipe – pipes and tweeds went so well together.

Mr. Julian wasn't on the corner. I wondered if he had decided, after all, to collect me at the stage door. I crossed the street and stood under the light, planning my next move.

'Mistress Maya?'

I turned, happy to be relieved of the problem. A small, very wiry old man was standing before me. His eyes were large and black and glistening. His bald head looked greased under the streetlight. He was smiling a row of decidedly polished metal teeth. And he wore a Kelly green suit.

'Mistress Maya, it's that I'm being Mr. Julian.'

If he was a swimming champion the match took place in 1910.

'Yes, Mr. Julian. How are you?' I offered him my hand and he took it, stroked the back of it, turned it over and kissed the palm.

He mumbled, 'I am loving you.'

I said, 'Yes.' And, 'How about that coffee?'

If Martha or Ethel or Lillian caught a glimpse of my athletic lover, I'd never be allowed to live it down.

'I can't go far, I must be in the hotel before curfew, you know.'

He didn't understand the word 'curfew' and I didn't have the time to stand on the corner explaining it.

'Let's go to the café up the street. Is that all right?'

We sat at a small table silently. Each conversational opening I tried was blocked by his statements of undying love. His bright eyes watched me drink coffee. He observed my lips so intently, I had the sensation that his gaze was following each sip slide over my tongue, through the esophagus and into my stomach.

I gulped the last swallow and stood up. 'Thank you, Mr. Julian. I must get back to the theater or the bus will leave me.'

'I will take you to your hotel.' His eyes were begging.

'No, thanks. The buses have to take us. Sorry.'

'It's that I will walk you back to the theater. I am loving you.'

'Absolutely not! No, thank you. I appreciate the coffee and the thought, but I'd like to remember you right here, having coffee with cream.' I didn't offer him my hand again. 'Thank you. Please stay. Good-bye, Mr. Julian.'

I walked slowly out of the café, but when I closed the door I broke into a run that would have impressed Jesse Owens. The bus was loading as I reached the theater.

As I climbed aboard, Martha said, 'Whatever else Mr. Julian is, I can tell he's fast.'

Lillian said, 'I've got something for you, Maya. You left it in your dressing room and I felt I'd better bring it to you. Your life would not be the same without it.'

She handed me a package. It was Mr. Julian's heart.

23

The singers were hardened to the discomfort of travel and the sense of dislocation. Yet the Yugoslavia trip put an unusual amount of pressure on us all. The cold weather, gray and dreary, and the incommodious hotel with its grim corridors and heavy odors pressed weightily on our spirits. The unhappy people in their ugly, thick clothes and the restrictions on our freedom of movement all combined to make us impatient to put the dour place behind us and to bask in the sunshine of North Africa.

Ethel, Martha, Barbara Ann, Lillian and I crowded our personal belongings into the two overhead racks of our compartment. It was seven o'clock on a dark morning. The cast had begun to assemble at the train station at six and we had boarded the fabled Orient Express as soon as Ella Gerber and Bob Dustin completed their head count and were satisfied that no member of the company was still sleeping at the Moskva. Belgradians crowded around the train steps. Some Yugoslavian women sniffled and dried their eyes as male singers embraced them, checked their watches and boarded the train. A few female singers waved good-bye to some native men, who wept openly.

My friends and I nestled down, anxious for the train to move. We were chatting when a noise alerted us. We looked up to see Mr. Julian standing in the doorway of the compartment, holding a small package.

'Mistress Maya?' Tears trickled down his face. 'Mistress Maya, I am wishing you joy, happiness and wictory.' With that emotional outcry he threw the package in my lap, slammed the door and leaped off the train.

Lillian asked, 'That was Mr. Julian?'

Ethel said unbelievingly, 'No, surely not?'

Barbara Ann asked, 'But when was he a swimming champion?'

Martha shifted her small head and said, 'He looks like he'd have a hard time floating across a bathtub.'

Before I could retort, his face was at the window. He waved his hands in a beckoning motion and the train began to move slowly. Mr. Julian kept up with our window for a while, but as the train gained momentum his face and all the other faces of those left behind began to slide from our view. In a few minutes we were in open country, looking out on lonely farmhouses and sullen fields.

Ned Wright pulled the door open and offered a bottle of slivovitz.

'Here we are, me darlings. Long gone and away. Tito can keep his Yugoslavia. I am meant to sit under sunny skies and sing. What the hell are you crying for, Maya?'

Ethel said it couldn't be for Mr. Julian. 'Did you see him?'

Martha laughed, 'He looked like a mile of country road in the winter in North Carolina.'

I said, 'But he persevered. And he was nice. I mean, he never failed to call and he had to get up very early to be at the station before we left. I admire that in anyone.'

Ethel asked, 'Would you like to go back to Belgrade?'

I didn't have to choose an answer. I said, 'No. Pass me the slivovitz!'

The train sped all day through the glowering provinces and we took our meals in an old dining car which smelled like our last hotel. Some of the cast took naps or wrote letters home. We played games of rise and fly bid whist in our compartment with all the passion of addicted gamblers. When the gray afternoon finally surrendered to night, a porter made our beds and we slept.

I awakened to find Martha and Ethel chittering like crickets. The sunlight came boldly through the windows and their faces were lit with a gaiety I hadn't seen for weeks.

'Maya, girl, you're going to sleep all day? Look out the window.' Martha edged over and made room for me. The countryside had changed. In one night we had passed from bleak winter to spring. Cows grazed on abundant green foliage and the farmhouses were painted in so many vivid colors the scene resembled a large Matisse painting.

Grownups, smiling broadly, waved at the train, and children bounced, laughing their excitement. The picture touched me so violently that I was startled, and in an instant I realized that I had not seen giddy children since Venice. The Parisian youngsters were so neat in dress and manner they might have been family ornaments created and maintained to

245

adorn. The children I saw in Yugoslavia appeared sensible and level-headed without the buoyancy of childhood. Here were children I could understand. Although their voices didn't carry over the distance and through our windowpane, I was certain they were shouting, yelling and screaming, and I was just as certain that the mothers were saying 'Be quiet,' 'Stop that' and 'Hush.'

I got up and excused myself. The longing for my own son threatened to engulf me. As I walked down the corridor, controlling the emotional deluge that swelled in my mind, I passed compartments where other members of the company sat close to their windows, absorbed.

We caught brief glimpses of the white buildings and green hills of Athens, then boarded buses which were to take us to the port city of Piraeus. The road was high and winding, and our moods were high. We sang in full voice every song that was suggested and laughed when someone made the wrong harmonic change or forgot the lyrics.

At the waterfront, Dustin doled out cabin assignments and announced that Lee Gershwin was throwing a champagne party on the ship for the entire cast before lunch.

If only Yanko and Victor and Mitch could see me now. I had dredged up some Greek learned during my marriage and greeted the crew members. They were already excited by the cluster of black people, and when they heard me speaking their language they nearly saluted. Three men left their posts to help me find my quarters, where my suitcases, books and mandolin were already stacked on a table in the single room.

Martha, Lillian, Ethel and Barbara Ann came down the

passageway talking about the ship, the champagne party and the handsome Greek sailors.

I stopped them, and said, 'Hey, you guys, aren't you surprised that Lee Gershwin is inviting the humble nobodies to her affair?'

Martha said, 'Darling, Miss Fine Thing has never been humble, and for your information, she has always been Somebody. She shall grace the motley crew with her presence.' She grinned and flung her head back.

Lillian said, 'Dearie, there's going to be champagne?' She nodded, answering her own question. 'I'm going to drink Madame Gershwin's champagne.'

Barbara Ann said smoothly, 'Maya, you've never forgiven her for telling you and Joy what to wear in Venice, have you?' She shook her head and managed a sad smile. 'And I thought you were supposed to be a Christian. Shame, Maya, shame.'

They continued looking for their rooms and left me thinking about Lee Gershwin. She had approached me and Joy in Venice's Saint Mark's Square on our second day in Italy.

'Don't you girls know you shouldn't wear slacks in Italy? The Italians don't like it.' Her narrow face was sour with propriety. 'Be nice. Remember, we are all ambassadors.'

Joy had told her: 'One, it's cold. Two, I'm singing every night on a cold stage and changing in a cold dressing room, and three, I'm working six hours a day with the cast on their roles. Four, I shall continue to wear slacks and, if I need it, a parka!'

I simply looked at Lee. If I had given tongue to my voice, I'd have said too much. I simply continued to wear slacks when I thought it necessary, counting on my own sense of propriety to dictate what I should wear where and when. The incident had slipped from my consciousness, but once reminded of it I had to admit that Lee's maternalistic attitude had so infuriated me that, although she traveled with us, I had erased her from my thoughts.

I unpacked the clothes I would need for the three-night, two-day trip to Alexandria and changed into a dress for lunch.

When I walked up the stairs, stewards grinned and spoke to me in Greek, and as I entered the dining room a large, bushy-haired man in a black suit caught my arm.

'Mrs. Angelos?'

'Yes?'

'I am the purser.'

I couldn't dredge up one idea of what to expect.

'You speak Greek?' he asked.

'Yes. A little.'

'How did you learn?'

'My husband was Greek.'

'Ah.' And he grinned a broad approval. 'Mrs. Angelos, may I make a suggestion?' He turned his large body sideways and spoke out of the side of his mouth as if he were giving me the secret of building an atomic bomb.

'Yes.'

'There is a party. A champagne party.' He inclined his head toward the tables where members of the cast were already lifting glasses. 'We expect a very rough trip to Alexandria. It would be better if you didn't drink today. Or tonight. Not champagne. Not wine. Not water. Eat lightly. Bread. Biscuits. And no drinking.'

I thanked him and asked if he had warned anyone else.

He smiled, pulling his lips leftward to reveal a solid gold tooth.

He said, 'They are opera singers. I wouldn't try to tell them. But you' – again he grinned – 'you are nearly Greek' – he took my hand and kissed it – 'and you have my sympathy. Good-bye. Remember.'

Sympathy? He thought having married a Greek made me deserving of his compassion? Strange.

My friends had saved a chair for me at their table.

'Miss Thing, hold your glass.' Martha held the champagne ready to pour.

'No, I'm not drinking.' I told them of the warning.

Lillian said, 'I've never been seasick in my life.'

Martha and Ethel seconded her. They shared the wine and giggled, paying no attention to my admonition. Every table was filled with happy flutters. Even the few nondrinkers were in a party mood. I only half believed the purser, but was glad for an excuse not to participate. I liked to pay for my own drink or at least choose the sponsor who treated me.

'Mother Afrique, your long-lost daughter is returning home . . .' Lillian was composing another toast and no one was waiting for her to complete it.

'Cheers.'

'*Salute.*'

'*À votre santé.*'

'*Doz vedanya.*'

'*Skoal.*'

An officer at the captain's table stood up, kissed the women's hands, bowed to the men and began to pick his way out of the dining room. He was tall and moved gracefully, hardly shaking the braid that looped across his wide shoulders. He turned his head and looked at our table. He had the most sensuous face I had ever seen. His lips were dark rose and pouted, and his nostrils flared as if he were breathing heavily through them. But his eyes were the most arresting feature. They were the 'bedroom eyes' sung about in old blues – heavy-lidded, as if he were en route at that moment to the boudoir of the sexiest woman in the world.

'Mart, Ethel, look at that,' I said.

My friends, who usually had a high appreciation of male beauty, were so occupied with their party that they gave the officer only a cursory look.

Ethel said, 'Yeah, he's cute.'

Martha said, 'I'll check him out later. Pour a little more of the bubbly into my slipper, please, for I am Queen of the May.'

I watched the man leave the dining salon and knew that when the sexy women in our company got around to noticing him, they would take some of the arrogance out of his swinging shoulders and lessen the bounce in his narrow hips.

After lunch I returned to my cabin, leaving the party in full hilarity. By midafternoon when we were well away from the coast of Greece, the ship began to shudder under the attack of a storm. My luggage shot back and forth across the tiny space between my bunk and the wall, and had I not stood up I would have been thrown out of bed. I shoved my bags tightly into the closet and jammed a chair under the closet's door-knob. I took a book and headed for the main deck.

In the passageway I met my suddenly sober and suddenly sick fellow singers. Those who were able to talk said the party had broken up as drinkers and players became too ill to continue; the waiters had removed all bottles and glasses and were tying the tables down.

The dining room was empty and dark, and I struggled, rolling from wall to wall, up the passageway to a small red sign which invited: BAR. The door opened on a small, empty but lighted room. I sat at a table, trying to glue my mind to the plot and away from the roiling sea. After an hour or so, a young crew member came in, saw me and was surprised. He asked if I was all right. I lied and told him in Greek that I was. He looked at me, astonished for a second, then left hurriedly. A few moments later the purser arrived.

'Mrs. Angelos, are you well?'

'Yes, of course.' My composure was paper-thin, but it covered the fear.

'You didn't drink. I noticed.' He was proud of himself and of me.

'No. I ate bread and a piece of cold chicken.'

'Very good. It is going to be worse tonight, but tomorrow will be calmer. You are not to worry. We have a doctor, but he is very busy. Both the opera company and the movie company are sick and he is kept running between the two.'

I didn't know about the movie company. 'Who are they? From America?'

'No. They are English. Except the star is French. Brigitte Bardot. They are all in their cabins and I don't expect to see either the singers or actors until we reach Alexandria.'

He took my hand. 'Mrs. Angelos, if you want me, please ring this bell' – he pointed to a button on the wall – 'and tell anyone to come for me. I will be with you immediately.' He kissed my hand and departed.

A waiter entered and said tea was being served in the dining room. I thanked him and said I wouldn't have anything.

The ship pitched and rolled and quivered and sometimes leaped, seeming to withdraw entirely from the surface of the water. I was frightened at the violence and my inability to control any part of the experience except myself and there was no certainty that my mental discipline would outlast the physical anxiety. But at least I wasn't ill.

The purser pushed his head in the door. 'Dinner is being served. I suggest that you eat. Again the plain bread. And again a small piece of meat. No wine. No water.' His head disappeared as the vessel rolled over on its side.

Although I had no appetite I decided to continue following his suggestions. The dining room was not quite empty. The captain and his officers sat quietly in their corner; a few teetotalers from *Porgy and Bess* were at separate tables; and two men whose faces I recognized from British movies occupied a table near the wall. I joined Ruby Green and Barbara Ann and ate sparingly.

Barbara asked, 'Where have you been? You haven't been sick?'

I told her I'd been reading and I wasn't sick because I didn't drink the champagne.

'You ought to see downstairs. Everybody's sick. I mean, people are moaning like they're dying. The poor doctor no sooner leaves one room than they call him to another. That man's got his work cut out for him. See, here he comes now. Poor thing. Just now getting a chance to eat his dinner.'

I looked up, following her gaze, and saw the voluptuous face that had startled me at lunchtime.

'That's the doctor?' I would have more easily believed him to be a gigolo, a professional Casanova.

'Yes. And he's very courteous. He gives the same attention to the men that he gives to the women.'

I looked at his retreating back and wondered if Barbara in her naïveté had described the man better than she could have imagined.

After a somber dinner we went below, where the groans of suffering escaped mournfully from each room. I paused before my friends' doors, but I knew I could do nothing for them except sympathize and I could do that without disturbing their agony.

There was a soft rap on my door. When I opened it and saw the purser, I thought he expected me to compensate him for my sound health. I held the door and asked icily, 'Yes, what do you want?'

He said meekly, 'Mrs. Angelos, I want to show you how to strap yourself in the bed so that you won't fall out and be hurt.'

I started to let him in and thought better of it. 'No, thanks. I was planning to sleep on the floor. I'll be all right. Thanks, anyway.'

He shot his hand in the narrow door opening and grabbed my arm.

'Mrs. Angelos, thank you. You are very sad and very beautiful.' He bowed and kissed my hand and released it. I slammed the door. How could he tell I was sad? That was a strange romantic come-on.

I made my actions fit the lie. I stripped mattress and covers from the bed and lay down on the floor to sleep in miserable fits and starts.

The morning was dreary and wet, but the sea was more restrained. The purser was waiting for me outside the dining room door.

'Mrs. Angelos, good morning. You may eat a full breakfast. We will have good weather by evening.' He looked at me lovingly, concern seeping out of his pores. 'How did you sleep?'

'Beautifully, thank you. Just beautifully.'

Some members of our company who had survived the storm exchanged stories of the night before.

'Honey, I was so sick I tried to jump overboard!'

'Did you hear Betty? She prayed half the night, then she got mad and screamed, "Jesus Christ, this ain't no way for you to act so close to your birthday!"'

My visits to Martha's and Lillian's cabins were not welcome, so I made them brief, staying only long enough to see that although their faces were the color of old leather boots, they would survive. I walked around the ship, enjoying the luxury of solitude. For the first time, there was a tender behind the bar and I ordered an apéritif. The very large British movie actor and his companion came in, ordered and sat near me.

'So you're a sailor too, are you?' The man's gruff voice was directed to me.

'I suppose so.'

'But the rest of your company have no sea legs?' He laughed and his eyes nearly closed beneath dark, thick eyebrows.

'Some have been a little sick,' I said. The man always played friendly characters, so without knowing his real personality, I felt friendly toward him. 'But they're better now.'

'My name is James Robertson Justice.'

Of course I knew the name and had thought it fitted his

giant size and huge laughter. He pointed to his smaller, quieter friend. 'And this is Geoffrey Keen.'

We talked about opera and movie making and I felt decidedly international. I was on a Greek ship, talking to English movie stars, en route to the African continent.

I ate lunch and dinner alone, but joined Ned Wright and Bey in the bar after dinner. James Robertson Justice was there again and the three men exchanged stories. They all laughed together, but it was not clear if they understood each other. Ned tended to talk and snap his fingers in the air like a flamenco dancer, meanwhile wiggling his head. Bey grumbled in a bass-baritone without moving his lips. Justice spoke in all the British accents, gamboling from upper class, middle class to Welsh and Irish like a skittish lamb on the heath.

I left the men laughing and talking loudly and walked down the passageway. The doctor passed me, lips distended and full, his eyes low and dense.

'Good evening,' he said.

I said 'Good evening,' and wished vainly that he would stop. The purser knocked at my door. I opened it a crack.

'Mrs. Angelos, we will dock at eleven. Everyone will be asked to come to passport control. There will be a crowd. I suggest that you meet me after breakfast, at nine o'clock, and I will see that your passport is stamped first.'

'Thank you.' I held on to the door. 'Thank you very much. Good night.' I closed the door firmly.

At nine o'clock the next morning he met me outside the dining room. He took my elbow and guided me to the upper deck. An official handed me my stamped passport and medical documents. The purser led me away.

'Now, Mrs. Angelos, I suggest you get your belongings, not your luggage, but handbags and other things you want to carry. Bring them on deck and then you will not have to stand in line with the others.' He kissed my hand and gave me a lingering look.

When the two companies lined up on the main deck and on the stairs leading to the officials' temporary office, I stood beside the rail watching the coast of Africa. The ship was being pulled into the harbor by a small, powerful tugboat.

The sea was a beautiful blue, and the tall white buildings on the shore belied the old statement that all Africans lived in trees like monkeys. Alexandria was beautiful.

I had all my hand luggage and was eager to step out on Egyptian soil. A camera swung from my right side, a shoulder bag from the left. I carried my mandolin and Mr. Julian's heart (I was too ashamed of my treatment of him to throw the thing away), and at my feet was a make-up case and a small box of books.

As the ship neared land, streets and the details of buildings became more visible in the bright sunlight, and I fantasized the Africans who designed the houses and laid out the streets. Tall and dark-brown-skinned. Proud and handsome like my father. Bitter-chocolate black like my brother, lightly made and graceful. Or chunky and muscular, resembling my Uncle Tommy. Thick and sturdy, walking with a roll to their hips like boxers or gandy dancers. The fantasy was mesmerizing, and before I knew it men were lashing the ship to the dock.

Except for their long gowns and little skullcaps, the men did look like my father and brother and uncle, and there appeared to be thousands of them, screaming and shouting and running up and down the pier. From my high perch I tried to distinguish the differences between these Africans who had not been bought, sold or stolen and my people who were still enduring a painful diaspora. But I was either too far away or they moved too fast for my purpose. Still, I was determined and kept my gaze fastened on the area below.

'Mrs. Angelos.'

I turned and was face-to-face with the doctor.

'Mrs. Angelos, what are your first impressions of your native continent?'

I retrieved my thoughts and longings and made a snappy remark. 'It is colorful. And noisy. And the sun shines on Africa.'

He fished two cigarettes from a package and lighted them simultaneously (he had seen *Now Voyager* too, and I wondered how often he had imitated Paul Henreid). He put one between my lips.

'Where are you staying in Alexandria?'

I told him the company was booked at the Savoy.

'Will you honor me with dinner? They have a decent dining room and you won't have to leave your hotel.'

I quickly weighed his lips, shoulders, hips and eyes against the chances of finding an interested Egyptian man on the first day. The sea had been smooth for nearly twenty-four hours, which meant that the huntresses were feeling well and would be back in the chase and any available men would be at a premium. 'I'd be delighted,' I said.

His eyes smoldered wonderful promises; then he tried a smile that was incongruous on the lascivious face. 'My name is Geracimos Vlachos. I am called Maki. Expect me at eight o'clock. Until then.' He bowed and kissed my hand.

Martha said, 'You got him, you fast thing, you. Took advantage of all your sick sisters and snatched that man while everybody was flat on their backs. Dying in the hold.'

We were lined up at the rails, ready to disembark.

Lillian nudged us. 'Look at the people, will you? Africans. My God. Now I have lived. Real Africans.'

Ethel and Barbara were a little more reserved, but just as excited. Our voices nearly equaled in volume the shouts and yells of the dock workers.

I saw that the older singers were as fascinated as we. Katherine Ayres, Georgia Burke, Eloise Uggams, Annabelle Ross and Rhoda Boggs stood facing Bob Dustin, but their eyes continued to steal away to the dock and to the people who were unloading the vessel. When they walked between the gowned stevedores on the way to the buses, their usually reserved smiles broadened into happy grins, and they doled out money, whose value they had not really considered, to the beggars who stretched out their hands.

In the hotel we deposited our hand luggage then raced back to the lobby to look at the Africans. It took less than five minutes to discover that the bellhops, porters, doormen and busboys were black and brown and beige, and that the desk clerk, head waiters, bartenders and hotel manager were white. As far as we knew, they might have all been African, but the distribution of jobs by skin color was not lost on us. The sweetness of our arrival in Africa was diluted, but not totally spoiled.

After all, Gamal Abdel Nasser was the President and every photograph showed him to be brown-skinned. Darker than Lena Horne, Billy Daniels and Dorothy Dandridge. Without a doubt, he was one of us.

258

We sat in the lounge and ordered drinks. Ned had thrown his cape rakishly across his shoulders and Joe Attles had donned a new and colorful ascot to protect his throat.

Ned asked, 'Does anyone want to go with us? We're going to look at The Dark Continent and bring back a sphinx.'

We all laughed and clapped our hands. Servants ran out into the lounge and bowed, waiting. We looked at them and each other. If we wore the same clothing no one would be able to say we were not members of the same family, yet we couldn't hold a conversation. (Europeans and white Americans are not surprised to see their look-alikes speaking foreign languages; but except for meeting a few African students in Europe, we had never seen a large group of black people whose culture, language and life styles were different from our own.)

Martha asked in French if they wanted something. One man answered in French that when he heard us clap our hands, he thought we wanted something. We learned that day, although we slipped up now and then, not to clap our hands at a joke, and that if we wanted to talk across the centuries that separated us from our brothers in Egypt, we had to use French, a language that was beautiful but more attuned to the thin lips of Europeans – it lacked the rhythms of Ned Wright popping his fingers and Martha Flowers swinging her hips. The knowledge made me sullen and I excused myself and went to my room.

The cast assembled for the evening meal. The large dining room was decorated with palm trees and paper ribbons swinging from slow-moving ceiling fans. Alexandria's playboys were present in evening finery, sending champagne to the women and occasionally to a man who caught their fancy. They introduced themselves from table to table, kissed hands, bowed and offered their calling cards. A few women in low-cut satin dresses ogled the male singers; when they netted a man's attention, their red lips split in a smile to welcome a pharaoh. It was sexually stimulating to be the object of such desire, even if the desire was general and the object collective.

I was so busy flirting and watching my friends that I had forgotten about my date with the doctor. He appeared out of nowhere and stood before me.

'Mrs. Angelos, my I present my cousin and cousin-in-law? They live in Alexandria.'

I shook hands with a tall, attractive woman and her short, pudgy husband. Maki asked me to join their table. When I excused myself from my friends, they raised their eyes.

We made small talk in a mixture of French and Greek. The tables were cleared, and a small band arranged itself at the back of the room. The men played Greek and Arabic music on instruments I had never seen before. When the belly dancer appeared, tasseled and sequined, our company exploded in approval.

'Yeah, baby. Shake that thing!' And she did. Her hips quivered and trembled and her breasts threatened to jiggle out of the skimpy satin-cup restraints. She bumped so hard she had to be cautioned, 'Throw it, but don't throw it away, baby.' Her skin was pale brown and her hair straight, and we were all flabbergasted; no white woman we'd ever seen could move that way.

'Shake it, but don't break it.'

'It must be jelly 'cause jam don't shake that way.'

Later the orchestra played popular songs for dancing and Maki invited me to dance. He held me close and whispered heavily accented words. I gave the appearance of listening, but in fact I was looking around the dance floor for my friends. As busy as they were with their own flirtations they still kept me within sight. I had posed too long as Goody Two-shoes and they weren't going to let me slip without a detailed inspection of my fall. Unity and friendship when needed is reassuring, but sometimes can become an obtrusive and nosy intrusion.

I asked Maki if he knew somewhere else where we might dance. He said he would drop his relatives at their home and we could go to his hotel. 'There is an accordion player who specializes in romantic Greek songs. I would like you to hear him.'

At once the object of my life was to be in Maki's arms and beyond the scrutiny of my colleagues. I told him I would meet him in front of the hotel. I shook hands with him and his relatives and they rose to go.

Someone at the table said, 'Going to let him slide, huh, Maya?'

I said I was going to bed – all the noise had given me a headache. They watched me leave, bemused.

Maki had a taxi waiting, and after we dropped his relatives at their house, near my hotel, we rode in silence for what seemed to be hours. Finally he ushered me into a mean little pension, which would have fitted well on San Francisco's skid row. An unshaven desk clerk handed a key to Maki, who said, 'I had forgotten. The accordion player is off tonight. But let us go to my room. I will sing for you.'

I considered my options. I didn't know where I was. I didn't speak the language. I was attracted to him. I wasn't married or being unfaithful, for I had no lover. He wouldn't hurt me – after all, he was a doctor, Hippocratic oath and all.

I followed him to the room and his songs were glorious. Early the next morning he said we were only a few blocks from my hotel and he would take a cab and drop me, then return to his ship. I wanted to walk and look at the city. The frivolous night was over; I had enjoyed it. But I needed to think great thoughts about myself and Africa and slavery and Islam; I didn't want a white man at my side – in fact, I didn't want anyone distracting me.

Maki was reluctant to let me go alone. I said, 'It's daybreak. And, after all, I am home.'

'You do not know this country, Maya.'

'I come from this country. I am only returning home.'

He said we would meet in two weeks, since his ship was to pick us up again in Alexandria after we finished our run at the Cairo Opera House. He said he loved me and I should think about that; he was married, but would get a divorce and come back to the United States with me; doctors made very good money in the United States and it was difficult to get a visa, but if he was married to an American citizen . . .

I walked out into a beautiful morning and struggled with a bitter thought. The very country that denied Negroes equality at home provided them with documents that made them attractive abroad. Mr. Julian and Maki, in my case, and hundreds of European men and women who tagged the coattails of black servicemen and singers and musicians might have found them much less appealing if they claimed West Indian

262

or African citizenship, but since they hailed from 'God's country,' the 'home of democracy' and the richest nation on earth, men were ready to leave their wives and women their husbands for entry into the land of plenty. Avarice cripples virtue and lies in ambush for honesty.

My footsteps disturbed a group of people wrapped in filthy rags and huddled in a doorway. Two small brown children awakened first; they punched and probed in the bundle of clothing until a man's head emerged. When he saw me he began bellowing and a woman sat upright. I was rooted to the pavement, watching the unfolding scene. The two children, joined by two smaller tykes, made their way to me; the mother and father followed, dragging the tatters of cloth that had once covered them. They encircled me, their hands outstretched. The man and woman clutched their fingers together and brought them to their mouths in a jabbing motion, then they stabbed the bunched hands at their stomachs. They were hungry, but I wasn't sure if it was safe to open my purse. Suppose they grabbed it from me, what could I do?

My inaction called for drama from the adults. The mother grabbed the smallest boy and wedged him between her knees facing me. The father took the child's chin roughly and forced it away from the chest. I looked at the baby's face in the soft morning sunlight. It was a biscuit topped with dusty black hair and, like a clean dinner plate, devoid of meaning except for a thick white substance which seeped from the closed eyes and slowly descended the cheeks. The parents held the boy's head for my view as if I had caused the condition, as if I had poked out the eyes with a nail and now I must pay for my deed.

I fished out my advance from my purse and peeled off a bill.

When I offered it to the child the man snatched it, and the woman flung her blind offspring behind her dirty skirts and grabbed another boy. They showed me his severed arm. The stump looked as blind and final as the diseased eyes. I gave them another bill. When they began to line up the whole family, I said in French, 'I have no more money,' and turned to walk toward my hotel.

They followed, running beside and behind me. I opened up my stride, and the man ran in front, talking loudly, gesturing and screaming, as if I had just evicted them from their home.

Their noise awakened other beggars who had found sleeping accommodations in doorways, on porches and next to roofless buildings. Their supplications, loud and cacophonous, merged; the adults wept and pushed crippled children in my path, ripping the filthy clothes to show the extent of the horror.

Egypt had stumbled under the imperialist and colonial yokes for two thousand years, and finally in 1953 achieved true independence as a republic. But success in gaining self-rule had not yet affected the lives of the poor. Much remained to be done.

I knew that and journalists in the local newspapers knew it, too. I had read magazine articles analyzing the depth of the problems of the country and I was distressed. But sympathy did not lessen my sense of guilt. I was healthy and, compared to the horde of beggars, rich. I was young, talented, well-dressed, and whether I would take pride in the fact publicly or not, I was an American.

The crowd followed me to the hotel where a large uniformed doorman spied me. He rushed to meet me halfway down the block. Then he began screaming and hitting out at the beggars. Occasionally his heavy fists connected and there was a thud of flesh on bone or bone on bone. I called to the man to stop, but he kept flailing his fists and arms until the beggars took to their heels, their shreds of clothing floating behind them like dirty smoke.

'Never mind, mademoiselle. Never mind.' His composure was so complete it seemed as if it had never been ruffled. My father had been a doorman in Long Beach, California, during the great depression. I wondered if he had ever had to chase beggars and hobos from the door. Were they black? Did he feel no more for them than the Savoy doorman felt for his fellow Egyptians?

Martha was sitting in the lobby when I entered. She still wore the dress from the night before. It was impossible to tell whether she had just come in seconds before me or had sat in the same chair all night.

'Good morning, Miss Thing. First night in Africa take the headache away?'

I told her to take a flying leap and went to bed.

24

We stayed in Alexandria two days before moving on to Cairo, but I would not leave the hotel again and refused to explain my seclusion. My close friends thought I had fallen in love with the doctor and I accepted their teasing without comment.

We were driven to Cairo, and thrown into another world. More black-skinned people held positions of authority. The desk clerk at the Continental Hotel was the color of cinnamon; the manager was beige but had tight crinkly hair. The woman who supervised the running of the house was small and energetic and her complexion would never have allowed her to pass for white.

Beggars still hounded our footsteps and the audiences which shouted Bravos at our performances were largely European, but I felt I was at last in Africa – in a continent at the moment reeling yet rising, released from the weight of colonialism, which had ridden its back for generations.

We toured the city and went en masse to the pyramids. We rode camels and had our photographs taken in front of the

Sphinx, but I couldn't satisfy my longing to breathe in the entire country.

I went again to the pyramids, alone. I used the few Arabic words I had picked up to tell the camel drivers and guides that I wanted to be alone. I took off my shoes and dug my feet into the hot sand.

Go down Moses, way down in Egypt land,
Tell old Pharaoh, to let my people go.

A Pharaonic tomb rose above my head and I shivered. Israelites and Nubians and slaves from Carthage and Mesopotamia had built it, sweating, bleeding, and finally dying for the mass of stones which would become in the twentieth century no more than the focus for tourists' cameras.

My grandmother had been a member of a secret black American female society, and my mother and father were both active participants in the Masons and Eastern Star organizations. Their symbols, which I found hidden in linen closets and night stands, were drawings of the Pyramid at Giza, or Cheops' tomb.

I tried to think of a prayer or at least some dramatic words to say to the spirits of long-dead ancestors. But nothing apt came to mind. When the sun became unbearable, I took a taxi back to town.

North Africa made me more reflective. Other members of the cast reacted similarly to the Egyptian experience.

Ethel and Martha were invited to a private party and they asked Lillian and me to come along. A well-to-do Arab came to the hotel and when he saw that his original invitation had expanded to include four women, he ordered a second horse-drawn carriage. We were driven to a large, lighted villa in Heliopolis, and when we started to climb out of the buggies, he stopped us and shouted at two men who stood by the wide wrought-iron gates. They emerged from the shadows bowing, touching their foreheads and chests like extras in a bad Hollywood film. They were as black as the night which closed in on us.

The host said, 'You are not to walk. These servants will carry you.' He stepped aside as one of the men walked up to the buggy, his arms outstretched.

Lillian said, 'Maya, you let him carry you. I'll walk.'

I said, 'No. Uh uh. I'll walk with you.'

Martha shouted from the other carriage, 'Have you ever heard of anything so foul? My dear, Miss Fine's never had to be carried to a party. Come on, Ethel, we'll walk.'

We stepped out into mud that oozed up over the tops of our shoes and walked on as if we were doing the most ordinary thing in the world.

We rejected the offer to have house blacks clean our feet, but accepted towels and wiped away the mud ourselves, chatting vapidly about the pretty villa and the lovely furnishings.

The hosts and other guests were shocked at our refusal to be tended to, not realizing that auction blocks and whipping posts were too recent in our history for us to be comfortable around slavish servants. The party flopped despite flowing champagne and brittle laughter, probably because we couldn't keep our eyes away from the black men who stood like barefoot sentinels at every door, dressed in old galibiyas, waiting with obsequious smiles on their handsome faces.

When we walked to the door to leave, we found that planks of wood had been laid over the wet walkway that led to the drive. There was only one carriage; we were told that our escort was obliged to stay with the other guests, but that the driver would see us safely back in our hotel.

We were obviously too democratic for the company's comfort and they too feudal for ours.

A sign in the hotel elevator read:

Défrisage
MONSIEUR PIERRE
Reservations Made at Hotel Desk

Martha, Ethel, Gloria and I decided to have our hair straightened by chemicals and be rid for a while, at least, of the heavy iron combs heated over cans of sterno that made our hotel rooms smell.

We sat side by side in a luxurious beauty salon and accepted hot cups of sweet black coffee from a young barefoot boy. Monsieur was visibly French: he pooched out his mouth, rolled his eyes and danced pantomimes with his long, thin fingers. Martha and Ethel were lathered down first; then I was taken into a booth. When the assistant put a green foam on my hair, it trickled down to my scalp and began to sting. I tried to sit still and say nothing – after all, my friends were receiving the same treatment without comment – but when my entire head started burning intensely I screamed, 'Take it out! Take this out of my hair!'

'*Qu'est-ce que vous dites?*' Monsieur rounded the corner, pushing the assistant out of the way.

I shouted, 'I said take this crap out of my hair.'

Ethel said from the next stall, 'Oooh, Maya, don't be such a crybaby.'

I turned on the water and pushed my head under the faucet. 'It's burning me.'

The hairdresser, prompted by my loud shouting, hurriedly rinsed out the chemicals. My hair was still wet when I stalked angrily out into the streets, followed by my friends' snickers.

That evening Gloria's hair was so straight and airy that it flew around her head each time she moved. Ethel, Martha and other singers who had endured the process had only to shake their heads and their hair would bounce up and down and sideways with a sinuous smoothness.

A week passed and the hair that moved so freely began to move completely off the women's heads. Bare patches of scalp the size of small coins appeared at first, then enlarged until they could no longer be covered by an adept combing and plastering and pinning of hair from another side of the head.

A few weeks later my mother wrote me, 'I read in Dorothy Kilgallen's column that all the young women in *Porgy and Bess* are wearing wigs. What on earth did you do to your hair?' I did my best not to laugh and sent my mother a photograph taken in a coin-operated booth. I was looking into the lens and had both hands to my head, pulling my healthy kinky hair.

Undeniably, Egypt impressed every member of the group. Irving Barnes, his wife and eight-year-old-daughter, Gail, spent whole days in museums and art galleries. The child who had put on grown-up airs, throwing her tiny hips as she tried to imitate the strut of a provocative Bess, became a little girl again, intrigued by African toys.

Paul Harris forgot his extraordinary good looks for a while and allowed his plump ego to deflate of its own accord. He semi-adopted two young beggars and they hung around the stage door and the hotel entrance until he emerged. He bought the urchins clothes and shoes and took them to restaurants for belly-distending meals.

Earl Jackson, our street-wise Sportin' Life, underwent the most startling personality change. Where he had used colorful profanity to shock the university-schooled and proper singers, he now substituted kind words, softly spoken. His romantic preferences for the local good-time women shifted and focused on the prim soprano of the group. He was to be found in the wings talking low to Miss Helen Thigpen, or finding a chair for Miss Thigpen in the hotel lobby, or rushing to be first on a bus to save a window seat for the quiet and reserved singer. He had begun to act, for all the world to see, like a man in love. And Thigpen, who had only been excited by recitals and her own repertoire, bloomed under the attention.

We left Egypt undeniably changed. The exposure to extreme wealth and shocking poverty forced the frivolous to be level-headed and encouraged the sober to enjoy what they had taken for granted.

Replicas of the Sphinx and the pyramids were packed along with three-inch busts of Nefertiti and small stuffed camels. Ned acquired a carved walking stick, which he kept at hand for the next six months, and Bey bought a red tasseled fez, which, with the giant congo drum that he never let out of his sight, made him look like a Sudanese musician on a pilgrimage to Mecca.

We boarded our Greek ship in Alexandria and the captain welcomed us. Maki smiled when he saw me, but the purser scowled, glum-browed and mean. He arrived at my cabin a moment after I entered.

'Mrs. Angelos.' His voice was nearly closed with accusation.

'Yes?'

'Why did you lie to me?'

'I beg your pardon? I don't lie to anyone.' I might not tell the truth, but I did draw the line at outright falsehood.

'You said you were a widow?'

'What? When did I say that?'

'I asked you how you had learned Greek and you said your dead husband taught you.' He was pointing his finger at me as if he had caught me stealing the gold out of his mouth.

'I said to you my husband was Greek.'

'Exactly.' His smile was malevolent with satisfaction. 'So he's dead?'

'No. I mean, he was my husband.'

'But he's still alive?' Confusion and disappointment shifted his features.

'Very much so.'

'Then why did you say he was Greek? Anyone who is Greek will be Greek until he dies.'

I thought about that and thought about my husband who had intended to lock me into the apologetic female role, which he understood was proper for wives.

272

'Yes. You're right. He is Greek and will be that until he dies. But he is no longer my husband.' I wanted to apologize to the purser for the misunderstanding, but I couldn't bring myself to ask for pardon.

'Vlachos loves you now?'

God, men talk about women gossiping. 'I don't know. I hardly know him.'

The frown was gathering again beneath his overhanging brow. 'He said you were going to take him to the United States . . .'

Lillian knocked at the door. 'Hey, Maya, let's have a drink.'

I opened the door and the purser gave Lillian a little bow, put his hat on and left the cabin.

'Girl, you don't wait, do you? Well, they say there's no time like the present.' She laughed.

I knew there was no use explaining the scene, and I knew that even if I stuck to Lillian's side like white on rice, the incident would be company knowledge before dinner.

'Thanks, I'm going to wait. The doctor ought to be coming soon and I have a few thousand words for him.'

She blew air out of her cheeks. 'Whew. You're a busy lady.' She pulled the door slowly, closing it on her grin.

Maki came to the cabin, his eyes wild. 'Maya, I have told my wife everything.' He reached for me.

I said, 'Hold it a minute.' I pushed him away. 'Listen, I don't know you. You don't know me.'

'But I love you. I want to marry you. I will come with you to the United States.'

'No, you won't.' I opened the door. 'You're nice. I guess. But I'm not marrying anyone. And surely not another Greek.'

273

'But I'm in love with you.'

'Really? Could we live in Greece after you married me?'

'You don't understand. Greece is a poor country. In America I could make money and . . .'

'Mister, my suggestion is that you keep the wife you've got.' I walked out into the passageway and held the door open with my foot. 'I think you'd better go.'

He put his hat on and stepped out of the room. His face was downcast and he was going to say something, but Martha walked by.

'Good morning, Doctor. Good morning, Miss Thing. Still at it, huh?'

I called after her. 'Wait, Mart. I'll go up with you.'

Except for what I had come to think of as only a reasonable amount of teasing, the rest of the cruise was uneventful.

25

The opera was well received in Athens. We photographed each other at the Acropolis and drank retsina late at night in small bars. I dodged Maki in the hotel lobby and tore up the letters he sent me without opening them.

I could have been wrong. It was just possible that he did like me a little. But I knew I would never marry again, nor would I be the cause of a marriage breaking up. I couldn't introduce another non-black to my son and family (although my mother might have accepted this one more heartily because at least he was a doctor). But what made marriage impossible was the fact I would have been embarrassed even if I loved the man (which I didn't). No amount of kindness or fidelity on his part would erase the idea that I had bought a mate with a license that gave me little personal gratification: American citizenship.

We flew from Athens to Tel Aviv. The bright sun that pleased us in Egypt shone on Israel too. The palm trees and white sand and tropical flowers were identical, but the streets were washed clean and there was a total absence of beggars. We were met by English-speaking fans who seemed to have drawn our individual names from lots and immediately became our companions and guides.

The very religious among our company visited Jerusalem, the Wailing Wall, the Mount of Olives and the Dead Sea. The rest were satisfied to buy vials of sand from the Holy Land and agate beads from tourist shops.

Lionel Hampton's band had just finished an engagement in Tel Aviv and we met at a party given by the American embassy and the Israeli government. The *Porgy and Bess* company had not seen such a gathering of American Negroes in months. We fell on the musicians as if they were bowls of black-eyed peas.

In the United States – or anywhere else, for that matter – jazz musicians and opera singers would find few topics of mutual interest. Their vocabularies have no unanimity and even their approach to the common musical scales are as different as odds and evens. But at the foreign official welcoming party we were indisputably siblings.

Helen Ferguson talked with a giant baritone sax player. He bent double to listen to her. Lillian and Ethel laughed with the frenetic drummer who pushed his words over and around a wad of chewing gum.

Gloria Davy and Delores Swan listened attentively as Hamp staccatoed his remarks: 'Yeah. Ha, ha. Yeah. Great. Yeah. Great. Ha, ha.'

Joe Jones and Merrit were telling stories to the brass section. I had my eyes on Sonny Parker, the male band singer. We had known each other slightly, but never as well as I wished.

'Sonny, who would have thought we'd meet in Israel?' I batted my eyes and tried to convey that I'd be happy to meet him anywhere.

'Yeah, baby. That's life, though. Yeah. Life's like that. Hey, Maya, who is that sharp chick?'

I said, 'Barbara Ann Webb,' but was too chagrined to add that she was so in love with her husband that when asked how she liked the weather, she would respond with 'Richard says . . .'

I left Sonny and walked around, rustling myself in the sounds and feasting my eyes on the tasty colors of my people.

I met Arik Lavy, who had the tawny hair and open-mouthed laugh of Victor Di Suvero. He introduced himself and his girl friend to me and told me they were both Sabras, persons born in Israel. Each evening in Tel Aviv after the performance I joined them in an open-air café. The Sabras taught me Hebrew folk songs and I sang spirituals in exchange, always thinking that the real Jordan River was only a few miles away and my audience was composed of the very Israelites mentioned in my lyrics.

I made an arrangement with a dance teacher to give classes in modern ballet and African movement for three weeks in exchange for lessons in Middle Eastern dance.

We boarded a plane for Morocco where we would give a concert and continue to Spain. I was downcast at leaving Tel Aviv. I had felt an emotional attachment to Egypt and made an intellectual identification with Israel. The Jews were reclaiming a land which had surrendered its substance to the relentless sun centuries before. They brought to my mind grammar school stories of pioneer families and wagon trains.

277

The dislodged Palestinians in the desert were as remote in my thoughts as the native Americans whose lives had been stifled by the whites' trek across the plains of America.

In Barcelona we were tired. Too many planes, hotel rooms and restaurant meals were exacting a toll on the company's spirits. But the Spaniards had no way of telling the extent of exhaustion the singers experienced. Years of training sustained the quality of performance, and an affection which bordered on kinship reduced the exhibition of ill humor which lay just under everyone's skin.

We went to Lausanne, Switzerland, performed and left, associating the white and icily beautiful town only with one more stop to be checked off our list. Our interests narrowed into petty little concerns and the cities and countries were beginning to melt together.

Genoa was quaint with its narrow streets and sailors – but were sweaters cheaper in Naples? Florence had Michelangelo statues and the Ponte Vecchio, but why didn't the clothes come back from the cleaners really clean?

In Marseilles, Gloria Davy and I tried to lift our spirits. Our birthdays were only two days apart, and we decided to give ourselves a treat. We bought a box lunch and took a small boat to the Château d'If. It turned out to be a dungeon built into the rocks, from which we were told no one had ever escaped, except the fictional Count of Monte Cristo. The guide wanted to show us where prisoners were chained to the walls. We refused and stood aside, gazing wistfully back at the mainland while other tourists ducked their heads and trooped through the small, low opening. I didn't relate the story to my friends because I knew they were too moody to hear another sour tale.

When we reached Turin the company was a drab lot. Merriment had seeped out of our repertoire and we fabricated joy on stage. Sullen and quiet, we went separately to our hotel rooms.

Helen Thigpen announced that she was giving a birthday party for Earl Jackson and everyone was invited. The statement sparked the first light of common interest I had seen in months. We had all noticed that Helen and Earl had become inseparable and had exchanged some character traits. He was more contained and the wise hopping walk had given way to more erect posture, while her reserve had thawed and she smiled more frequently.

Lillian and I made a bet with Martha and Ethel that the lovers were going to announce their engagement at the party. Ned held the bet, declining to join either side.

Helen had taken over the top floor of a restaurant near the hotel. Every table held a bottle of expensive whiskey, and waiters, assigned to our party exclusively, brought food and wine. I sat with Martha and Ethel and her mother, who had just arrived to spend a month with her daughter.

The party began like any party, coolly and dryly at first, but the sounds of a good time increased in direct proportion to the absorption of food and drink. Joy sat down at the piano and Leslie Scott stood to deliver a rich 'Blue Moon.' We applauded happily. Laverne Hutchinson, without being urged, sang another sentimental song, trying to outdo Leslie. Martha, who was sipping no less steadily than the rest of us, submitted to requests and honored the gathering with a song a cappella. When she finished, another singer took her place. Between songs we talked. People who had found it hard to smile for weeks were suddenly reminding each other of old stories and sharing the hilarious memories. It was a much needed festival.

Rhoda Boggs, at five foot eight inches and nearly two hundred pounds, was called 'one of the big women in the company.' She wore a mink capelet to all formal affairs, hats that quivered with large silk roses and high-heeled baby-doll shoes, the straps sinking deep into her ankles. She had the lyrical voice and artistic temperament of almost every classical soprano. As the party reached a peak, Rhoda clutched her capelet to her large bosom and started across the small dance floor to share stories with friends at another table. At the same time, Billy Johnson, waspish, impish and balding, decided to traverse the small space en route to another destination. The two collided midway. Rhoda stumbled at the shock while Billy almost fell under the impact. Rhoda was the first to recover. She looked down at the associate conductor as if he were a street urchin laying obstacles in the route of her parade. She rushed to the nearest table.

'Did you see him? Did you see that?' Her indignant voice was sounded like a flute played in anger. 'Did you see that he struck Rhoda Boggs?' She went quickly but gracefully to the next table. 'Did you see him actually strike Rhoda Boggs? Oh, my dear.' She patted her breast and sang a little mean 'Where does he live? Oh, where does he stay?' She carried her outrage from table to table, the roses on her hat nodding wildly in agreement at the affront.

Billy Johnson was still wondering in the center of the dance floor when Earl Jackson approached. Rhoda had relayed her news to the hostess and host, and although under Helen's influence Earl had mellowed, it was not safe to think he had ripened.

He caught Billy's lapels and pulled him out of the stupor. 'What the hell you trying to do, hittin' that woman? You trying to be funny?' His voice carried over the room to Rhoda who was fanning her face with her hat. 'This is my party, you sonna bitch!'

And then he pushed Billy away with his left hand and slapped him with the right. The loud smack pulled us all to our feet, but Billy Johnson spun and dove a full gainer onto the highly polished wood. All movement and sound were suspended for a second and we heard Billy drawl in his plain Oklahoma accent, 'That's the first time a man has really ever hit me.'

The moment was so brief, there was no time to decide whether the pronouncement was a complaint or a compliment. Some people laughed out of nervousness, others because it was a funny scene, and a few began to down the last of the free drinks and collect their coats.

Behind my chair I heard a waiter say 'Carabinieri.' I told Ethel to get her mother and I would find Martha, that we should leave at once because the police had been called. I found Martha in a group sympathizing with Rhoda Boggs.

'Mart, we'd better go. The waiters have called the police.'

'You're so smart, Miss Thing.' Partying and excitement had thickened her tongue.

'Here's your coat.' I helped her put it on. 'Come on.'

I started toward the stairs and she followed me.

'Maya Angelou.'

I turned and looked back. Martha was on the landing and I was four steps below her.

'Maya Angelou, you're a smart-ass! Miss Fine Thing doesn't like smart-asses.'

281

Obviously, excitement after such a long period of dullness had intoxicated us all.

I opened my mouth to speak just as she threw the contents of her glass in my face. All the pious self-placating words – 'Patience,' 'Tolerance,' 'Forgive, for that is the right thing to do' – fled from me as if I had never known them.

I could have gone back up the stairs and stomped her face flat into the floor until her features became part of the parquetry design. But she was so small. Five foot tall and absolutely too small to hit. Yet I couldn't just walk out with the whiskey dribbling down my cheeks and into my collar and down my neck.

I grabbed a handful of the hem of her coat and gave it a lusty jerk. Her feet shot out from under her and she came bumping down the stairs. When she settled, a step below me, I saw that her wig had jumped free from the pins and had been turned askew. Long, black, silky hair covered her face and the wig's part began somewhere behind her left ear.

When I reached the bottom of the stairs I looked back. Ned Wright was bent over the woman. 'Oh, my dearie. Someone pushed Miss Fine Thing down the stairs? Do let Uncle Ned help you up.'

The soprano had both hands on her wig. In one move she snatched it around straight on her head and composed her face. She smoothed the hair down to her shoulders, fingering the curls that lay on her collar.

'No one pushed Miss Fine Thing,' she said, jaw lifted as she struck a pose on the steps. 'I fell.'

The next day I sat sulking in my room, feeling betrayed and friendless. I told myself the time had come to go home. I missed my son and he needed me. His letters, printed in large letters, arrived regularly, and each one ended: 'When are you coming home, Mother? Or can I come to visit you?'

Breen and Bob Dustin had offered to send for him and give me an allowance for his upkeep. But there were many male homosexuals in the company, and while I wasn't afraid that they might molest him I did know he was at an impressionable age. He would see the soft-as-butter men, moving like women, and receiving the world's applause. I wasn't certain that Clyde wouldn't try to imitate their gestures in a childish attempt to win admiration. Everyone wants acceptance.

No matter what it cost in loneliness, I was doing the good-mother thing to leave my son at home. Thus I had soothed my guilt, never admitting that I was reveling in the freedom from the constant nuisance of a small child's chatter. When the travel had been good, it had been very good. I could send money home, write sad and somehow true letters reporting my loneliness and then stay up all night past daybreak partying with my friends. There were no breakfasts to either prepare or worry about. I could wear my hangovers openly, like emblems of sophistication, without fear of judgment.

The truth was, I had used the aloneness, loving it. Of course, I had to work, but dancing and singing every night with sixty people was more like a party than a chore. And I had my friends.

I thought about Martha and knew I'd never speak to her again. Or to Lillian, or Ned, or any of the others. They had been friends before I came along and I was certain they were closing ranks to push me out, even as I sat in the miserable hotel room. I had lunch sent to my room and made up my mind to hand in my resignation. It was time for me to go. The greatest party of my life was over.

That night I barely grumbled hello to the singers backstage, and when we took our places and the overture began, I was working hard at holding back the tears.

The curtain rose on Bey, Ned, Joe Jones, Joe Attles and John Curry shooting dice. Ned, as Robbins, sang his lyrical tenor line, 'Nine to make. Come nine,' and won the pot. Crown, angered by the game's outcome, took the baling hook and a fight began. In the struggle, Crown stabbed Robbins with the weapon. Robbins screamed as always and turned upstage to face the company. A small gasp of surprise raced around the stage. He had always played the death scene to the audience, milking the moment for every drop of drama. Now he clutched his chest where the hook was supposed to have struck and said aloud, 'He struck me. Oooh! He struck me. Did you see that? He struck Ned Wright.'

He stumbled across the stage from right to left. He asked Joy McClain and Delores Swann, 'Where does he live? Where is he staying?' He then hurtled over to Freddie Marshall and Ruby Green, 'Did you see that? He actually struck me. Oooh weee!'

The company was supposed to be shocked into silence by the murder, and the music rests during the scene, but when Ned began imitating the disaster of the night before, a few soft giggles could be heard onstage.

After thrusting, clutching and stumbling, Ned finally went down to the floor. He then sat up absolutely straight, putting one fist at the back of his head and another to his forehead, gave a vigorous tug, slipping both hands around until they were directly over his ears.

He said prissily, in a loud whisper, 'No one struck Ned Wright. I fell.' Only then did he lie down and close his eyes.

The giggles might never have increased except that Ned was hunched face down while his body jumped and shook with convulsions, and Bey let out a bass shout of such pure glee that we were all pulled along into uncontrollable laughter.

The conductor looked up from the pit, aghast. He lifted both hands, cueing the singers to begin the dirge; not one voice followed his signal. He lifted his hands higher, imperiously pointing his baton at the stage, but the sopranos had buried their faces in their aprons and the men had covered their mouths with their hats, their shoulders shaking with laughter.

Alexander Smallens' face darkened with fury. He held his baton between his fingers like a pencil and made short stabbing motions at the singers. The orchestra played the entire passage alone. On the cue for the cast to exit stage left in a wild attempt to escape a white policeman who enters stage right, we tripped over each other, falling into the wings.

People leaned on the walls or clung together – some even held on to the curtain – trying to keep laughter under control. Rhoda Boggs wiped the tears from her round face; she managed to steal a breath from her spasms and said, 'That Ned Wright. Uh uh. That Ned Wright. He's crazy.'

Someone caught me and pulled me around. It was Martha. She looked at me and I wasn't sure if her wide grin was meant to be an attempt to apologize. Suddenly she put her hands on her wig and pulled it askew. Then she shoved it back to the correct position.

'Miss Fine Thing didn't fall. Somebody pushed her.'

I bent low, laughing, and she put her arms around my neck. Neither begged the other's pardon. We picked up our friendship as if it had not fallen but had only stumbled. A few weeks later she shed the wig. A black beautician in Rome curled her newly grown hair in a high and luxuriant coiffure, and we never mentioned the incident again.

26

Porgy and Bess was to be the first American opera sung at La Scala. Famous white sopranos, tenors and baritones from the United States had soloed at Milan's renowned opera house; now an entire cast of Negro singers were nervously rehearsing on the legendary stage.

Photographers and journalists lounged around the stage door and waited in our hotel lobbies.

'Miss Davy, how does it feel to be the star of the first . . .?'

'I am honored, of course, but then, we all work hard. I am just one of the Besses.'

'Mr. Scott, are you nervous about singing at La Scala?'

'Nervous? No. I am excited, yes, but then, I am excited each time I sing.'

'Miss Flowers, did you ever think you would have the opportunity to sing in Milan? At the world's most prestigious opera house?'

'Certainly. I do believe in the work ethic. Work hard and be prepared. Naturally, we are all pleased.'

Oh, I was so proud of them. Their hands were knotted with tension and their brows moist with perspiration, but they acted cool.

We were told that La Scala audiences reacted to singers in the same way patrons of the Apollo in Harlem responded to the acts. That warning didn't need to be spelled out. The Apollo audiences were famous for shouting mediocre performers out of the theater or joining the entertainers on the stage to show them how a dance should be danced and how a song should be sung.

On opening night the backstage silence was unusual and ominous. Dressing-room doors were not only closed but locked. When the five-minute call was given we all went quietly to our places; not even a whisper floated over the dark stage. The rustling audience was stilled by the gradually darkening lights; they applauded the conductor's entrance and the overture began. The cast remained apart and I felt a little afraid. Suppose Gloria lost her voice, or Annabelle couldn't hit her high coloratura note. Just suppose I tripped over someone's foot on my entrance. I was coiled tight like a spring and realized as the curtain rose that every other member of the cast had also wound themselves up taut for a shattering release.

The moment the curtain opened the singers in concert pulled the elegant first-night audience into the harshness of black Southern life. When Robbins was killed, the moans were real (didn't we all know people who, unable to talk back to authority, killed a friend over fifty cents?). The entrance of the white policeman was met with actual fear (wasn't the law always on the side of the mighty and weren't the jackals always at our heels?). The love story unfolded with such tenderness that the singers wept visible tears. (Who could deny this story? How many black men had been crippled by the American oppression and had lost the women they loved and who loved them, because they hadn't the strength to fight? How often had the women submitted to loveless arrangements for the sake of bare survival?)

The first smiles of the evening were shared during our bows. We had sung gloriously. Although we faced the audience – which was on its feet, yelling and applauding – we bowed to compliment each other. We had performed *Porgy and Bess* as never before, and if the La Scala patrons loved us, it was only fitting because we certainly performed as if we were in love with one another.

We arrived in Rome on a late spring afternoon. I arranged my bags in the hotel room and went downstairs to find a telephone directory. In Paris, Bernard Hassel had told me to go to Bricktop's if I ever got to Rome. She was a living legend. He said Bricktop, Josephine Baker and Mabel Mercer had been the high-yellow toasts of Europe in the thirties. They hobnobbed with the rich and the royal, and although Mabel had gone to the United States and Josephine was semiretired, Bricktop still owned the most fashionable night club in Rome.

When night fell I walked down the Via Veneto, past the outdoor tables of Doney's Restaurant and into the next block where a small simple sign BRICKTOP'S hung over the door.

I opened the door and found myself standing behind a pudgy broad-shouldered man and a heavily made up woman whose brown hair was frosted blond. A small, very light-skinned, freckled woman with thin red hair stood facing the couple.

'On dit que vous avez bu trop en Cannes. (They say you've

289

been drinking too much in Cannes).' She frowned and her French accent was as Southern and sweet as pecan pie.

The man said, 'Please, Brickie. I promise not to drink tonight. My word of honor.'

Her scowl relaxed when the man's companion added, 'I won't let him have a thing, Brickie. We'll just watch the show.'

Bricktop called a waiter. 'Come here and take King Farouk to a table.' My ears almost rejected the name. 'But don't give him a drop. Not one *goutte*.'

The couple followed the waiter and Bricktop signaled to me. Her face was closed.

'Are you alone?'

I said, 'Yes.'

'I'm sorry, miss. But I don't allow ladies in here unescorted.' She started to turn away.

I said, 'Miss Bricktop, I am sorry too. I have been waiting for six months to come here and meet you.' It was flattery, but it was also the truth.

She walked closer to me and stood straight. 'What are you doing in Rome?' The question was asked cynically, as if she thought I might be a traveling prostitute, and her eyes said she had heard every version of every lie ever told.

'I'm with *Porgy and Bess*. I am a dancer-singer.'

'Uh-huh.' I could see her defenses relax. 'When did you get in?'

'About two hours ago.'

She nodded, appreciating that her place had been my first stop. She turned and lifted her hand. A waiter came scuttling to her.

'Take mademoiselle to a table.' She said to me, 'Go and sit down. I'll be over to talk to you pretty soon.'

The club had thick carpets and heavy chandeliers, and the waiters dressed as handsomely as the customers. Bricktop was a Negro woman away from the United States thirty years, and still her Southern accent was unmistakable. I was even more amazed when she later told me she wasn't Southern at all, but had come from Chicago.

When she finally came to my table, she asked where I was from.

I said, 'San Francisco.'

'How do you feel, being so far from home?'

I said, 'There is no place God is not.'

Her face crinkled in a little-girl grin. 'Oh, you're going to be my baby. Did you know that I've converted to Catholicism?'

I said I hadn't heard.

She leaned across the table, her eyes sparkling. 'I have friends who ask me why. They found out I go to Mass every day and they're shocked. I say, "Look, for thirty years you saw me running in and out of bars every day and you never tried to stop me and it didn't shock you. Why do you want to stop me now?"' She sat back in the chair and smiled smugly. 'Don't you reckon that stopped them?'

She invited me to the club whenever I wanted to come and promised to cook a dinner of black-eyed peas. 'I know where to find them in this town. Fact is I know where to find anything and everyone in Rome.'

I looked around the room at some famous American and European faces, and at the line of people waiting inside the doorway for tables. I didn't doubt that Brickie had the keys necessary to open the Eternal City.

27

After a few weeks in Rome I received a disturbing letter from Mother. Wilkie had moved out into his own studio. Lottie was looking for a housekeeping job because Mr. Hot Dog was losing money. And mother was planning to become a dealer in a Las Vegas Negro casino – which meant there would be no one to take care of Clyde, who missed me more than ever. He had developed a severe rash that resisted every medical treatment. I wrote immediately, saying I would be home in a month. I was obliged by union rules to give two weeks' notice, but since we were in Europe, it was only fair to allow the company four weeks to find another dancer-singer.

I went to Bob Dustin and explained that I would be leaving in one month and what a pleasure the tour had been. That evening he came to my dressing room, took a seat and looked at me solemnly.

'I am sorry, but I've got bad news for you. Since you're handing in your notice, we do not have to send you home.

You'll have to pay your own way. And you'll have to pay your replacement's fare, first class, from wherever we find her.'

The fares could come to over a thousand dollars! I had not seen that amount of cash since the war when I had kept the keys to my mother's money closet.

Bob left me alone with my tears. I told Martha and Lillian, who sympathized but had no money to lend me. Desperation began to build. I had to go to my son, but how could I find the money to do it?

Bricktop answered the private phone number she had given me. 'Well, now, stop crying and tell me what's the matter.'

I told her how I had left my son and that my family was down on its luck and that I needed to have another job to earn my fare home.

'That's nothing to cry about. I've heard of dancers crying because they were worked too hard, but never because they weren't worked enough. Put your faith in God and come down here this afternoon to rehearse with my pianist. You can start tonight.'

For the next two months I not only danced in the opera and sang at Bricktop's but also found daytime employment. Some dancers at the Rome Opera House asked me to give them classes in African movement. I charged them as much as they could afford and watched each penny carefully, so that my bankroll grew. Bricktop fed me often, and once when I was so depressed I could hardly speak she asked me to her house. When I entered the large foyer she lifted her skirt and showed me her knees. The light skin was bruised and scratched.

'I went up the holy stairs on my knees for your son. And I've been lighting a candle and praying to the Holy Mother for him every day. Now, will you please have faith and know that he is all right?'

I counted the money unbelievingly; every penny I needed was there. I made reservations on the *Cristoforo Colombo*. Martha and Ethel, Lillian, Barbara, Bey, Ned, the Joes (Attles and James) gave me a lavish farewell party.

Martha said, 'Miss Thing, why don't you fly home? The way you're going it'll take you two weeks to reach California.'

I was afraid. If the plane crashed my son would say all his life that his mother died on a tour in Europe, never knowing that I had taken the flight because I was nearly crazy to be with him.

Lillian made a face at Martha. 'Let her alone, Miss Fine Thing. She gets these hunches and sometimes they work. Let us not forget about the Cairo and the *défrisage*.' We all laughed at the good times in the past which were good enough when they happened but were much better upon reflection.

The nine-day trip from Naples to New York threatened to last forever. I seemed to have spent a month going to bed in the tiny cabin where sleep was an infrequent visitor. Uncomfortable thoughts kept me awake. I had left my son to go gallivanting in strange countries and had enjoyed every minute except the times when I thought about him. I had sent a letter saying I was coming two months before and had felt too guilty to write and explain my delay.

A barely adequate band played music in the second-class salon, and after the third restless night I started singing with them.

A very thin and delicate-looking man from first class introduced himself and sat every evening until the last song had been played and the musicians had covered their instruments. Without the band and his company the trip would have been totally unbearable.

My friend was a chronic insomniac, so we played gin rummy and talked until sunrise. He told me he was a friend of Tennessee Williams, and we discussed the future of drama. I recited some of my poetry, which he said was promising.

We exchanged addresses at the dock and I took a taxi to the train station. The three-day trip in a coach deposited me tired, frazzled, but happy at the Third and Townsend Station of the Southern Pacific in San Francisco.

28

Lottie answered the doorbell and gave a shout of welcome. In seconds the family closed around, kissing, stroking and hugging me. They guided me to the sofa, talking and asking questions that they didn't expect to be answered. When I sat down, Clyde jumped into my lap and snuggled his head under my chin. Every minute he would pull away to look at my face, then nestle again against my neck. Mother patted my hair and my cheek and laughed, wiping her eyes.

Lottie said, 'She needs a cup of coffee.'

'The prodigal daughter,' Mother said, 'That's who you are. The prodigal daughter returns home.'

Lottie, in the kitchen, said, 'Oh, baby. We've missed you.'

'If we lived on a farm,' Mother said, 'I'd kill the fatted calf. Oh, yes, baby.' She turned to my son. 'That's what the mother does when the prodigal daughter returns.'

Clyde's arms were wound around my neck.

'Clyde,' Mother said.

He murmured into my collar, 'Yes, Grandmother?'

'You're too big to sit in your mother's lap. You're a little man. Come on, get up and go find a fat calf. We'll kill it and cook it.'

His arms tightened.

I said, 'Mother, let him sit here awhile. It's O.K.'

The first day was spent dispensing gifts and telling each other snatches of stories. I talked about the company and some of the cities we visited. Mother and Lottie told me about losing the restaurant lease and how Clyde had missed me and how they had taken him to a dermatologist who recommended an expensive allergist, but nothing seemed to help.

Clyde had little to say. The loquacious, beautiful and bubbling child I had left had disappeared. In his place was a rough-skinned, shy boy who hung his head when spoken to and refused to maintain eye contact even when I held his chin and asked, 'Look at me.'

That evening I went in to hear him say his prayers dully, and when I bent to kiss him good night he clung to me with a fierceness that was frightening. In the very early hours of the morning I heard a faint knock at my door.

I turned on the light and said, 'Come in.'

My son tiptoed into the room. His face was puffy from crying. I sat upright. 'What's the matter?'

He came to my bed and looked at me directly for the first time since my return. He whispered, 'When are you going away again?'

I put my arms around him and he fell sobbing on my chest. I held him, but not my own tears.

'I swear to you, I'll never leave you again. If I go, when I go, you'll go with me or I won't go.'

He fell asleep in my arms and I picked him up and deposited him in his own bed.

29

Disorientation hung in my mind like a dense fog and I seemed to be unable to touch anyone or anything. Ivonne was happily married at last; she introduced me to her new husband, but my interest was merely casual. At home I played favorite records, but the music sounded thin and uninteresting. Lottie prepared elaborate meals especially for me, and the food lay heavily on my tongue – it had to be forced down a tight, unwilling throat. Mother and I showed each other the letters we had received from Bailey. The sadness I experienced in Europe when I read the mail had obviously been left abroad, and now rereading his poignant and poetic tales of prison life left me unmoved.

I was aware that I was not acting like the old Maya, but it didn't matter much. My responses to Clyde, however, did alarm me. I wanted to hold him every minute. To pick him up and carry his nine-year-old body through the streets, to the store, to the park. I had to clench my fists to keep my hands off his head and face whenever I sat near him or moved past him.

Clyde's skin flaked with scales and his bedclothes had to be changed each day in an attempt to prevent new contagion. I had ruined my beautiful son by neglect, and neither of us would ever forgive me. It was time to commit suicide, to put an end to accusations and guilt. And did I dare die alone? What would happen to my son? If my temporary absence in Europe caused such devastation to his mind and body, what would become of him if I was gone forever? I brought him into this world and I was responsible for his life. So must the thoughts wind around the minds of insane parents who kill their children and then themselves.

On the fifth day home I had a lucid moment, as clear as the clink of good crystal. I was going mad.

Clyde and I were alone in the house. I shouted at him. 'Get out. Go outside this moment.'

'Where, Mother?' He was stunned at the violence in my voice.

'Outside. And don't come back, even if I call you. Out.'

He ran down the stairs as I picked up the telephone. I ordered a taxi and telephoned the Langley Porter Psychiatric Clinic.

'I am sorry. There's no one here to see you.'

I said, 'Oh, yes. Someone will see me.'

'Madame, we have a six-month waiting list.'

'This is an emergency. My name is Maya Angelou. Someone will see me.'

I grabbed a coat and went to sit on the steps. Clyde came running around from the backyard when he heard the cab stop. He squinted his eyes as if he were about to cry.

'You're going away?'

I said, 'I'm just going to see a friend. You go back in the house. I'll be home in an hour or so.'

I saw him watching the taxi until we turned the corner.

The receptionist was not alarmed at my hysteria. 'Yes, Miss Angelou. Doctor will see you now, in there.' She showed me to a door.

A large, dark-haired white man sat behind the desk. He indicated a seat. 'Now, what seems to be the trouble?' He put his hands on the desk and laced his fingers. His nails were clean and clipped short. His good suit was freshly pressed. He looked muscular. I thought he's probably one of the tennis players who drive expensive sports cars and his wife has black servants who wash her underclothes and bring her breakfast on a tray.

'Are you troubled?'

I started to cry. Yes, I was troubled; why else would I be here? But what could I tell this man? Would he understand Arkansas, which I left, yet would never, could never, leave? Would he comprehend why my brilliant brother, who was the genius in our family, was doing time in Sing Sing on a charge of fencing stolen goods instead of sitting with clean fingernails in a tailor-made suit, listening to some poor mad person cry her blues out? How would he perceive a mother who, in a desperate thrust for freedom, left her only child, who became sick during her absence? A mother who, upon her return, felt so guilty she could think of nothing more productive than killing herself and possibly even the child?

I looked at the doctor and he looked at me, saying nothing. Waiting.

I used up my Kleenex and took more from my purse. No, I

couldn't tell him about living inside a skin that was hated or feared by the majority of one's fellow citizens or about the sensation of getting on a bus on a lovely morning, feeling happy and suddenly seeing the passengers curl their lips in distaste or avert their eyes in revulsion. No, I had nothing to say to the doctor. I stood up.

'Thank you for seeing me.'

'If you'd like to make another appointment—'

I closed his door and asked the receptionist to call a taxi.

I gave the driver the address of Wilkie's studio. I arrived in the middle of a lesson. He took one look at me and said, 'Go into my bedroom. There's a bottle of scotch. I have another student after this one, then I'll cancel for the rest of the afternoon.'

I sat on his bed and drank the whiskey neat and listened to the vocalizing in the next room. I didn't know what I was going to say to Wilkie, but I knew I would feel better talking to him than to that doctor, to whom I would be another case of Negro paranoia. I telephoned home and told Lottie where I was and that I'd be home soon.

The piano was finally silent and Wilkie opened the bedroom door. 'O.K., old sweet nappy-head thing. Come on and talk to Uncle Wilkie.'

I walked out into the studio and collapsed in his arms.

'Wilkie, I can't see any reason for living. I went to a psychiatrist and it was no good. I couldn't talk. I'm so unhappy. And I have done such harm to Clyde . . .'

He held me until I finished my babbling.

'Are you finished? Are you finished?' His voice was stern and unsympathetic.

I said, 'Well, I guess so.'

'Sit down at that desk.'

I sat.

'Now, see that yellow tablet?' There was a legal-size yellow pad on the blotter. 'See that pencil?'

I saw it.

'Now, write down what you have to be thankful for.'

'Wilkie, I don't want silly answers.'

'Start to write.' His voice was cold and unbending. 'And I mean start now! First, write that you heard me tell you that. So you have the sense of hearing. And that you could tell the taxi driver where to bring you and then tell me what was wrong with you, so you have the sense of speech. You can read and write. You have a son who needs nothing but you. Write, dammit! I mean write.'

I picked up the pencil and began.

> 'I can hear.
>
> I can speak.
>
> I have a son.
>
> I have a mother.
>
> I have a brother.
>
> I can dance.
>
> I can sing.
>
> I can cook.
>
> I can read.
>
> I can write.'

When I reached the end of the page I began to feel silly. I was alive and healthy. What on earth did I have to complain about? For two months in Rome I had said all I wanted was to be with my son. And now I could hug and kiss him anytime the need arose. What the hell was I whining about?

Wilkie said, 'Now write, "I am blessed. And I am grateful."'

I wrote the line.

'It's time for you to go to work. I'll call you a cab. Stop at the theatrical agency on your way home and tell them you're ready to go to work. Anywhere, anytime, and for any decent amount of money.'

When he walked me to the door he put his arm around my shoulders. 'Maya, you're a good mother. If you weren't, Clyde wouldn't have missed you so much. And let Uncle Wilkie tell you one last thing. Don't ask God to forgive you, for that's already done. Forgive yourself. You're the only person you can forgive. You've done nothing wrong. So forgive yourself.'

I told the agent I would accept any job and the only stipulation was that I had to have transportation and accommodation for my son. He was surprised at the unusual request, but we signed contracts and I went home.

My lighter mood influenced everyone. I told funny stories about the singers and stopped lying about how miserable I had been.

Mother said, 'Well, at least. I knew you had to have some good times.'

Lottie was cheered by my new appetite and planned even more elaborate meals for my pleasure. And Clyde began to tell me secrets again. He resurrected Fluke and the two of them held interminable conversations in the house's one bathroom. I took him out of school for a week and we spent days riding bikes in Golden Gate Park and having picnics on the grass.

Before my eyes a physical and mental metamorphosis began as gradually and inexorably as a seasonal change. At first the myriad bumps dried and no fresh ones erupted. His skin slowly regained its smoothness and color. Then I noticed that he no longer rushed panting to my room to assure himself that I was still there. And when I left the house to shop we both took the parting normally, with a casual 'See you in a minute.' His shoulders began to ride high again and he had opinions about everything from the planning of meals to what he wanted to be called.

'Mother, I've changed my name.'

I'm certain that I didn't look up. 'Good. What is it today?'

In the space of one month, he had told Fluke and the rest of the family to call him Rock, Robin, Rex and Les.

'My name is Guy.'

'That's nice. Guy is a nice name.'

'I mean it, Mother.'

'Good, dear. It's quite a nice name.'

When I called to him later in the day, he refused to answer. I stood in the doorway of his room watching him spraddled on the bed.

'Clyde, I called you. Didn't you hear me?'

He had always been rambunctious, but never outright sassy.

'I heard you calling Clyde, Mother, but my name is Guy. Did you want me?'

He gave me a mischievous grin.

Mother, Lottie and I failed for a time to remember his new name.

'Aunt Lottie, if you want me, call for Guy.'

'Grandmother, I have named myself Guy. Please don't forget.'

One day I asked him quietly why he didn't like Clyde. He said it sounded mushy. I told him about the Clyde River in Scotland, but its strength and soberness didn't impress him.

'It's an O.K. name for a river, but my name is Guy.' He looked straight into my eyes. 'Please tell your friends that I never want to be called Clyde again. And, Mother, don't you do it either.' He remembered 'Please.'

Whenever anyone in the family called him Clyde, he would sigh like a teacher trying to educate a group of stubborn kindergarten students and would say wearily, 'My name is Guy.'

It took him only one month to train us. He became Guy and we could hardly remember ever calling him anything else.

30

I received a telegram from Hawaii:

OPENING FOR YOU THE CLOUDS. $350 DOLLAR WEEKLY,
FOUR WEEKS. TWO WEEK OPTION. TRANSPORTATION AND
ACCOMMODATION YOU AND SON. REPLY AT ONCE.

The three women who owned the hotel and night club met
us at the airport dressed in long, colorful Hawaiian dresses.
They were white Americans, but years in the islands had
tanned their skins and loosened their inhibitions. Ann, a tall
blonde and one-time professional swimmer, smiled warmly
and draped fresh leis around our necks. Verne, the shortest of
the trio, kissed us, while Betty, handsome and rugged, clapped
our backs, grabbed our bags and herded the company into a
car.

On the drive to Waikiki I imagined Bing Crosby and a
saronged Dorothy Lamour standing under palm trees, singing
'Lovely Hula Hands.' The air was warm and moist and the

perfume of our flowers filled the car. Guy asked how deep I thought the ocean was and if there were any sharks. And did they have any life guards?

The Clouds was near the sea, at an angle from the vast and elegant Queen's Surf Hotel, which jutted pink stucco towers near Diamond Head.

We were shown to our separate rooms with a connecting bath and invited to have our first dinner with my employers.

Guy and I took a walk and happiness wound him up so tight he chattered incessantly. We went along the beach and he ran forward and back, laughing to himself, grabbing my hand to pull me along faster, then letting go in impatience and racing off alone.

After dinner and after his prayers, he told me he had left Fluke at home, because Fluke couldn't swim. I reminded him to wake me in the morning and after we had breakfast I'd change a traveler's check so that he'd have some cash. After he went to sleep, I found Ann and Betty. They showed me the club and we drank and talked late into the night.

I awakened and looked at my watch. It was ten-thirty. I thought the long plane trip had exhausted Guy because he usually got up before seven. There was no answer when I knocked on our connecting door. I tried the knob, but the lock had been turned. I went out and tried the hall door leading to his room. It, too, was locked. I called the maid and explained that my young son was sleeping and I was unable to wake him. She unlocked the door. The room was empty. I didn't panic at first. I thought he had decided to let me sleep and one of the owners had taken him downstairs to eat in the hotel restaurant.

I asked the waiter where I could find my son. He said no children had been in the restaurant that morning. Betty was in her office. She said Verne and Ann were still asleep and she hadn't seen him but I shouldn't worry – he'd probably just gone for a walk.

I thanked her and went back to the rooms. Betty didn't know Guy. He might have decided to spare waking me and he might have gone for a stroll, but there was one sure thing – he would have eaten. Even when he had been seriously upset and physically ill my son's large appetite never slackened. His normal daily breakfast consisted of oatmeal, bacon, eggs, toast, jam, orange juice and milk. On special days he ate hot biscuits and fried potatoes as well.

The maid let me in his room again. The clothes he had worn on the journey were hanging in the closet and his suit-case was open, but the contents looked undisturbed. His pajamas were at the foot of the bed.

Could he have been kidnapped? Why? I had no money. Could some sex maniac have taken my beautiful son? How could he have gotten him out of the hotel naked? Guy would have fought and screamed. I walked down to the beach, but all the children looked like my little boy. They all had tawny skin and dark eyes. I went back to the hotel and called the police.

Two large Oriental men appeared in the lobby. One of them asked, 'What was he wearing, Miss Angelou?'

'Oh, nothing as far as I can deduce. All his clothes are in his room.'

'What does he look like?'

I showed them a photograph.

'We'll find him, don't worry.'

Don't worry?

I went to the bar and ordered gin and nodded when Verne, Betty and then Ann sympathetically repeated, 'Don't worry.'

This was the way the whole world ended. One child disappears and the sun slips out of the sky. The moon melts down in blood. The earth ripples like a dark ocean. I had another gin and tried to blank out the headlines that rushed behind my eyes: *Child's Body Found in Alley, Boy Kidnapped under Mysterious Circumstances*.

I had just found a seat in the lobby when Guy walked in flanked by the policemen. He had on swim trunks and was completely covered with sand. Weak with relief, I couldn't have stood up even for a moment. He saw me and rushed away from his escorts to stand in front of me.

'Mom' – his voice was loud and concerned – 'what's the matter? Are you all right?'

I said yes, I was all right, because I couldn't think of anything else to say.

'Whew!' He blew out his breath. 'Gee, I was worried for a minute.'

I pulled enough strength from some hidden resource to stand. I thanked the officers and shook hands. They ran their hands over Guy's head, and sand fell to the carpet like brown snow. 'Don't worry your mother like that again, hear?'

They left and I fell back in the chair. 'Guy, where have you been?'

'Swimming, Mother.'

'Where did you get the swimsuit?'

'Grandmother gave it to me. But why were you worried?'

309

'You didn't have breakfast. That's why.'

'But I did.'

'The waiter said you hadn't been in this morning.'

'I didn't eat here. I ate at the Queen's Surf.'

'But you didn't have any money. Who paid?'

'No one. I signed my name.'

I was flabbergasted.

'But they didn't know you. I mean, they just accepted your signature?' That was incredible.

He looked at me as if I wasn't quite as bright as he would have liked.

'Mom, you know your name is up on that thing outside?'

I had noticed when we arrived that a large sign proclaimed MAYA ANGELOU. I said, 'Yes. I saw it.'

'Well, after I finished breakfast I pointed to it and said I would like to sign the check and that Maya Angelou is a great singer and she is my mother.'

I nodded.

He was partially right. Although I was not a great singer I was his mother, and he was my wonderful, dependently independent son.